Student Book

D0743733

American Headway 3

Liz and John Soars

OXFORD
UNIVERSITY PRESS

OXFORD
UNIVERSITY PRESS

198 Madison Avenue
New York, NY 10016 USA

Great Clarendon Street
Oxford OX2 6DP England

Oxford New York

Auckland Bangkok Buenos Aires Cape Town
Chennai Dar es Salaam Delhi Hong Kong Istanbul
Karachi Kolkata Kuala Lumpur Madrid Melbourne
Mexico City Mumbai Nairobi São Paulo Shanghai
Taipei Tokyo Toronto

OXFORD is a trademark of Oxford University Press.

ISBN 0-19-435383-4

American Headway Student Book 3:
Editorial Manager: Nancy Leonhardt
Managing Editor: Jeff Krum
Senior Production Editor: Joseph McGasko
Associate Production Editor: Nova Ren Suma
Art Director: Lynn Luchetti
Designer: Claudia Carlson
Page Composition: Shelley Himmelstein
Senior Art Buyer/Picture Researcher: Jodi Waxman
Art Buyer: Elizabeth Blomster
Production Manager: Shanta Persaud
Production Coordinator: Eve Wong

Printing (last digit): 10 9 8 7 6 5 4

Printed in China.

Acknowledgments

Cover concept: Rowie Christopher
Cover design: Rowie Christopher and Silver Editions

Illustrations by:
Marc Burckhardt; Carlos Castellanos; Mary Chandler; Kasia Charko; Jim DeLapine; Florentina/Piranha Represents; Stephen Foster; Lee Montgomery/Illustrationweb.com; Roger Penwill; Rodica Prato; Carlotta Tormey/Wilkinson Studios

Handwriting and realia by: Claudia Carlson; Karen Minot

Location and studio photography by: Dennis Kitchen Studio; Jodi Waxman/OUP

The publishers would like to thank the following for their permission to reproduce photographs:

Garry Adams/Index Stock, AFP/Corbis, Alaska Stock, Bartomeu Amengual/AgeFotostock, Tony Anderson/Getty Images, Archive Photos, Asia Images, Bill Bachmann/Index Stock, Shama Balfour/ Gallo Images/CORBIS, Scott Barrow Inc./International Stock, Bettmann/Corbis, Walter Bibikow/Index Stock, Harrod Blank/www.artcaragency.com, James Blank/Index Stock, Maryelizabeth Blomster, Matthew Borkoski/Index Stock, Michael Brennan/Corbis, BSIP Agency/Index Stock, Burke/Triolo Productions /Foodpix, Claudia Carlson, Myrleen Cate/Index Stock, Jason Childs/FPG, Cleo Freelance/Index Stock, Stewart Cohen/Index Stock, Pedro Coll/AgeFotostock, Comstock Images, Corbis, Pablo Corral/Corbis, Mitch Diamond/Index Stock, George B. Diebold/The Stockmarket, Robert Discalfani/Photonica, Mark Downey/Index Stock, Steve Dunwell Photography Inc./Index Stock, Kenneth Ehlers/International Stock, Eyewire Collection/Getty Images, James Fly/Index Stock, David Frazier/Index Stock, Larry Gatz/AgeFotostock, Deborah Gilbert/The Image Bank, Mark Giolas/Index Stock, Michael Goldman/FPG, Rob Goldman/AgeFotostock, Great American Stock/Index Stock, Peter Gridley/Getty Images, Tom Grill/AgeFotostock, Northrop Grumman/Index Stock, Jacob Halaska/Index Stock, Jan Halaska/Index Stock, George Hall/Corbis, David Hanover/Getty Images, Robert Harding Picture Library, John Henley/The Stockmarket, Robert Holmes/Corbis, Hulton Archive/Getty Images, Richard Hutchings/Corbis, Tomoko Inanami/Photonica, Andrew Itkoff, Johner/Photonica, Dewitt Jones/Corbis, Henry Kaiser/Index Stock, Bill Keefrey/Index Stock, Michael Keller/Index Stock, Michael Keller/The Stockmarket, Bob Krist/Corbis, Claudia Kunin/Corbis, James Lafayette/Index Stock, Bill Lai/Index Stock, Larry Lawfer/Index Stock, John Lawrence/International Stock, Lifestyles Productions/Index Stock, Lightscapes Inc./The Stockmarket, A. Littlejohn/Harstock, Larry Luxner, Steve Mason/Getty Images, Masterfile/Masterfilc, Ryan McVay/Getty Images, Doug Menuez/Getty Images, Zoran Milich/Getty Images, Juan G. Montanes/AgeFotostock, Bruno Morandi/AgeFotostock, Museo Nacional Centro de Arte Reina Sofia, Madrid, Spain/Bridgeman Art Library, J. P. NACIVET/Getty Images, NASA/Index Stock, National Enquirer, Vincent Oliver/Getty Images, Omni Photo Communications Inc./Index Stock, Stuart Pearce/AgeFotostock, Photodisc, photolibrary.com/Index Stock, Phyllis Picardi/International Stock, Picturebank/Harstock, Todd Powell/Index Stock, Roger Ressmeyer/Corbis, Reuters, Reuters New Media Inc./Corbis, Jon Riley/Index Stock, David Samuel Robbins/Corbis, Chris M. Rogers/Getty Images, Kim Sayer/Corbis, Juan Silva/Getty Images, Kevin Sink/Midweststock, L. Smith/Harstock, Paul A. Souders/Corbis, Mary Steinbacher/Photonica, Stock Montage/Index Stock, Lynn Stone/Index Stock, Keren Su/Index Stock, Superstock, SW Production/Index Stock, Jas. Townsend and Son, Inc., Ken Usami/Photodisc, John Wang/Getty Images, Kennan Ward/Corbis, Simon Warren/Corbis, Jodi Waxman/OUP, Karl Weatherly/Corbis, Wirepix/Pizza Hut Inc., Alan Wycheck/Harstock, Jeff Zaruba/The Stockmarket, ZEFA FAST FORWARD/Photonica

Special thanks to: Justin and Lucinda Baines; Mike Buttinger; Stan Czyzk at the National Weather Service; Andrea Levitt; Alan Marriott; Jeff Norman; Jeff Perkins; Dennis Woodruff; Bob Issacson and John Harvi at City University Television (CUNY–TV)

The publishers would also like to thank the following for their help:
p. 12 Adapted from "College Grad Loves Life as a $60,000-a-Year Paperboy" from *The National Enquirer,* January 23, 2001. Used by permission.
p. 62 "Who Wants to Be a Millionaire?" by Cole Porter. ©1956 Warner Chappell Music. Used by permission.
p. 65 Amnesty International logo and text Copyright ©Amnesty International. Used by permission.
World Wildlife Fund logo and text ©World Wildlife Fund. Used by permission.
Save the Children logo and text ©Save the Children. Used by permission.
p. 95 "Funeral Blues" copyright 1940 and renewed 1968 by W.H. Auden, from *W.H. Auden: The Collected Poems* by W.H. Auden. Used by permission of Random House, Inc.
p. 96 "My Way" by Paul Anka, Jacques Revaux, Claude Francois, Giles Thibault. ©1969. Used by permission.

Contents

SCOPE AND SEQUENCE

Unit	Grammar	Vocabulary	Everyday English
1 It's a wonderful world! page 2	**Auxiliary verbs** *do, be, have* p. 2 **Naming the tenses** Present, Past, Present Perfect p. 3 **Questions and negatives** *What did you do last night? Cows don't eat meat.* p. 3 **Short answers** *Yes, I did.* p. 4	Learning vocabulary Meaning Pronunciation Word formation Words that go together Keeping vocabulary records p. 8	Social expressions *Don't worry about it! Take care! You must be kidding!* p. 9
2 Happiness page 10	**Present tenses** Present Simple *Does she work in a bank?* p. 11 Present Continuous *Is he working in Mexico right now?* p. 11 Present Simple versus Continuous *She usually drives to work, but today she isn't driving. She's walking.* p. 13 Present Passive *He is paid a lot.* p. 14	Verbs with sports and leisure activities *play tennis go skiing do aerobics* p. 16	Numbers and dates *Money, fractions, decimals, percentages, phone numbers, dates* p. 17
3 Telling tales page 18	**Past tenses** Past Simple and Continuous *He danced and sang. He was laughing when he saw the baby.* p. 19 Past Simple and Past Perfect *I didn't laugh at his joke. Why? Had you heard it before?* p. 20 Past Passive *A Farewell to Arms was written by Ernest Hemingway.* p. 23	Art and literature *painter poet* p. 21 Collocations *paint a picture read a poem* p. 21	Giving opinions *What did you think of the play? It was so boring I fell asleep!* p. 25

Stop and Check 1   Teacher's Book p. 123

Unit	Grammar	Vocabulary	Everyday English
4 Doing the right thing page 26	**Modal verbs 1** *can, be allowed to, have to* *He can do what he likes.* p. 27 *Children have to go to school.* p. 27 *You're not allowed to smoke in here.* p. 28 *should, must* *We should take traveler's checks.* p. 29 *Passengers must have a valid ticket.* p. 29	Countries and adjectives *the United States American* *China Chinese* Nationalities *Brazil the Brazilians* *Japan the Japanese* p. 32	Requests and offers *Could you ...? Can you ...? I'll ... Should I ...?* p. 33
5 On the move page 34	**Future forms** *going to* and *will* *I'm going to buy some. I'll pick up a loaf.* p. 35 Present Continuous, *might* *We're playing tennis this afternoon. I might stop at Nick's.* p. 35	The weather *It's sunny. sunshine The sun's shining.* p. 40	Traveling around Using public transportation Requests in a hotel p. 41
6 I just love it! page 42	**Questions with** *like* *What's she like? What does she look like? What does she like to do?* p. 43 **Verb patterns** *I love cooking. I wanted to go home early. She made him go to bed, but she let him read for a while.* p. 45	Describing food, places, and people *fresh polluted sophisticated* p. 48 Words that go together *fresh food historic towns elderly people* p. 48	Sights and sounds *Dry clean only Just looking, thanks.* p. 49

Stop and Check 2   Teacher's Book p. 125

1

It's a wonderful world!

Tenses · Auxiliary verbs · Short answers · Learning vocabulary · Social expressions

► TEST YOUR GRAMMAR

1 Make questions with *you* from the sentences.

1. I come from Japan. *(Where?)*

Where do you come from?

2. I was born in São Paulo in 1984. *(Where? When?)*

Where were you born? When …?

3. I live in Montreal. *(Where?)*
4. I speak three languages. *(How many?)*
5. I'm studying English because I need it for my job. *(Why?)*
6. I've been to the United States, Canada, Japan, and Australia. *(Which countries?)*
7. I've been studying English for three years. *(How long?)*
8. I watched a movie with some friends last night. *(What?)*

2 Ask and answer the questions with a partner.

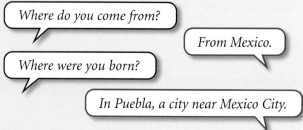

Where do you come from?

From Mexico.

Where were you born?

In Puebla, a city near Mexico City.

3 Tell the class about your partner.

Enrique comes from Mexico. He was born in Puebla in 1985, but now he lives in Mexico City.

WHAT DO YOU KNOW?
Tenses and auxiliary verbs

1 Answer the questions in the quiz.

GENERAL KNOWLEDGE
QUIZ

1. When did the modern Olympic Games start?
   a. 1806
   b. 1896
   c. 1922

2. How long does it take for the sun's rays to reach Earth?
   a. 8 minutes   b. 8 hours   c. 8 days

3. What was Neil Armstrong doing when he said in 1969, "That's one small step for a man, one giant leap for mankind"?

4. What doesn't a vegetarian eat?

5. If you are flying over the International Date Line, which ocean is below you?
   a. the Atlantic Ocean
   b. the Pacific Ocean
   c. the Indian Ocean

6. What does VIP stand for?

2 [T 1.1] Listen and check.

GRAMMAR SPOT

1 Which questions in the quiz contain the following tenses?

Present Simple	Past Simple	Present Perfect Simple
Present Continuous	Past Continuous	Present Perfect Continuous
Present Passive	Past Passive	

2 Which tenses use the auxiliary verbs *do/does/did* to make the question and negative?

Which tenses are formed with *have*?

Which tenses are formed with *be*?

▶▶ **Grammar Reference 1.1–1.3 p. 136**

3 In groups, write some general knowledge questions. Ask the other groups.

---

7. **Which language is spoken by the most people in the world?**
  a. Spanish   b. Chinese   c. English

8. **Where were glasses invented?**
  a. Mexico
  b. Italy
  c. China

9. **How many times has Brazil won the World Cup?**

10. **Why didn't Nelson Mandela become president of South Africa until he was 76 years old?**

11. **What was Abraham Lincoln doing when he was assassinated?**
  a. Giving a speech
  b. Watching a play
  c. Playing cards

12. **How long has Nintendo been selling video games?**
  a. Since 1968
  b. Since 1978
  c. Since 1988

PRACTICE

Negatives and pronunciation

1 Correct the information in the sentences.

  1. The sun rises in the west.
  2. Cows eat meat.
  3. Mercedes-Benz cars are made in Canada.
  4. Neil Armstrong landed on the moon in 1989.
  5. Abraham Lincoln was giving a speech when he was assassinated.
  6. The Pyramids were built by the Chinese.
  7. We've been in class for one month.
  8. We're studying Japanese.

> *The sun doesn't rise in the west! It rises in the east!*

[T 1.2] Listen and compare your answers.

Talking about you

2 Complete the questions.

  1. **A** What ___did you do___ last night?
     B I stayed home and watched television.
  2. **A** What kind of books _____ like to read?
     B Horror stories and science fiction.
  3. **A** _____ ever been to the United States?
     B Yes, I have. I went there last year.
     A _____ like it?
     B Yes, I really enjoyed it.
  4. **A** What _____ the teacher _____ ?
     B He's helping Maria with this exercise.
  5. **A** _____ your mother do?
     B She works in a bank.
  6. **A** _____ do your homework last night?
     B No, I didn't. I didn't feel well.
  7. **A** What _____ doing next weekend?
     B I'm going to a party.
  8. **A** _____ have a TV in your bedroom?
     B No, I don't. Just a CD player.

[T 1.3] Listen and check. Then with a partner, ask and answer the questions about you.

is and *has*

3 [T 1.4] Listen to the sentences. They all contain *'s*. Write *is* or *has*.

  1. ___is___   4. _____   7. _____
  2. _____   5. _____   8. _____
  3. _____   6. _____

MAKING CONVERSATION
Short answers

1 **T 1.5** Listen to the breakfast conversation. How does Pam feel?

Dad Good morning! Did you have a nice time last night?
Pam Yes.
Dad Do you want breakfast?
Pam No.
Dad Have you had any coffee?
Pam Yes.
Dad Is Bill coming over tonight?
Pam No.
Dad OK. Are you leaving for school soon?
Pam Yes. Bye!

2 **T 1.6** Listen to a similar conversation. What are the differences?

3 Complete the conversation.

Dad Good morning! Did you have a nice time last night?
Pam Yes, ____I did____ . I went to the movies with Bill.
Dad Do you want breakfast?
Pam No, _____ , thanks. I'm not hungry.
Dad Have you had any coffee?
Pam Yes, _____ . I don't want any more, thanks.
Dad Is Bill coming over tonight?
Pam No, _____ . He's going out with his friends.
Dad OK. Are you leaving for school soon?
Pam Yes, _____ . I'm going right now. Bye!

T 1.6 Listen again and check.

4 Close your books. Try to remember the conversation.

GRAMMAR SPOT

1 We use short answers in English conversation. It helps if you can add some information.

> Did you watch the game last night?

> Yes, I did. It was great!

2 Reply to these questions using a short answer. Add some information.

   Do you like cooking?
   No, I don't. But I like to eat!
   Do you have any brothers or sisters?
   Is it cold out today?
   Are you working hard?
   Did you go out last night?
   Have you ever been to Singapore?

▶▶ **Grammar Reference 1.4 p. 137**

5 **T 1.7** Listen and answer the questions with a short answer.

PRACTICE

Conversations

1 Match a line in **A** with a short answer in **B** and a line in **C**.

A	B	C
1. Do you like studying English?	No, I haven't.	It's rainy and cold.
2. Is it a nice day today?	Yes, I am.	It's my favorite subject.
3. Have you seen my pen?	Yes, I do.	I couldn't afford to.
4. Are you staying home this evening?	No, I didn't.	Do you want to come over?
5. Did you take a vacation last year?	No, it isn't.	You can borrow mine if you want.

T1.8 Listen and check. Practice the conversations with a partner.

2 Stand up! Ask three students the Yes/No questions in the chart below. Add one or two questions of your own. Put **Y** for *yes* and **N** for *no* in the columns. Give short answers in your reply, and add some information.

CLASS SURVEY	S1	S2	S3
1 Do you have a computer at home?			
2 Are you going out tonight?			
3 Do you play a musical instrument?			
4 Did you watch TV last night?			
5 Have you seen any good movies lately?			
6 Are you going to have coffee after class?			
7 _____			
8 _____			

Getting information

3 The United Nations invites celebrities from all over the world to be Goodwill Ambassadors. Work with a partner. You each have different information about Kaori Sato, who works for the UN. Ask and answer questions.

Student A Go to page 98.
Student B Go to page 100.

READING
Wonders of the modern world

1 Match each topic in **A** with two items in **B**.

A	B
International travel	solar system airlines
Medical science	competition online wheat
the Internet	health care drug abuse
Agriculture	
Space travel	penicillin famine galaxies
the Olympic Games	abroad web site

2 Read the text on the right. Put a topic from **A** into the paragraph headings 1–6.

3 Answer the questions.

1. What has changed because of the Internet? What will happen with the Internet?
2. What has happened in space exploration since 1969?
3. What is the most noticeable result of better health care?
4. X = the number of people who traveled abroad in the nineteenth century. What does X also equal?
5. What are the good and bad things about the Olympics?
6. What was Senator Everett trying to say about planting wheat?
7. "We are still here." Why is this a wonder?
8. What do these numbers refer to?

47	50
billions	1994
1969	half a billion
millions of people	4

What do you think?

In groups, discuss one of these questions.

- What are your favorite web sites?
- When did you last take a plane trip? Where were you going?
- Are there any stories about health care in the news right now?
- What sporting events are taking place now or in the near future?

Wonders

I don't believe that today's wonders are similar in kind to the wonders of the Ancient World. They were all buildings, such as the Pyramids in Egypt, or other architectural structures. In the past 100 years, we have seen amazing technological and scientific achievements. These are surely our modern wonders.

of the modern world
by Ann Halliday

1

It is everywhere. More than half a billion people use it, and the number of people who are online increases by 100 million every year. In 1994 there were only a few hundred web pages. Today there are billions.

It has revolutionized the way we live and work. But we are still in the early days. Soon there will be more and more interactivity between the user and the web site, and we will be able to give instructions using speech.

2

In 1969, Neil Armstrong stepped out of his space capsule onto the surface of the moon and made his famous statement: "That's one small step for a man, one giant leap for mankind." Since then, there have been space probes to Mars, Jupiter, Saturn, and even the sun. A space observatory will someday study how the first stars and galaxies began.

So far, it seems that we are alone in the universe. There are no signs yet that there is intelligent life outside our own solar system. But who knows what the future holds?

3

Surely nothing has done more for the comfort and happiness of the human race than the advances in health care! How many millions of people have benefited from the humble aspirin? How many lives has penicillin saved? Average life expectancy worldwide has risen dramatically over the past 100 years, from about 47 years in 1900 to about 77 years today.

4

We are a world on the move. Airlines carry more than 1.5 billion people to their destinations every year. It is estimated that at any one time these days there are more people in airplanes than the total number of people who traveled abroad in the whole of the nineteenth century .(but I have no idea how they figured this out!).

5

It is true that they are now commercialized, and there is greed and drug abuse. However, it is a competition in which every country in the world takes part. Every four years, for a brief moment, we see these countries come together in peace and friendship. We feel hope again for the future of mankind.

6

In 1855, an American senator named Edward Everett said, "Drop a grain of California gold into the ground, and there it will lie unchanged until the end of time. Drop a grain of wheat into the ground and—lo!—a mystery."

Farming has played an important role in the economies of the United States and Canada. Nowadays, we can't eat all the food we produce. If only politicians could find a way to share it with those parts of the world where there is famine.

7 We are still here!

The last wonder of the modern world is simply that we are still here.

We have had nuclear weapons for over 50 years that could destroy the world, but we haven't used them to do it. This is surely the greatest wonder of all.

LISTENING AND SPEAKING
My wonders

1 **T 1.9** Listen to three people from the same family giving their ideas of the wonders of the modern world. Complete the chart.

	What is the wonder?	What's good about it?	Are there any problems?
Sam	air travel		
Kelly			
Peter			

2 Work in pairs. Which of the inventions do you think is the most important? Which has changed the world the most? Mark them *1* for the most important to *8* for the least important.

____ the computer	____ nuclear weapons
____ the car	____ the space rocket
____ the television	____ the cellular telephone
____ the airplane	____ the space satellite

3 Work in groups of four. Work together to agree on the three most important inventions!

4 Talk together as a class. What other machines, inventions, or discoveries would you add to the list?

VOCABULARY
Learning vocabulary

These exercises will help you think about how you learn vocabulary.

Meaning

1 These sentences all contain the nonsense word *oggy*. Is *oggy* used as a verb, an adjective, a noun, or an adverb?

1. I couldn't hear the movie because the man next to me was eating his *oggy* so loudly.
2. There was a lot of snow on the ground. Unfortunately, I *oggied* on some ice and crashed into a tree.
3. When Pierre and Madeleine met, they fell *oggily* in love and got married one month later.
4. After an *oggy* day at work, with meetings and phone calls all day, I was ready for a quiet evening.

Can you guess what *oggy* means in the four sentences? Which real English word goes in each sentence?

passionately	skidded	hectic	popcorn

Pronunciation

2 Underline the word with the different vowel sound.

1. good   <u>food</u>   wood   stood
2. bread   head   read (present)   read (past)
3. paid   made   played   said
4. done   phone   son   won
5. dear   hear   bear   near

T 1.10 Listen and check.

Word formation

3 Complete the sentences with a suffix from the box.

-or	-ion	-ing	-ive	-ivities

1. My brother's an act **_or_** . He's making a movie now.
2. My grandmother is 89, but she's still very act____ .
3. This is not a time to do nothing. It is a time for act____ .
4. Act____ is not usually a well-paid job.
5. We do a lot of act____ in class to learn English.

Words that go together

4 Match a word in **A** with a word in **B**.

A	B
strong	carefully
full-time	coffee
movie	in love
drive	a sweater
fall	star
try on	job

(strong — coffee, full-time — job lines shown)

Keeping vocabulary records

5 Discuss with your teacher and the other students how they keep vocabulary records.

- Do you have a special notebook? Do you write the translation? What about pronunciation?
- Do you write a sentence with the new word?

STUDENT Notebook

subject *Vocabulary*

9¾ in. x 7¾ in.   50 Leaves

WRITING: Correcting mistakes
▶▶ Go to page 110

EVERYDAY ENGLISH
Social expressions

1 When we're talking with friends, we use a lot of idiomatic expressions!

> *Hurry up, we're late!*

> *Hang on. I have to go to the bathroom first.*

Match a line in **A** with a line in **B**.

1. __c__   4. ____   7. ____   10.____

2. ____   5. ____   8. ____

3. ____   6. ____   9. ____

A	B
1. Sorry I'm late. I got stuck in traffic.	a. That sounds like a good idea. You need a break.
2. Bye, Mom! I'm going to school now.	b. So am I. I can't stand all this rain.
3. Have you heard that Jenny's going out with Pete?	c. Don't worry about it. You're here now. Come and sit down.
4. How long did it take you to do the homework?	d. Ages! How about you?
5. I don't know about you, but I'm sick and tired of this weather.	e. Yes, it cost a fortune!
6. Who was that I saw you with last night?	f. Really? I don't know what she sees in him.
7. I'm tired. I'm taking next week off.	g. I'm sorry. I can't make it then. How about a little later?
8. Hey! Let's go running in the park!	h. Take care, Honey. Have a nice day!
9. Can we get together this afternoon at 3:00?	i. Me? Run? You must be kidding!
10. What a gorgeous coat! Was it expensive?	j. None of your business!

2 **T 1.11** Listen and check.
Memorize some of the conversations. Close your books and practice them in pairs.

3 **T 1.12** Listen to the sentences. Reply using one of the lines in **B** in Exercise 1. You will have to change some of them a little.

4 Choose some of the conversations and continue them.

A What a gorgeous coat! Was it expensive?
B It cost a fortune. But the material's beautiful, don't you think?
A Wow! Where did you get it?
B I saw it in the window of that new store on Main Street, you know, it's called "Chic."
A Yes, I know it. They have some really nice stuff.

2 Happiness

Present tenses · Passive · Simple vs Continuous · Sports · Numbers and dates

TEST YOUR GRAMMAR

Look at the pairs of sentences. Which one is correct? Why?

1. ☐ She speaks five languages.
   ☐ She's speaking five languages.

2. ☐ Don't turn off the TV! I watch it.
   ☐ Don't turn off the TV! I'm watching it.

3. ☐ They have a teenage son.
   ☐ They're having a teenage son.

4. ☐ Do you understand Spanish?
   ☐ Are you understanding Spanish?

5. ☐ We're thinking opera is boring.
   ☐ We think opera is boring.

6. ☐ English speaks all over the world.
   ☐ English is spoken all over the world.

THE BEST YEARS OF YOUR LIFE
Present tenses

1 What do you think is the happiest time of a person's life—when you are young or when you are old?

2 A research organization analyzed data from over 5,000 people to find out which age groups are the happiest. Here are the results of the survey:

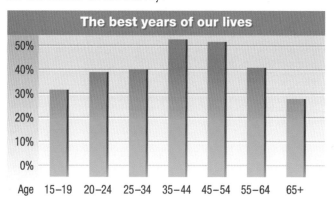

At what time in their lives are most people happiest? When are they least happy? Why do you think this is?

3 **T 2.1** Listen and read about Sidney Fisk.

"I don't know if I'm happy." —Sidney Fisk, 45

Work
Sidney Fisk is a lawyer. He's paid very well, but he usually has to work long hours. He works for an international company in Dallas, Texas, so he travels a lot in his job. Right now he's working in Mexico, and next week he's traveling to France.

Home life
Sidney is married and he has two children, ages 11 and 14. He rarely sees his children as much as he would like to because so much of his time is spent away from home. He has a beautiful house in a suburb of Dallas. It's very big, with eight bedrooms. His wife is an interior designer.

Leisure time
If he's at home on the weekend, he and his wife sometimes play golf, but that doesn't happen very often. They never have much time to relax together.

Is he happy?
He says he doesn't know if he's happy. He's too busy to think about it.

Discuss these questions with the class.

- What do you think are the good and bad things about Sidney's life?
- Do you think his life is exciting or boring?
- Would you like to have a life like Sidney's?
- Do you know any people with similar lives? Are they happy?

GRAMMAR SPOT

1 What tense are most of the verbs in the above text? Why?

2 Find two examples each in the text of the Present Continuous and the Present Simple Passive. Which auxiliary verbs are used to form these?

3 Complete the questions and answers with the correct auxiliary verbs.

   a. **Does** he travel a lot?   Yes, he _____ .

   b. _____ she work in a bank?   No, she _____ .

   c. _____ they play golf?   Yes, they _____ .

   d. _____ you play tennis?   No, I _____ .

   e. _____ he working in   Yes, he _____ .
        Mexico right now?

   f. _____ he paid a lot?   Yes, he _____ .

4 Find these words in the text about Sidney Fisk: *usually, often, rarely, never.*
What kind of words are they?

▶▶ **Grammar Reference 2.1 and 2.2 pp. 137–138**

---

4 Complete the questions about Sidney. Then ask and answer them with a partner.

   Is he married?   *Yes, he is.*

- ... married?
- What ... do?
- Where ... live?
- Does ... any children?

- What ... his wife do?
- Which sports ... play?
- Where ... working right now?
- ... paid very well?

T 2.2 Listen and check.

5 Ask and answer similar questions with your partner.

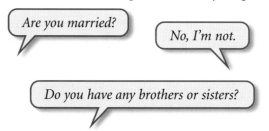

Are you married?   *No, I'm not.*

Do you have any brothers or sisters?

PRACTICE
Listening and speaking

1 [T 2.3] Look at the photos and listen to Jeff Norman. What's unusual about his lifestyle? Do you think he likes his job?

EXTRA! EXTRA!
Read all about it!
45-year-old college graduate makes $60,000 a year as a paperboy!

JEFF NORMAN from Iowa City, Iowa

2 Complete the sentences with the exact words Jeff uses.

1. I **'m paid** good money, $60,000 a year. And I often _____ $50 a week in tips.
2. I _____ _____ at 2 A.M. The first newspaper _____ _____ at 2:30 A.M.
3. I _____ a red Chevy Blazer and the newspapers _____ _____ into the back.
4. I _____ the peace and quiet.
5. Occasionally, I _____ a jogger.
6. I usually _____ back home by 7 A.M.
7. My wife _____ at the University of Iowa.
8. Some days I _____ my kids' baseball team, other days I _____ golf.
9. I _____ also _____ for my master's degree at the moment. I _____ to be a marriage counselor.
10. Some people _____ it's not much of a job, but when they _____ _____ in an office, I _____ _____ golf.

   [T 2.4] Listen and check.

3 Write notes about Jeff and Sidney in the columns.

JEFF NORMAN

Work	Home and family	Leisure

SIDNEY FISK

Work	Home and family	Leisure

Work with a partner. Compare Jeff's life with Sidney's. How old are they? How many things do they have in common? Who do you think is happier? Why?

WHAT DO YOU DO?
Simple vs Continuous

1 **T 2.5** Read and listen to the conversation.

A What do you do?
B I'm an interior designer. I decorate people's homes and give them ideas for furniture and lighting.
A And what are you working on these days?
B Well, I'm not working on a home right now. I'm working on a hotel. I'm designing a new lobby for the Plaza.
A Do you like your job?
B Yes, I love it.

Memorize the conversation and practice with a partner.

2 Work in pairs. Make up similar conversations with some of the following jobs.

> a journalist   an artist   an architect   a movie director
> a rock musician   an actor   a research scientist
> a web page designer   a zookeeper   a soccer player

Ask each other about your own jobs or studies.

GRAMMAR SPOT

1 Some verbs are used in both Simple and Continuous.

She usually **drives** to work, but today she **isn't driving**. She's **walking**.

These are called action verbs.

2 Some verbs are almost never used in the Continuous tenses. These are called stative verbs.

I **like** black coffee. (NOT I'm liking black coffee.)

3 Seven of these verbs are not usually used in the Present Continuous. Underline them.

> like   know   work   understand   enjoy
> come   want   think (= opinion)   play
> have (= possession)   love

▶▶ **Grammar Reference 2.3 p. 138**

PRACTICE

Discussing grammar

1 Are these sentences correct (✓) or incorrect (✗)? Correct the mistakes.
1. ☑ What do you want to drink?
2. ☒ I'm not understanding this word.
   I don't understand this word.
3. ☐ I'm loving you a lot.
4. ☐ Do you think Michiko plays golf well?
5. ☐ I'm sorry. I'm not knowing the answer.
6. ☐ We're enjoying the class very much. We're working hard.
7. ☐ I'm thinking you speak English very well.
8. ☐ The lions are fed once a day. They're being fed right now.

2 Complete the pairs of sentences using the verb in *italics*. Use the Present Simple for one and the Present Continuous for the other.

1. *come*
   Alec and Marie are Canadian. They ___**come**___ from Montreal.
   They'll be here very soon. They **'re coming** by car.

2. *have*
   Lisa can't come to the phone. She _____ dinner now.
   She _____ a beautiful new car.

3. *think*
   I _____ that all politicians tell lies.
   I _____ about my girlfriend at the moment. She's in Mexico.

4. *not enjoy*
   We _____ this party at all. The music is too loud.
   We _____ big parties.

5. *watch*
   Be quiet! I _____ my favorite program.
   I always _____ it on Thursday evenings.

6. *see*
   Joe isn't here. He _____ the doctor right now.
   I _____ your problem, but I can't help you. I'm sorry.

7. *use* (passive)
   This room _____ often _____ for parties.
   This room _____ being _____ for a party tonight.

READING AND SPEAKING
I'm a clown doctor!

1 What does a doctor do? What does a clown do? Write down three things for each. Tell the class your ideas.

2 Which of the following did you think of? Which do clowns do? Which do doctors do? Which do both do?

> wear funny clothes   wear white coats   tell jokes
> make children feel better   do magic tricks
> perform operations   give shots   make funny faces

3 Peggy Volz is a clown doctor. What do you think a clown doctor does? Now read what Peggy says about her job.

4 Answer the questions.

1. Where does Peggy work?
2. In what ways is her job "extremely silly"? Give some examples.
3. Why was she often in trouble at school?
4. What did she do after she left school?
5. How did she become a clown doctor?
6. What does she wear?
7. Who is always in her thoughts at the moment?
8. Why does she eat in the hospital cafeteria?
9. Does she earn a lot of money?
10. What does she do after work?
11. What is a typical working day for Peggy?

> *She arrives in the hospital and puts on …*
> *Then she goes into the wards and …*
> *At lunchtime, she …*

GRAMMAR SPOT

1 What tense is this sentence from the text?
We**'re** not **paid** like millionaires, but we**'re** **rewarded** in other ways.

2 Complete the sentences using the Present Simple Passive.
a. They pay him a lot.
He __is__ __paid__ a lot.
b. They tell her what to do.
She _____ _____ what to do.
c. People of all ages love clowns.
Clowns _____ _____ by people of all ages.
d. Teachers don't wear white coats.
White coats _____ _____ by teachers.

▶▶ **Grammar Reference 2.4 and 2.5 p. 139**

THE CLOWN

PEGGY VOLZ is 31 and works as a "clown doctor" for the Magdalena's Children's Trust.

I'M A CLOWN DOCTOR; I call myself "Dr. Banana." I spend my time in children's hospitals being extremely silly. I make funny faces, tell jokes, and do magic tricks. I blow bubbles as I walk into the wards, shake hands with the kids. I carry a "funky" radio and microphone, so I can do karaoke with children who are well enough to sing. We often meet kids who look really sick one week, but who are racing around yelling, "Hi, Dr. Banana!" when we go back a week later.

I'm naturally a very cheerful person. I've always been a clown. In school I was always in trouble for being the joker in class. After school I worked in a daycare center, taught drama, and traveled the world. I became a clown doctor because of a chance meeting with someone who works for Aid for Sick Children. I knew it was just the job for me. I still feel like a teenager in my work. I wear a big red coat, a striped shirt, and tights with big colored dots on them. Also I have a red rubber nose and a plastic banana in my hair.

Being a clown in a hospital is very tiring, both physically and emotionally. You learn not to show your feelings, otherwise you'd be no help at all.

DOCTOR

Clown doctors are sensitive, but it's not a side you often see. To other people we're happy all the time. I'm still learning to allow myself to feel sad occasionally. There are special kids you get really close to. Right now I'm working with a very sick little girl from Costa Rica. We don't have a common language, but we communicate through laughter. She's been in and out of the hospital so many times for operations. She's always in my thoughts.

At lunchtime we eat in the hospital cafeteria. That's good because we meet the nurses and doctors. They tell us about particular kids who they think would benefit from a visit from us. We're there to help the nurses too. If a child is frightened—perhaps they're getting a shot or some nasty medicine—we can distract them so the nurses can do their job.

Being a clown doctor makes the worries of everyday life seem small. We're not paid like millionaires, but we're rewarded in other ways. For me, this is definitely a millionaire job.

At six o'clock I take off all my makeup and change my clothes. I'm totally exhausted. Sometimes I have a girls' night out with my friends. I love my life. At night I really come alive and party. I'm a 17-hour-a-day girl. Then bang! I fall into bed and I'm out like a light.

Language work

5 Find phrases or sentences in the text that mean the same as the following.

1. They're running around shouting.
2. I have a happy personality.
3. I happened to meet someone.
4. I'm always thinking about her.
5. We don't earn much money, but it's a very rewarding job.
6. I go to bed and immediately fall into a deep sleep.

6 Read the interview with Peggy (**P**). Complete the Interviewer's (**I**) questions.

1. **I** Do _you like your job?_ _____

   P Oh, yes, I do. I enjoy my job very much.

2. **I** Why _____ so much?

   P Because I love working with children and making them laugh.

3. **I** What _____ ?

   P I wear crazy clothes. I wear a big red coat, a striped shirt, and tights with big colored dots on them.

4. **I** Who _____ ? Anyone special?

   P Well, at the moment I'm working with a very sick little girl from Costa Rica. She's had so many operations. She's very special to me.

5. **I** Don't _____ ?

   P Yes, I do feel sad sometimes, but it's important not to show it. And then again there are some very special moments.

6. **I** Isn't _____ ?

   P Yes, it is. It's very tiring. I'm always exhausted at the end of the day.

7. **I** What _____ ?
   Do you just go home and relax?

   P No, I don't. Sometimes I go out with friends. I love to go out. I love life. I have the best friends and the best job in the world.

T 2.6 Listen and check. Are your questions exactly the same? What are the differences?

What do you think?

Discuss the questions in groups.

- When are you happiest? At work? At home? With friends and family? In your leisure time?
- What are your favorite activities?
- What were your happiest days last year?

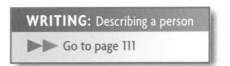

WRITING: Describing a person
▶▶ Go to page 111

VOCABULARY AND LISTENING
Sports verbs—*play*, *go*, and *do*

1 Make a list of as many sports and leisure activities
you can think of. Use the pictures to help you.

3 Choose some of the sports or activities from your list and
fill in the columns below.

Use a dictionary to look up any new words that you need.

Sport/ Activity	Go, play, or do?	People	Place	Equipment needed
baseball	play baseball	player catcher pitcher umpire	stadium field ballpark	ball bat glove bases

2 Write *play* (x4), *go* (x3), or *do* (x2).

1. **play** tennis   4. ____ exercises   7. ____ swimming
2. ____ baseball   5. ____ golf   8. ____ soccer
3. ____ skiing   6. ____ aerobics   9. ____ jogging

4 **T 2.7** Listen to three people talking about their favorite sports and take notes.

John

Suzanne

Kurt

	Kurt	John	Suzanne
1. Which sport are they talking about?			
2. How often do they do it?			
3. Where do they do it?			
4. What equipment do they use?			
5. Are they good at it?			

5 Work in pairs. Ask and answer questions.
- What sports do you play?
- How often ... ?
- Where ... ?
- What equipment ... ?
- Are you good at ... ?

EVERYDAY ENGLISH
Numbers and dates

2006
$4.95
1978
2/3
.33
$1,999.99
1/3/02
50¢
3.14
65%

1 Read these numbers aloud.

15	50	406	72	128
90	19	850	1,520	36
247	5,000	100,000	2,000,000

T 2.8 Listen and practice.

2 Read these numbers aloud.

Money					
$400	50¢	$9.40	$47.99	¥5,000	£100

Fractions				
$1/4$	$3/4$	$2/3$	$7/8$	$12 1/2$

Decimals and percentages				
6.2	17.25	50%	75.7%	100%

Dates				
1995	2020	1789	7/15/94	10/30/02

Phone numbers		
(800) 451-7545	(919) 677-1303	44-01865-556890

T 2.9 Listen and practice.

3 **T 2.10** Listen and write the numbers you hear.
1. _fifteenth, twenty-fourth_ 4. _____
2. _____ 5. _____
3. _____

Discuss what each number refers to with your partner.
The 15th and the 24th are dates.

3

Telling tales

Past tenses · Passive · Past Perfect · Art and literature · Giving opinions

1 Match a picture with a sentence.

   a. When Judy arrived home, Eric cooked dinner.
   b. When Judy arrived home, Eric was cooking dinner.
   c. When Judy arrived home, Eric had cooked dinner.

2 What is the difference in meaning?

A NATIVE AMERICAN FOLKTALE
Past tenses

1 Look at the pictures. They tell the story of Gluskap, a warrior from the Algonquian tribe of North America. What can you see? What do you think the story is about?

2 Read the story on page 19 and the phrases below. The phrases are taken from the story. Where do they fit?

   a. had run a few miles
   b. had fought and won so many battles
   c. was still yelling
   d. had never heard such a terrible noise
   e. was sitting and sucking a piece of sugar
   f. had never heard of Wasis

3 **T 3.1** Listen and check.

GRAMMAR SPOT

1 Which tense is used in these two sentences? Which verbs are regular? Which are irregular?

He **laughed** and **walked** up to the baby.
He **danced** and **sang**.

Find more examples of this tense in the story of Gluskap.

2 What is the difference in meaning among these three sentences? What are the tenses?

He **laughed** when he **saw** the baby.
He **was laughing** when he **saw** the baby.
He **laughed** when **he'd seen** the baby.   (he'd = he had)

3 Find two examples of the Past Passive in the story.

▶▶ **Grammar Reference 3.1–3.4 pp. 139–141**

4 Work with a partner. These 12 Past Simple verbs are all from "The Tale of Gluskap and the Baby." Write them in the correct column according to the pronunciation of the -ed ending.

| laughed | covered | wanted | stopped | shouted | listened |
| opened | boasted | looked | danced | screamed | pointed |

/t/	/d/	/ɪd/
• laughed	• covered	• wanted
•	•	•
•	•	•
•	•	•

T 3.2 Listen and check. Practice saying the words.

THE TALE OF GLUSKAP AND THE BABY

Gluskap the warrior was very pleased with himself because he (1) ___b___ . He boasted to a woman friend: "Nobody can beat me!"

"Really?" said the woman. "I know someone who can beat you. His name is Wasis." Gluskap (2) _____ . He immediately wanted to meet him and fight him. So he was taken to the woman's village. The woman pointed to a baby who (3) _____ on the floor of a teepee.

"There," she said. "That is Wasis. He is little, but he is very strong." Gluskap laughed and walked up to the baby. "I am Gluskap. Fight me!" he shouted. Little Wasis looked at him for a moment, then he opened his mouth. "Waaah! Waaah!" he yelled. Gluskap (4) _____ . He danced a war dance and sang some war songs. Wasis screamed louder. "Waaah! Waaah! Waaah!" Gluskap covered his ears and ran out of the teepee. After he (5) _____ , he stopped and listened. The baby (6) _____ . Gluskap the fearless was terrified. He ran on and was never seen again in the woman's village.

PRACTICE

What was she doing?

1 Judy works for MicroSmart Computers in Boston. Read about what she did yesterday.

6:30	got up
6:45–7:15	packed her suitcase
7:30–8:30	drove to the airport
9:20–10:15	flew to Chicago
11:00–12:45	had a meeting
1:00–2:15	had lunch
2:30–4:15	visited Dot Com Enterprises
5:30–6:15	wrote a report on the plane
8:00–8:45	put the baby to bed
9:00–11:00	relaxed and listened to music

2 Work with a partner. Ask and answer questions about what Judy was doing at these times.

> 7:00 A.M.   8:00 A.M.   10:00 A.M.   11:30 A.M.   1:30 P.M.
> 3:00 P.M.   6:00 P.M.   8:30 P.M.   10:00 P.M.

What was she doing at 7 A.M.?

She was packing her suitcase.

T 3.3 Listen and check.

3 Write a similar list about what you did yesterday. Ask and answer questions with your partner about different times of day.

What were you doing at 7 A.M.?

I was taking a bath.

Had you heard it before?

4 Work with a partner.

Student A Read aloud a statement from your box.
Student B Answer with the correct response from your box.

STUDENT A

1. I didn't laugh at his joke.
2. Were you surprised by the ending of the movie?
3. I went to the airport, but I couldn't get on the plane.
4. I was homesick the whole time I was living in France.
5. The hotel where we stayed on our vacation was awful!
6. I met my girlfriend's parents for the first time last Sunday.
7. My grandfather had two sons from his first marriage.

STUDENT B

- Why? Had you left your passport at home?
- Why? Had you heard it before?
- That's too bad. Hadn't you stayed there before?
- Really? I didn't know he'd been married before.
- Really? I thought you'd met them before.
- No, I'd read the book, so I already knew the story.
- That's really sad! Had you ever lived abroad before?

T 3.4 Listen and check.

5 Change roles and practice the conversations again. Make some of them into longer conversations.

I didn't laugh at his joke.

Why? Had you heard it before?

No, I hadn't. I just didn't think it was very funny. That's all.

Really? I thought it was hilarious!

An amazing thing happened!

6 Wanda and Roy had an amazing story to tell about their vacation. Work with a partner.

Student A Read the story on page 99.
Student B Read the story on page 101.

7 Wanda is telling a friend, Lim, what happened. Work with a partner. One of you is Wanda and the other is Lim. Continue their conversation.

> **L** Hi, Wanda. Did you have a good vacation?
> **W** Oh, yeah, we had a great time. But I have to tell you—the most *amazing* thing happened!
> **L** Really? What was that?
> **W** Well, Roy and I were swimming …

T 3.5 Listen and compare the conversations.

Discussing grammar

8 Complete the sentences with *was*, *were*, *did*, or *had*. Check your answers with a partner. Discuss the differences in meaning.

1. When I arrived at the barbecue, they ___**were**___ eating hot dogs.
   When I arrived at the barbecue, they _____ eaten all the hot dogs.
2. We thanked our teacher for everything she _____ doing to help us pass the test.
   We thanked our teacher for everything she _____ done to help us pass the test.
3. He told me that they _____ staying at the Plaza Hotel.
   He told me that they _____ stayed at the Plaza Hotel before.
4. _____ you learn Italian when you went to Italy?
   _____ you already learned Italian when you went to Italy?
5. _____ Shakespeare write *Hamlet*?
   _____ *Hamlet* written by Shakespeare?

VOCABULARY AND PRONUNCIATION
Art and literature

1 Look at the nouns in the box and write them in the correct column. Which word goes in both columns?

> painter   author   poet   poem   sculpture   novel
> picture   brush   palette   chapter   biography
> exhibition   fairy tale   portrait   play   art gallery
> novelist   masterpiece   sketch

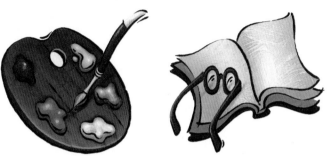

ART	LITERATURE
painter	

2 Which of the following verbs can go with the nouns in Exercise 1?

> read   write   paint   draw   go to

Read a poem, read a novel …

3 Fill in each blank with a noun or a verb from Exercises 1 and 2. Put the verb in the correct form.

1. Shakespeare ___**wrote**___ many famous _____ and poems.
2. I couldn't put the book down until I'd _____ the last _____ .
3. I love _____ about the lives of famous people so I always buy _____ .
4. _____ often begin with the words "Once upon a time."
5. My friend's a great artist. He _____ my _____ and it looked just like me.
6. We went to an _____ of Picasso's paintings and _____ .

READING AND SPEAKING
The writer and the painter

1 Who are or were the most famous writers and painters in your country?

2 You are going to read about the lives of Ernest Hemingway and Pablo Picasso. Discuss these questions.
- Why are they famous?
- What nationality were they?
- Which century were they born in?
- Do you know the names of any of their works?
- Do you know anything about their lives?

3 The sentences below appear in the texts. Which sentences go with which man? Write **P** or **H** next to each one.

1. __H__ He had wanted to become a soldier, but couldn't because he had poor eyesight.

2. ____ His first word was *lapiz* (Spanish for pencil) and he could draw before he could talk.

3. ____ His portraits of people were often made up of triangles and squares with their features in the wrong places.

4. ____ In the 1930s, he became a war correspondent in the Spanish Civil War and World War II.

5. ____ He was awarded the Nobel Prize in literature, but he was too sick to receive it in person.

6. ____ At the age of 90 he was honored by an exhibition in the Louvre in Paris.

4 Work in two groups.

Group A Read about Ernest Hemingway.
Group B Read about Pablo Picasso.

Read about your person and check your answers to Exercise 3.

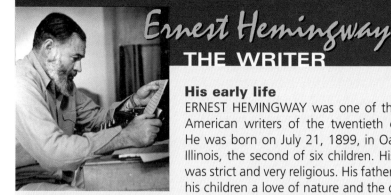

Ernest Hemingway
THE WRITER

His early life
ERNEST HEMINGWAY was one of the great American writers of the twentieth century. He was born on July 21, 1899, in Oak Park, Illinois, the second of six children. His family was strict and very religious. His father taught his children a love of nature and the outdoor life. Ernest caught his first fish at the age of three, and was given a shotgun for his twelfth birthday. His mother taught him a love of music and art. At school, he was good at English and wrote for the school newspaper. He graduated in 1917, but he didn't go to college. He went to Kansas City and worked as a journalist for the *Star* newspaper. He learned a lot, but left after only six months to go to war.

Hemingway and war
Hemingway was fascinated by war. He had wanted to become a soldier, but couldn't because he had poor eyesight. Instead, in the First World War, he became an ambulance driver and was sent to Italy, where he was wounded in 1918. After the war, he went to live in Paris, where he was encouraged in his work by the American writer Gertrude Stein. In the 1930s, he became a war correspondent in the Spanish Civil War and World War II. Many of his books were about war. His most successful book, *For Whom the Bell Tolls*, was written in 1940 and is about the Spanish Civil War. Another novel, *A Farewell to Arms*, is about the futility of war.

His personal life
Hemingway's success in writing was not mirrored by similar success in his personal life. He married four times. His first wife divorced him in 1927. He immediately married again and moved to Key West, Florida, where he enjoyed hunting, fishing, and drinking, but he also suffered from depression. This wasn't helped when, in 1928, his father committed suicide. Hemingway's health was not good and he had many accidents. Two more marriages failed and he began to drink heavily. In 1954, he had two plane crashes. In October of the same year he was awarded the Nobel Prize in literature, but he was too sick to receive it in person.

His final years
His final years were taken up with health problems and alcohol. He began to lose his memory and he couldn't write anymore. On Sunday, July 2, 1961, Hemingway killed himself with a shotgun, just as his father had done before him.

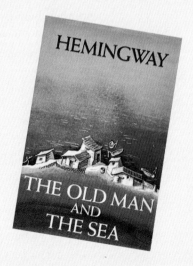

Pablo Picasso
THE PAINTER

His early life

On October 25, 1881, a baby boy was born in Malaga, Spain. It was a difficult birth and to help him breathe, cigar smoke was blown into his nose! This baby grew up to be one of the twentieth century's greatest painters—PABLO PICASSO.

Picasso showed his genius from a very young age. His first word was *lapiz* (Spanish for pencil) and he could draw before he could talk. He was the only son in the family, so he was thoroughly spoiled. He hated school and often refused to go unless he was allowed to take one of his father's pet pigeons with him!

Apart from pigeons, his great love was art. When in 1891 his father got a job as an art teacher, Pablo went with him to work and watched him paint. Sometimes he was allowed to help. One evening, his father was painting a picture of their pigeons when he had to leave the room. When he returned, Pablo had completed the picture. It was so beautiful and lifelike that he gave his son his palette and brushes and never painted again. Pablo was just 13.

His life as an artist

His genius as an artist was soon recognized by many people, but others were shocked by his strange and powerful paintings. He is probably best known for his Cubist pictures. His portraits of people were often made up of triangles and squares with their features in the wrong places. One of his most famous portraits was of the American writer Gertrude Stein, who he met after he'd moved to Paris in 1904.

His work changed ideas about art around the world, and to millions of people, modern art means the work of Picasso. *Guernica*, which he painted in 1937, records the bombing of that small Basque town during the Spanish Civil War, and is undoubtedly one of the masterpieces of modern painting.

His final years

Picasso married twice and also had many girlfriends. He had four children. The last, Paloma, was born in 1949 when he was 68 years old. At the age of 90 he was honored by an exhibition in the Louvre in Paris. He was the first living artist to be shown there.

Picasso created over 6,000 paintings, drawings, and sculptures. Today, a Picasso costs millions of dollars. Once when the French Minister of Culture was visiting Picasso, the artist accidentally spilled some paint on the Minister's pants. Picasso apologized and wanted to pay for them to be cleaned, but the Minister said, "Non! Please. Monsieur Picasso, just sign my pants!"

Picasso died of heart failure during an attack of influenza in 1973.

Guernica

5 Answer the questions.

1. Where and when was he born? When and how did he die?
2. What kind of family life did he have?
3. How did his parents play a part in his career?
4. What do you think were the most important events in his early life?
5. When did he move to Paris? Who did he meet there?
6. How did war play a part in his life?
7. What did you learn about his personal relationships?
8. Which of the following dates relate to your person? What do they refer to?

1891	1904	1917	1918	1927
1928	1937	1940	1949	1954

6 Find a partner from the other group and go through the questions in Exercise 5 together. What similarities and differences can you find between the two men?

They were both born in the nineteenth century.

GRAMMAR SPOT

1 What tense are these verb forms?

Guernica **was painted** by Pablo Picasso.

A Farewell to Arms and *For Whom the Bell Tolls* **were written** by Ernest Hemingway.

Find more examples of this tense in the texts and underline them.

2 Put the auxiliaries *was*, *were*, or *had* into the blanks.

a. Pablo's father left the room. When he returned, Pablo ____ completed the painting.
b. Picasso ____ given his father's palette and brushes.
c. Both Hemingway and Picasso ____ living in Paris when they met Gertrude Stein.
d. Both men ____ honored in their lifetimes.

▶▶ **Grammar Reference 3.5 p. 141**

LISTENING AND WRITING
Books and movies

1 Work in groups. Do you have a favorite book or movie? Why do you like it? Think about it for a minute. Tell your group about it.

2 Look at the list of books and movies. Which ones do you know?

- ☐ Ragtime
- ☐ The Godfather
- ☐ The Old Man and the Sea
- ☐ A Tree Grows in Brooklyn
- ☐ Star Wars
- ☐ Lord of the Rings
- ☐ Titanic
- ☐ Angela's Ashes
- ☐ A Farewell to Arms
- ☐ Toy Story
- ☐ Harry Potter and the Sorcerer's Stone

3 **T 3.6** Listen to four friends having lunch together. Their conversation turns to their favorite books and movies. Put a check (✓) next to the titles in Exercise 2 that they mention. What do they say about these titles? Discuss with your group, then with the class.

4 Choose a book or movie that you know and like. Write some notes about it. Use these questions to help you. Discuss your notes with a partner.
- What's it called?
- Who wrote it?/Who starred in it?
- Where does it take place?
- Who and what is it about?
- Why do you like it?

5 Write about the book or movie that you chose.

> **WRITING:** Telling tales
> ▶▶ Go to page 112

EVERYDAY ENGLISH
Giving opinions

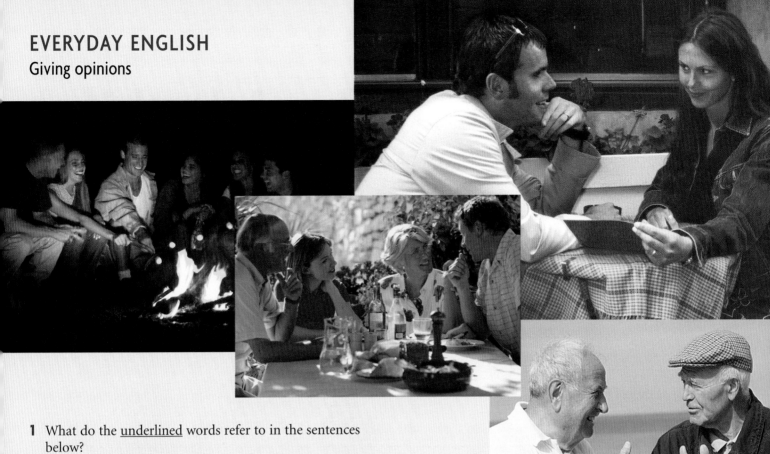

1 What do the <u>underlined</u> words refer to in the sentences below?

   a. <u>It</u> was really boring! I fell asleep during the first act.
     a play

   b. I didn't like his last <u>one</u>, but I couldn't put his new one down until the last page.

   c. <u>It</u> was excellent. Have you seen it yet? It stars Julia Roberts and Antonio Banderas.

   d. <u>She's</u> usually good, but I don't think she was right for this part.

   e. I think they spoil <u>them</u>. They always give <u>them</u> whatever they want.

   f. <u>It</u> was a nice break, but the weather wasn't very good.

   g. <u>They</u> were delicious. John had turkey and cheese and I had tuna salad.

   h. <u>It</u> was really exciting, especially when Michael Jordan scored in the last second.

2 The following questions all ask for opinions. Match them with the opinions in Exercise 1.

   1. Did you like the movie?   c

   2. What did you think of the play?   ____

   3. Did you like your sandwiches?   ____

   4. Do you like Stephen King's novels?   ____

   5. What do you think of their children? ____

   6. What was your vacation like?   ____

   7. What did you think of Jennifer Lopez? ____

   8. How was the game?   ____

T 3.7 Listen and check. Practice the questions and answers with a partner.

3 Write down some things you did, places you went, and people you met last week. Work with a partner and ask for and give opinions about them.

I went to a party.

Really? How was it?

Great! I really enjoyed it.

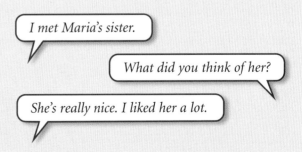

I met Maria's sister.

What did you think of her?

She's really nice. I liked her a lot.

4 Doing the right thing

Modal verbs 1 · *can/allowed to* · Nationality words · Requests and offers

---

TEST YOUR GRAMMAR

Look at the sentences.

I	can should have to	go.

Make the sentences negative.

Make them into questions.

Make them into the third person singular *(He/she ...)*.

Which verb is different?

I'm sorry, but I have to go now.

TEENAGERS AND PARENTS
have (got) to, can, allowed to

1 **T 4.1** Listen to Sarah and Lindsey, ages 14 and 15. What are some of the things they like and don't like about being teenagers?

2 What did they say? Fill in the blanks.

1. You __don't have to__ go to work.
2. You _____ pay bills.
3. You _____ go out with your friends.
4. I always _____ tell my Mom and Dad where I'm going.
5. What time _____ get back home?
6. You _____ buy whatever you want.
7. We _____ wear makeup.
8. I _____ go. I _____ do my homework.

T 4.2 Listen and check. Practice saying the sentences.

3 Lindsey's parents' names are Peter and Diane. What are some of the things they have to do, and some of the things they don't have to do?

Diane doesn't have to work full-time.
Peter has to drive over 500 miles a week.

GRAMMAR SPOT

1 Put *have to* or *don't have to* in the blanks.

Children _____ go to school.
Millionaires _____ work.
You _____ go to the United States if you want to learn English.
In England, you _____ drive on the left.

2 *Have got to* means the same thing as *have to*, but we use it more in spoken English than in written English.

I've got to go now. Bye!

▶▶ **Grammar Reference 4.1 p. 141**

PRACTICE

Discussing grammar

1 Put these sentences into the negative, the question, and the Past.

1. Henry can swim.
   Henry can't swim. Can Henry swim? Henry could swim.
2. I have to go.
3. She has to work hard.
4. He can do what he likes.
5. We're allowed to wear jeans.

Talking about you

2 Look at the chart. Make true sentences about you and your family.

I don't have to do the cooking.

A	B	C
I	has to	go to work.
My parents	have to	get up early.
My mother	doesn't have to	go shopping.
My father	don't have to	clean my room.
My sister	had to	do the cooking.
My brother	didn't have to	take out the garbage.
My grandparents		do the laundry.
My husband/wife		do the dishes.

Compare your sentences with a partner.

3 Complete the sentences with *has/have to* and a line from **C** in Exercise 2.

1. Where's my briefcase? I __**have to go to work.**__
2. Look at those dirty plates! We _____ .
3. Pam and Chuck don't have any food in their house. They _____ .
4. John needs to get an alarm clock. He _____ .
5. I don't have any clean socks. I _____ .
6. My mother comes home late from work, so I _____ .

T 4.3 Listen and check. Practice saying the sentences.

4 Work in groups. Talk about your school.
- Are/Were your teachers strict?
- What are/were you allowed to do?
- What are/were you *not* allowed to do?

Signs

5 What do these signs mean?

Adults $5.00 Children FREE

Adults have to pay $5, but children don't have to pay anything.

You can't smoke in here. You aren't allowed to smoke in here.

What do you think?

Is it the same in your country?

In the United States …

- you can get married when you're 16.
- you can't drink alcohol until you're 21.
- you have to wear a seat belt in the front seat of a car.
- you can vote when you're 18.
- young men don't have to do military service.
- there are lots of public places where you aren't allowed to smoke.

PLANNING A TRIP
should and *must*

1 **T 4.4** Brad and his friend, George, are going to travel around Asia. Listen to them talking about their trip. What two decisions do they make?

Practice the conversation.

B I'm so excited. I can't stop thinking about this trip.
G Me, too. I spend all my time just looking at maps.
B What do you think? Should we take cash or traveler's checks?
G I think we should take traveler's checks. It'll be safer.
B Yeah, I think you're right.
G When should we go to Thailand?
B Well, I don't think we should go during the rainy season. I'd rather go in February or March, when it's drier.
G Sounds like a good idea to me. I can't wait to get going!

2 Use *I think we should …* or *I don't think we should …* to make more suggestions. Match a line in **A** with a sentence in **B**.

I think we should buy some guidebooks. They'll give us a lot of information.

A	B
1. … buy some guidebooks.	Our bags will be too heavy to carry.
2. … take plenty of sunscreen.	I have some friends there.
3. … pack too many clothes.	We don't want to get sick.
4. … take anything valuable.	It'll be really hot.
5. … go to Japan first.	That would be really stupid.
6. … go anywhere dangerous.	They'll give us a lot of information.
7. … get some vaccinations.	We might lose it.

Passengers must report
to the boarding gate
at least 30 minutes
before departure

Passengers
must have a
valid ticket
to board
train

RIGHT LANE
MUST
TURN RIGHT

You must keep
your luggage
with you
at all times

3 Brad and George see these signs and notices
as they travel. Are they … ?

- in a train station
- on a highway
- at an airport
- at a bus station

GRAMMAR SPOT

1 Look at the sentences below.

We **should** take traveler's checks.
Passengers **must** have a valid ticket.

Which sentence expresses strong
obligation?
Which sentence expresses a suggestion?

2 What type of verbs are *should* and *must*?

▶▶ **Grammar Reference 4.2 p. 142**

PRACTICE

Suggestions and rules

1 Make suggestions. Use *I think … should* or *I don't think … should*.

  1. Peter has the flu.
     I think he should go to bed. I don't think he should go to work.
  2. I lost my checkbook and credit cards.
  3. Tony got his driver's license last week, and now he wants to drive from Los Angeles to New York.
  4. My sister doesn't get out of bed until noon.
  5. I never have any money!
  6. Jane and Paul are only 16, but they say they want to get married.
  7. I'm really sick of my job.
  8. My grandparents complain that they don't go out enough.

  Do you have any problems? Ask the class for advice.

2 Write some rules for your school.

  Students must pay their tuition by the first week of the semester.

A new job

3 **T 4.5** Dave is about to start a new job. Listen to him talking to the manager. What's the new job?

4 Work in pairs. Choose a job. Then ask and answer questions about the responsibilities, hours, breaks, etc.

Student A You are going to start the job next week.

Student B You are the boss.

What time do I have to start?

Do I have to wear a uniform?

When can I take a break?

Check it

5 There is a mistake in each sentence. Find and correct it.

  1. Do you can help me?
  2. What time have you to start work?
  3. We no allowed to wear jeans at school.
  4. We no can do what we want.
  5. My mother have to work very hard six days a week.
  6. You no should smoke. Is bad for your health.
  7. Passengers must to have a ticket.

WRITING: Filling out a form
 Go to page 113

READING AND SPEAKING
How to behave abroad

1 Are these statements true (✔) or false (✗) for people in your country?

    1. ☐ When we meet someone for the first time, we shake hands.

    2. ☐ Friends kiss on both cheeks when they meet or when they say good-bye.

    3. ☐ We often invite people to our home for a meal.

    4. ☐ If you have arranged to do something with friends, it's OK to be a little late.

    5. ☐ You shouldn't yawn in public.

    6. ☐ We call most people by their first names.

2 Read the text "A World Guide to Good Manners." These lines have been taken out of the text. Where do they go?

    a. many people prefer not to discuss business while eating

    b. some businesses close in the early afternoon for a couple of hours

    c. for greeting, eating, or drinking

    d. the deeper you should bow

    e. should wear long-sleeved blouses and skirts below the knee

3 Answer the questions.

    1. What nationality are the people in the pictures? How do you know?

    2. What are the two differences between the American and the Japanese greeting?

    3. Is your main meal of the day the same as in Latin America?

    4. In which countries do they prefer not to discuss business during meals?

    5. List some of the clothes you think women shouldn't wear in Asian and Muslim countries.

    6. What are some of the rules about business cards?

    7. Why is it not a good idea to say to your Japanese business colleagues, "I don't feel like staying out late tonight"?

    8. Which Extra Tips are about food and drink? Which ones are about general behavior?

What do you think?

Discuss these questions in groups.

- There is a saying in English, "When in Rome, do as the Romans do." What does it mean? Do you agree? Do you have a similar saying in your language?

- Think of one or two examples of bad manners in your country. For example, in the United States it is considered impolite to ask very personal questions such as "How much do you earn?" or "Why aren't you married?" You should be careful if you talk about politics and religion.

- What advice would you give somebody coming to live and work in your country?

A WORLD GUIDE TO GOOD MANNERS
How not to behave badly abroad
by Eva Vorderman

Traveling to all corners of the world gets easier and easier. We live in a global village, but this doesn't mean that we all behave the same way.

Greetings

How should you behave when you meet someone for the first time? An American or Canadian shakes your hand firmly while looking you straight in the eyes. In many parts of Asia, there is no physical contact at all. In Japan, you should bow, and the more respect you want to show, (1) _____ . In Thailand, the greeting is made by pressing both hands together at the chest, as if you are praying, and bowing your head slightly. In both countries, eye contact is avoided as a sign of respect.

Food and drink

In Italy, Spain, and Latin America, lunch is the biggest meal of the day, and can last two or three hours. For this reason many people eat a light breakfast and a late dinner. In the United States, you might have a business lunch and do business as you eat. In Mexico and Japan, (2) _____ . Lunch is a time to relax and socialize, and the Japanese rarely drink alcohol at lunchtime. In the United States and Britain, it's not unusual to have a business meeting over breakfast, and in China it's common to have business banquets, but you shouldn't discuss business during the meal.

Clothes

Many countries have rules about what you should and shouldn't wear. In Asian and Muslim countries, you shouldn't reveal the body, especially women who (3) _____ . In Japan, you should take off your shoes when entering a house or a restaurant. Remember to place them neatly together facing the door you came in. This is also true in China, Korea, and Thailand.

Doing business

In most countries, an exchange of business cards is essential for all introductions. You should include your company name and your position. If you are going to a country where your language is not widely spoken, you can get the reverse side of your card printed in the local language. In Japan, you must present your card with both hands, with the writing facing the person you are giving it to.

In many countries, business hours are from 9 or 10 A.M. to 5 or 6 P.M. However in some countries, such as Greece, Italy, and Spain, (4) _____ then remain open until the evening.

Japanese business people consider it their professional duty to go out after work with colleagues to restaurants, bars, or nightclubs. If you are invited, you shouldn't refuse, even if you don't feel like staying out late.

Extra Tips

Here are some extra tips before you travel:

- In many Asian cultures, it is acceptable to smack your lips when you eat. It means that the food is good.

- In Thailand, you should never point your foot at anyone—it is considered rude.

- In India and the Middle East, you must never use the left hand (5) _____ .

- The Chinese generally do not use their hands when speaking and become distracted by speakers who do.

- Most South Americans and Mexicans like to stand very close to the person they're talking to. You shouldn't back away.

- In China, if you don't want refills of tea during a meal, you should leave some in your cup.

- In Indonesia, it is considered impolite to disagree, so people rarely say "no." One way to indicate a "no" is to suck air in through the teeth.

- In the Philippines, social events sometimes end with singing and dancing. You may be asked to sing.

- In Bulgaria, a nod means "no," and a shake of the head means "yes."

VOCABULARY
Nationality words

1 Complete the chart with the country and the nationality adjective. Put in the stress marks.

Country	Adjective
the U'nited 'States	A'merican
Ja'pan	
_____	Chi'nese
'Mexico	
_____	Ko'rean
Greece	
_____	Thai
Bra'zil	_____

T 4.6 Listen and check.

2 Match a line in **A** with a line in **B**. Notice the stress marks.

A	B
The I'talians	cook lots of noodles and rice.
The Chi'nese	produce champagne.
The 'British	eat raw fish.
The Ca'nadians	invented fish-and-chips.
The French	eat a lot of pasta.
The Japanese	watch ice hockey on TV.

> **!**
> **1** Notice that all nationality words have capital letters in English.
>
>   the French   the Mexicans   the Koreans
>
> **2** If the adjective ends in /s/, /z/, /ʃ/, or /tʃ/ there is no -s at the end of the people.
>
>   Japanese   the Japanese
>   Irish   the Irish

3 Complete the chart and mark the stress. Add some more countries.

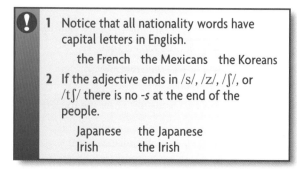

Country	Adjective	A sentence about the people
'Italy	I'talian	Italians like to eat pasta.
'Thailand		
Aust'ralia		
'Russia		
'Mexico		
the U'nited 'States		
'Britain		

LISTENING AND SPEAKING
Come over to my place!

1 Have you ever been a guest in someone's home in a foreign country? When? Why? What happened?

2 **T 4.7** Work in three groups. You will hear three people talking about what happens when they invite guests home for a meal. Listen and take notes.

Aya – Nagano, Japan	Mary – Columbus, Ohio	Lucas – Porto Alegre, Brazil

	Aya	Mary	Lucas
Formal or informal invitation?			
Day and time			
Preparations the host or hostess has to make			
What gifts guests usually bring			
The food and drink served			

3 Work with students from the other groups. Compare your information. What similarities and differences are there?

4 What happens when you invite guests home in your country? Is it usual to invite people to your home for a meal? What are such occasions like in your home?

EVERYDAY ENGLISH
Requests and offers

1 Match a line in **A** with a line in **B**. Who is talking to who? Where are the conversations taking place?

A	B
1. Could we have the check, please?	Diet or regular?
2. Could you fill it up, please?	No problem. It's stuffy in here.
3. Can I help you?	Sure. Should I check the oil, too?
4. Two large sodas, please.	That line's busy. Would you like to hold?
5. Can you tell me the city code for Seoul, please?	Yes, sir. I'll bring it right away.
6. Can I give you a ride?	One moment. I'll look it up.
7. Would you mind opening the window?	Just looking, thanks.
8. Could I have extension 238, please?	That would be great! Could you drop me off at the library?

2 **T 4.8** Listen and check. Which are requests? Which are offers? Practice the conversations, paying particular attention to intonation and stress.

▶▶ **Grammar Reference 4.3 and 4.4 pp. 142–143**

3 **T 4.9** Listen to the conversations. Where are the people? What is the relationship between them?

Where are they?	What's their relationship?
1.	
2.	
3.	
4.	

T 4.9 Listen again. What are the words used to make each request?

Could you ... ?

1. _____   3. _____
2. _____   4. _____

Role play

Work in pairs. Choose one of the situations and make up a conversation using the prompts.

Situation 1	Situation 2	Situation 3
Student A You are a customer in a restaurant. **Student B** You are a server. *Use these words:* • table near the window • menu • order • clean fork • dessert • check	**Student A** You are going away on vacation very soon. **Student B** Offer to help. *Use these words:* • pack • confirm flight • lock the suitcases • give me a ride • take care of the cat • water the plants	**Student A** You are cooking a meal for 20 people. **Student B** Offer to help. *Use these words:* • prepare the vegetables • make the salad • stir the sauce • check the meat • set the table

5 On the move

TEST YOUR GRAMMAR

1 Match a sentence in **A** with a sentence in **B**. <u>Underline</u> the verb forms that refer to the future. What is the difference between them?

A	B
1. The phone's ringing.	I think it's going to rain.
2. Look at those black clouds!	Don't worry! It'll be spring soon.
3. What are you doing tonight?	We might go to Florida, or we might go to Mexico.
4. I'm sick and tired of winter!	I'll get it!
5. Where are you going on your vacation?	I'm staying home. I'm going to watch a video.

I'll get it!

2 Answer the questions about you.
- What are you doing after class today?
- What's the weather forecast for tomorrow?
- Where are you going on your next vacation?

BILL'S LIST
Future forms

1 Bill always writes a list at the beginning of the day. Read his list on page 35. Where's he going today? What's he going to do?

He's going to get a haircut.
He's going to fill up the car with gas.
He's going to buy some sugar.

Things to do
haircut
gas
electric bill—bank
tickets—travel agent
library
visit Nick?

Things to buy
sugar
yogurt
milk
tennis balls

2 **T 5.1** Listen and complete the conversation between Bill and Alice.

B I'm going shopping. Do we need anything?

A I don't think so. … Oh, wait. We don't have any sugar.

B It's OK, it's on my list. I _____ some.

A What about bread?

B Good idea! I _____ a loaf.

A What time will you be back?

B I don't know. I might stop at Nick's. It depends on how much time I have.

A Don't forget, we _____ tennis with David and Pam this afternoon.

B Don't worry. I _____ forget. I _____ back before then.

A OK. See you later, Honey.

In pairs, memorize the conversation. Close your books and practice the conversation.

3 Alice also asks Bill to get these things.

- stamps
- two steaks
- some shampoo
- some film for my camera
- a newspaper
- a can of white paint
- a video
- a CD

Which stores will Bill go to? Work with a partner to make conversations.

Can you get some stamps, please, Honey?

OK. I'll go to the post office.

And we need some … . Don't forget …

GRAMMAR SPOT

1 Look at these future forms from the conversation:
It's on my list. **I'm going to buy** some.
Good idea! **I'll pick up** a loaf.

In one case, Bill made the decision before speaking. In the other case, he made the decision at the moment of speaking. Which is which?

2 Which of the following sentences expresses …

- a future possibility?
- a future arrangement?

We**'re playing** tennis this afternoon.
I **might stop** at Nick's.

▶▶ **Grammar Reference 5.1 p. 143**

PRACTICE

Going on vacation

1 **T 5.2** Listen to Mike and Cindy talking. Are they …

- on vacation?
- getting ready to go on vacation?
- talking about where to go on vacation?

Make five sentences with *going to* about Mike and Cindy.

They're going to take a plane.

What do you think will happen?

2 Use the words in **A** to make sentences with *I think … will*. Match them with a sentence in **B**.

I think Jerry will win the tennis match. He's been playing really well lately.

A	B
1. Jerry/win the tennis match	—— But we'd better get going.
2. it/be a nice day tomorrow	_1_ He's been playing really well lately.
3. I/pass my test on Friday	—— The forecast is for warm and dry weather.
4. you/like the movie	—— You have the right qualifications and plenty of experience.
5. we/get to the airport in time	—— It's a wonderful story, and the acting is excellent.
6. you/get the job	—— I've been studying for weeks.

T 5.3 Listen and check.

3 Make sentences with *I don't think … will* using the words in **A** in Exercise 2. Match them with a sentence in **C**.

I don't think Jerry will win the tennis match. He hasn't practiced for weeks.

C
____ There's too much traffic.
____ I haven't studied at all.
____ The forecast said rainy and windy.
_1_ He hasn't practiced for weeks.
____ They're looking for someone with more experience.
____ It's kind of boring.

T 5.4 Listen and check.

Talking about you

4 Make true sentences starting with *I think …* or *I don't think … .*

1. I/bath tonight
   I think I'll take a bath tonight.
   I don't think I'll take a bath tonight.
2. the teacher/give us a lot of homework
3. I/eat out tonight
4. it/rain tomorrow
5. I/go shopping this afternoon
6. I/be a millionaire someday
7. we/have a test this semester

Arranging to meet

5 **T 5.5** Two friends, Liz and Han, are making arrangements to meet over the weekend. What are they doing? Listen and complete the chart.

	Liz	Han
Friday	*going to a dance class*	
Saturday		

Where and what time do they manage to meet?

6 It is Friday morning. You need to arrange to meet a friend over the weekend. Fill in your calendar. What are you doing this weekend? When are you free?

FRIDAY
morning   afternoon   evening

SATURDAY
morning   afternoon   evening

SUNDAY
morning   afternoon   evening

7 In pairs, think of a reason to get together this weekend. Then arrange to meet.

> *What are you doing this afternoon?*

> *I'm going swimming. / I might get together with some friends in town.*

When you are finished, tell the class when and where you're meeting.

We're meeting on Sunday morning at my place. We're going to . . .

READING AND SPEAKING
My kind of vacation

1 Look at the photos of the three hotels and answer the questions.
- Which countries do you think they're in?
- What do you think people can do on vacation there?

The Ice Hotel

The Burj al-Arab

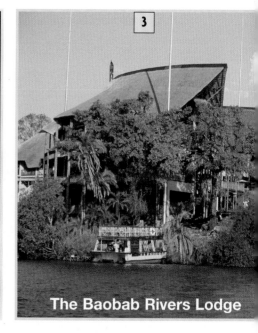

The Baobab Rivers Lodge

2 Write one more question about each hotel.

1 How do you keep warm at night?

_____ ?

2 What's that funny horizontal tube at the top?

_____ ?

3 How do you get there?

_____ ?

3 Read the article and hotel brochure on page 39. Answer the questions in Exercise 2. Then in pairs, answer the questions below.
- What is Karen's job?
- Why does she take working vacations?
- What is her idea of a perfect vacation?
- Why does she spend her vacations at home?
- Animals are mentioned. Which ones, and why?

4 Complete the chart about Karen's trips to Canada and Dubai.

Which country is she going to next?	Which hotel is she staying at?	How long is she staying there?	What's special about the hotel and her room?	What's she going to do there?
Canada				
Dubai				

5 In pairs, look at the brochure for the Baobab Rivers Lodge in Selous, Tanzania. Ask and answer questions about Karen's trip there.

Language work

6 Find words or expressions in the text with similar meanings.

Section 1
1. doing nothing *lazing*
2. stopping to look around in
3. I'm very interested in
4. move around without any hurry

Section 2
5. in an exciting and impressive way
6. something that should not be missed

What do you think?

- What is your ideal vacation?
- Where are you going for your next vacation?

WRITING: Making a reservation
▶▶ Go to page 114

My Kind of Vacation

She travels for her job, but when it's her own vacation, Karen Saunders stays home.

Karen Saunders has her own travel agency in San Francisco that sends people all over the world on their dream vacations. She needs to know where she's sending them, so she goes on working vacations four or five times a year.

My ideal vacation

My ideal vacation has a little bit of everything. I like lazing on a beach with a pile of books, but then I get bored and I need to do something. I love exploring new places, especially on foot, and poking around in churches, stores, museums, and restaurants. I'm very into cooking, so I love going around markets and food stores.

However, I must confess that my favorite "vacation resort" is home. I travel so much in my job that just waking up in my own bed is heaven. I putter around the house in my pajamas, read the paper, do some gardening, shop for some food, then make a delicious meal in the evening.

My business vacations

I have three trips coming up. I'm looking forward to going to Canada soon, where I'm staying for four nights at the Ice Hotel. This is a giant igloo situated in Montmorency Fall Park, just 20 minutes from downtown Quebec. It is made from 4,500 tons of snow and 250 tons of ice, and it takes 5 weeks to build. It will stay open for three months. When the spring arrives, it will melt. Then it will be built again for next year—maybe in a different location! Each room is supplied with a sleeping bag made from deer pelts. The hotel has two art galleries featuring ice sculptures, and an ice movie theater. It also has a bar where all the drinks come in glasses made of ice. Of course I'll visit them all!

In complete contrast to the Ice Hotel, I'm going to Dubai the following month, to stay a few days at the spectacular Burj al-Arab, which means the Arabian Tower. It's shaped like a giant sail, and it rises dramatically out of the Arabian Gulf. Each room has sea views. I really want to try the restaurant in the tube at the top next to the helipad. Other must-dos include shopping in the markets, called *souks*. (You can buy designer clothes, perfumes, and spices, but what I want is some gold jewelry.) I'm also going to visit the camel races.

The next trip, different ~~~~ ~~~~~~~~~~ rs,

The Baobab Rivers Lodge in Selous, Tanzania—so remote, you arrive by boat

What to see:

Each tree-top room has views over the vast forested banks of the Rufiji River, which runs through one of the largest game reserves in Africa

What to do:

Safari by Land Rover in search of elephants, rhinos, and lions; or by boat along the Rufiji River in search of crocodiles, hippos, and rare birds

LISTENING AND VOCABULARY
A weather forecast

1 Look at the map of the United States. What do you know about the places named on the map?

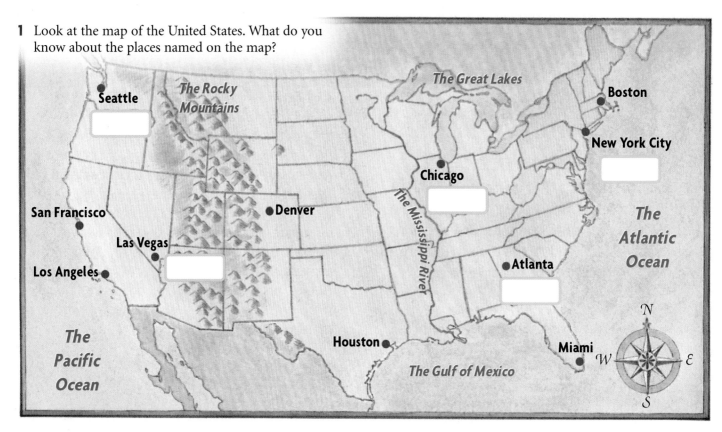

2 Put the adjectives about temperature in the right order.

cold	warm	freezing	chilly	hot

3 Complete the chart with words from the box.

sunny sunshine shining snowing windy wind fog
stormy ice blowing snowy icy cloud rain snow
raining storm/thunderstorm cloudy foggy rainy

4 **T 5.6** Listen to the weather forecast for the United States. Mark on the map what the weather will be like today. Use the words in Exercise 3, and write the temperatures next to the places on the map.

5 Work in pairs. Write a weather forecast for where you are. Read it to the rest of the class.

	Adjective	Noun	Verb
	It's _sunny._	_sunshine_	The sun's _shining._
	It's _____	_____	It's _____
	It's _____	_____	It's _____
	It's _____	_____	The wind is _____
	It's _____	_____	
	It's _____	_____	
	It's _____	_____	
	It's _____	_____	

EVERYDAY ENGLISH
Traveling around

1 Here are some lines from conversations on different kinds of transportation. Where does each conversation take place? Choose from the box.

car	bus	taxi	subway	train	plane	ferry

1. Do you think it'll be a rough crossing?
2. Excuse me, I think those seats facing the front are ours.
3. We're going to Market Street. Could you tell us when it's our stop?
4. Can you take us to the airport?
5. Can I take these bags on with me?
6. Here you go. Keep the change.
7. Excuse me, are we landing on time?
8. No, no! He said turn left at the light, not right!
9. Which line goes to Yankee Stadium?

2 Match a line in Exercise 1 with a reply.

<u>8</u> a. Look! *You* drive and *I'll* navigate from now on!

___ b. Sure. Hop in!

___ c. I'm sorry. Only one carry-on item per passenger.

___ d. Oh, I'm sorry. We didn't know they were reserved.

___ e. Yes. We're beginning our descent soon.

___ f. Well, the forecast is good, so it should be pretty smooth.

___ g. Just sit up front and I'll call it out.

___ h. Go downstairs and follow the signs for the number 4 train going uptown.

___ i. Thank you, sir. Can I help you with those bags?

T 5.7 Listen and check. Practice the conversations with a partner.

Role play

Work in pairs. You are in a hotel.

Student A You are the receptionist at the front desk.
Student B You are a guest.

The guest has several requests, and calls the front desk from his/her room. Change roles after three conversations.

Situation: There are no towels in the room.

A Can I help you?
B Yes, there are no towels in my room. Could you send some up, please?
A Certainly. I'll take care of it right away.
B Thanks. Bye.

Student B Use these situations:

- You'd like some coffee and a sandwich in your room.
- You want the telephone number of the train station.
- You want the front desk to recommend a good place to eat.
- You can't get the television to work.
- You want a wake-up call at 7:00 in the morning.
- You want to order a taxi to take you to the airport.

6 I just love it!

like · Verb patterns · Describing food, places, and people · Around town

TEST YOUR GRAMMAR

1 Complete these sentences about yourself.

I look just like my dog.

1. I like my coffee …
   I like my coffee black with no sugar.
2. I look just like my …
3. On Sundays, I like …
4. After this class, I'd like to …
5. When I'm on vacation, I enjoy …
6. Yesterday evening, I decided to …

2 Tell the class some of the things you wrote.

A STUDENT VISITOR
Questions with *like*

1 Many students come from other countries to study in the United States. They sometimes stay with an American family. Do you know anyone who has been to study in the United States?

2 Sandy's family has just welcomed Soon-hee, an exchange student from Seoul, South Korea, to their home in Ohio. Sandy is telling her friend Nina about Soon-hee. Put one of the questions from the box into each blank in the conversation.

> What does she like doing?   How is she?   What's she like?
> What does she look like?   What would she like to do?

Sandy Our student from Seoul arrived on Monday.
Nina What's her name?
Sandy Soon-hee.
Nina That's a pretty name! (1) __What's she like?__
Sandy She's really nice. I'm sure we'll get along well. We seem to have a lot in common.
Nina How do you know that already? (2) _____
Sandy Well, she likes dancing, and so do I. And we both like listening to the same kind of music.
Nina (3) _____
Sandy She's really pretty. She has big, brown eyes and long, dark hair.
Nina Why don't we do something with Soon-hee this weekend? What should we do? Get a pizza? Go to the movies? (4) _____
Sandy I'll ask her tonight. She was kind of homesick at first, so I'm pretty sure she'll want to go out and make some friends.
Nina (5) _____ now?
Sandy Oh, she's OK now. She called her folks back home and she felt much better after she spoke to them.
Nina Oh, that's good. I can't wait to meet her.

PRACTICE

Talking about you

1 Ask and answer the questions with a partner.
- What do you like doing on weekends?
- Who do you look like in your family?
- What is your best friend like?
- What's your school like?
- What does your teacher look like?
- How are your parents and grandparents?

Listening and asking questions

2 **T 6.2** Listen and put a check (✓) next to the question each person is answering.

1. ☐ Do you like Thai food?
   ☐ What's Thai food like?

2. ☐ Who does Bridget look like?
   ☐ What's Bridget like?

3. ☐ How's your father?
   ☐ What's your father like?

4. ☐ What does she like?
   ☐ What does she look like?

5. ☐ What's the weather like there?
   ☐ Do you like the weather there?

6. ☐ What does he look like?
   ☐ What's he like?

7. ☐ What do you like doing on vacation?
   ☐ What was your vacation like?

8. ☐ What kind of books do you like?
   ☐ What kind of books would you like?

3 **T 6.1** Listen and check. Practice the conversation with a partner.

GRAMMAR SPOT

1 Write a question from Exercise 2 next to the correct definition.

Question	Definition
a. **What's she like?**	= Tell me about her because I don't know anything about her.
b. _____	= Tell me about her physical appearance.
c. _____	= Tell me about her interests and hobbies.
d. _____	= Tell me about her preferences for tomorrow evening.
e. _____	= Tell me about her health or happiness.

2 In which questions above is *like* used as a verb, and in which is it used as a preposition?

▶▶ **Grammar Reference 6.1–6.3 p. 144**

A THANK YOU LETTER
Verb patterns

1 Soon-hee has returned home to Seoul. Read her letter and circle the correct verb form.

Sang-chul and me

SOON-HEE

Seoul
December 15

Dear Sandy and family,

I just wanted (1) (to say)/saying thank you for (2) to have/having me as your guest in your beautiful home. I had a great time. I really enjoyed (3) meeting/to meet your friends. You all made me (4) feel/to feel so welcome. You know how much I missed my family at first, but you were so kind that I soon stopped (5) to feel/feeling homesick. I can't find the words to tell you how grateful I am. I'd like (6) to call/calling you sometime. What's a good time to call?

You know that on my way home I stopped (7) to visit/visiting my aunt in Canada. Toronto was so cold. It snowed all the time, but I loved it. My aunt wanted (8) that I stay/me to stay longer, but I wanted (9) to see/seeing my parents and my brother. But my aunt has invited me (10) to go/going back and I'd love (11) to do/ to doing that. I'm thinking of (12) go/going next year.

Anyway, I'm looking forward to (13) hear/hearing from you very soon. Let me (14) to know/know if you ever want to visit Seoul. My brother and I could take you to a "nore bang" (a singing room). It's kind of like karaoke!

Love to you all,
Soon-hee
p.s. How do you like the picture of my brother and me?

rson
ia Drive
IN 46614
USA

2 **T 6.3** Listen and check.

Grammar Reference 6.4 p. 144

Verb Patterns p. 153

GRAMMAR SPOT

1 We use *-ing* after some verbs and after prepositions.
   I **love cooking** so I'm thinking **of taking** a cooking class.

2 We use the infinitive (*to* + Simple verb) after some verbs.
   I **wanted to go** home early.
   They **asked** me **to leave** the room.

3 *Make* and *let* are followed by the Simple verb.
   She **made** him **go** to bed, but she **let** him **read** for a while.

4 Match a sentence with a picture.
   ___ They stopped to talk to each other.
   ___ They stopped talking to each other.

PRACTICE

What's the pattern?

1 Fill in the columns with the verb patterns from Soon-hee's letter.

1	2	3	4	5
verb + *-ing*	verb + *to*	verb + person + *to*	verb + person + simple verb	verb + preposition + *-ing*
enjoyed meeting	wanted to say	wanted me to stay	made me feel	thank you for having

2 **T 6.4** Listen to the sentences and add the verbs to the correct columns in Exercise 1.

1. tell
2. promise
3. finish
4. help
5. forget
6. hate
7. can't stand
8. need
9. ask
10. succeed in

Look at the list of verb patterns on page 153 and check your answers.

Discussing grammar

3 In these sentences, two verbs are correct and one is not. Put a check (✓) next to the correct verbs.

1. My father _____ to fix my bike.
   a. ☑ promised   b. ☐ couldn't   c. ☑ tried

2. She _____ her son to turn down his music.
   a. ☐ asked   b. ☐ wanted   c. ☐ made

3. I _____ going on long walks.
   a. ☐ refuse   b. ☐ can't stand   c. ☐ love

4. We _____ to go shopping.
   a. ☐ need   b. ☐ 'd love   c. ☐ enjoy

5. She _____ me do the cooking.
   a. ☐ wanted   b. ☐ made   c. ☐ helped

6. I _____ working for the bank 20 years ago.
   a. ☐ started   b. ☐ stopped   c. ☐ decided

4 Make correct sentences using the other verbs in Exercise 3.
   My father couldn't fix my bike.

READING AND SPEAKING
The world's favorite food

1 Do you know any typical dishes from these countries? Discuss with your class.

- the United States
- Japan
- Italy
- Mexico
- India
- Brazil
- Australia
- China
- England

Can you think of any foods that might be popular in all of the countries above?

2 Which of the following are fish or seafood? How do you pronounce the words?

> anchovies   garlic   eel   oil   shrimp   bacon   squid
> salmon   peas   sweet corn   herring   pineapple   tuna

T 6.5 Listen and repeat the words.

3 Work in groups. Read the text quickly and find the foods listed above. How many other foods can you find?

4 Read the text again and answer the questions.
1. What are the similarities and differences between the hamburger and pizza?
2. What year was pizza invented?
3. Which came first, "picea" or "plakuntos"? How are they different from pizza?
4. Why are Mexico and Peru important in the development of pizza?
5. What do the Italian flag and a Pizza Margherita have in common?
6. When and how did pizza become really popular in the United States?

5 Work in groups. Read "Pizza Trivia" again and make questions. Use these question words.

How many ... ?   How much ... ?   Which month ... ?
Where and when ... ?   Which toppings ... ?

Close your books. Ask and answer questions.

What do you think?
- Which three facts in "Pizza Trivia" do you find most interesting? Why?
- Why do different countries prefer such different toppings?
- Do you like pizza? What are your favorite toppings?
- What are the most popular places to eat in your country? Why? Which is your favorite place to eat?

Language work

Study the text and find the following.
1. An example of *like* used as a verb and an example of *like* used as a preposition.
2. An example of a verb that is followed by an *-ing* form.
3. An example of a verb that is followed by an infinitive.
4. An example of an adjective + infinitive.

Naples, Italy

GLOBAL PIZZA

by Connie Odone

So you thought the hamburger was the world's most popular fast food? After all, McDonald's Golden Arches span the globe. But no, there is another truly universal fast food, the ultimate fast food. It's easy to make, easy to serve, much more varied than the hamburger, can be eaten with the hands, and it's delivered to your front door or served in fancy restaurants. It's been one of America's favorite foods for over 50 years. It is, of course, the pizza.

It's kind of silly to talk about the moment when pizza was "invented." It gradually evolved over the years, but one thing's for sure—it existed long before the discovery of the Americas. The idea of using pieces of flat, round bread as plates came from the Greeks. They called them "plakuntos" and ate them with various simple toppings such as oil, garlic, onions, and herbs. The Romans enjoyed eating something similar and called it "picea." By about 1000 A.D. in the city of Naples, "picea" had become "pizza" and people were experimenting with more toppings: cheese, ham, anchovies, and finally the tomato, brought to Italy from Mexico and Peru in the sixteenth century. Naples became the pizza capital of the world. In 1889, King Umberto I and Queen Margherita heard about pizza and asked to try it. They invited pizza maker Rafaele Esposito to make it for them. He decided to make the pizza like the Italian flag, so he used red tomatoes, white mozzarella cheese, and green basil leaves. The Queen loved it and the new pizza was named "Pizza Margherita" in her honor.

Pizza migrated to America with the Italians at the end of the nineteenth century. The first pizzeria in the United States was opened in 1905 at 53½ Spring Street, New York City, by Gennaro Lombardi. But the popularity of pizza really exploded when American soldiers returned from Italy after World War II and raved about "that great Italian dish." Americans are now the greatest producers and consumers of pizza in the world.

Pizza Trivia

1. Americans eat 350 slices of pizza per second.
2. There are 61,269 pizzerias in the United States.
3. Pizza is a $30 billion per year industry.
4. October is national pizza month.
5. The world's first pizzeria, the Antica Pizzeria Port'Alba, which opened in Naples in 1830, is still there.
6. Pizza Hut has over 12,000 restaurants and delivery/take-out units in over 90 countries.
7. In the United States, pepperoni is the favorite topping. Anchovies is the least favorite.
8. In Japan, eel, corn, and squid are favorites. In Russia, it's red herring, salmon, and onions.
9. In Brazil, green peas are popular on pizza; in Australia, shrimp and pineapple. Costa Ricans like coconut.
10. The French like bacon, onions, and fresh cream on theirs. The English like tuna and sweet corn.

VOCABULARY AND PRONUNCIATION
Adjectives for food, towns, and people

1 Look at the groups of words. In each diagram, four of the surrounding words cannot go with the noun in the center. Put an ✗ through them.

junk fresh fast delicious disgusting ~~disgusted~~ **FOOD** plain tasteless ~~tasteful~~ frozen rich homegrown vegetarian wealthy starving

excited exciting home old modern college polluted **TOWN** young busy antique capital cosmopolitan industrial historic agricultural small

young antique long elderly sophisticated expensive **PEOPLE** shy bored boring starving wealthy sociable reserved rude crowded tall

2 Fill in the blanks with adjectives from Exercise 1. Use a different word in each blank. If necessary, use the comparative or superlative forms.

1. **A** Tommy's really quiet and __shy__ . He didn't say a word.
    B Well, he's only three. He is the __youngest__ in the family.
2. **A** What is Carrie's brother like?
    B Well, he's _____ , dark, and handsome, but he's not very polite. In fact, he's even _____ than Carrie!
3. **A** How was your lunch?
    B Yuck! It was awful. The pizza was _____ . We were really _____ , but we still couldn't eat it!
4. **A** Mmm! These tomatoes are really _____ . Did you grow them yourselves?
    B Yes, we did. All our vegetables are _____ .
5. **A** Did you have a good time in London?
    B We had a great time. There's so much to do. It's a really _____ city. And there are so many people from all over the world. I think it's almost as _____ as New York.

T 6.6 Listen and compare your answers. Practice the conversations with a partner.

Talking about you

Go to page 102.

LISTENING AND SPEAKING
New York and London

1 Look at the pictures of New York and London. Write down what you know about these cities. Compare your lists as a class. Has anyone been to either city?

2 Work in two groups.

Group A `T 6.7` Listen to Justin and Cinda who live in New York.

They used to live and work in London. They moved to New York because of Justin's job. Listen and take notes.

Group B `T 6.8` Listen to Alan who lives in London.

Alan is an American who has lived and worked in London for the past 15 years. Listen and take notes.

What do they say about the following?
- the people
- places
- work, vacations, and holidays
- getting around
- stores
- food

Speaking

3 Find a partner from the other group. Compare your information.

WRITING: Describing a room
▶▶ Go to page 115

EVERYDAY ENGLISH
Sights and sounds

1 Where would you see the following?

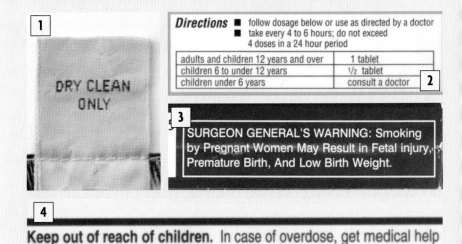

1 DRY CLEAN ONLY

Directions ■ follow dosage below or use as directed by a doctor
■ take every 4 to 6 hours; do not exceed 4 doses in a 24 hour period

adults and children 12 years and over	1 tablet
children 6 to under 12 years	½ tablet
children under 6 years	consult a doctor

2

3 SURGEON GENERAL'S WARNING: Smoking by Pregnant Women May Result in Fetal injury, Premature Birth, And Low Birth Weight.

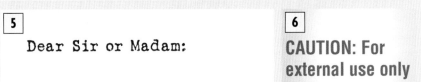

4 **Keep out of reach of children.** In case of overdose, get medical help or contact a Poison Control Center right away.

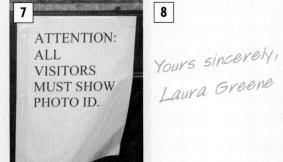

5 Dear Sir or Madam:

6 CAUTION: For external use only

7 ATTENTION: ALL VISITORS MUST SHOW PHOTO ID.

8 Yours sincerely, Laura Greene

9 BAGGAGE CLAIM

GROUND TRANSPORTATION

2 Where would you hear the following?

Coming up next—traffic, news, and the weather.

Please place your tray tables in their fully upright and locked positions.

Just looking, thanks.

A table for four, please.

Give my love to everyone at home.

7 The world of work

TEST YOUR GRAMMAR

1 Answer these questions about yourself.

What do you do?

PRESS

1. What do you do?
2. How long have you had your current job?
3. What did you do before that?
4. Which foreign countries have you been to?
5. When and why did you go there?

2 Ask and answer the questions in pairs. Tell the rest of the class about your partner.
Eun-mi is a student.
She's been at Seoul National University for ...
She's been to ...

3 What tenses are used in the questions?

THE JOB INTERVIEW
Present Perfect

1 Read the job advertisement. Do you have any of the qualifications?

BUSINESS JOURNALIST
WORLDWATCH AMERICAS

This international business magazine, with one million readers worldwide, is seeking a journalist, based in Santiago, Chile, to cover business news in Latin America.

Requirements:

- A bachelor's degree in journalism
- At least two years' experience in business journalism
- Fluent in Spanish and English. If possible, have some knowledge of Portuguese
- Excellent communication skills
- International travel experience is a plus

We offer a good salary, full benefits, and paid vacation.

Please send a resume to:

George Butler
WORLDWATCH AMERICAS
7950 Merritts Avenue
Overland Park, IL 51551

2 **T 7.1** Listen to Heather Mann being interviewed by George Butler. Do you think she will get the job? Why or why not?

3 Read the first part of Heather's interview. Complete the sentences with *do*, *did*, or *have*.

> **G** Who ___**do**___ you work for now, Heather?
>
> **H** I work for Intertec Publishing. We publish international business magazines.
>
> **G** I see. And how long _____ you worked there?
>
> **H** I _____ worked there for five years. Yes, exactly five years.
>
> **G** And how long _____ you been in charge of East Asia publications?
>
> **H** For two years.
>
> **G** And what _____ you do before you were at Intertec?
>
> **H** I worked as an interpreter for the United Nations.

T 7.1 Listen and check.

GRAMMAR SPOT

1 Does Heather still work for Intertec?
   Does she still work for the UN?

2 Heather says:
   *I **work** for Intertec Publishing.*
   *I**'ve worked** there for five years.*
   *I **worked** as an interpreter in Geneva.*

   What are the different tenses?
   Why are they used?

▶▶ **Grammar Reference 7.1 and 7.2 p. 145**

4 Read and complete the second part of the interview with *did*, *was*, or *have*.

> **G** As you know, this job is based in Santiago, Chile. ___**Have**___ you ever lived abroad before?
>
> **H** Oh, yes. Yes, I _____ .
>
> **G** And when _____ you live abroad?
>
> **H** Well, in fact, I _____ born in Colombia and I lived there until I was 11. Also, I lived in Geneva for one year when I _____ working for the UN.
>
> **G** That's interesting. _____ you traveled much?
>
> **H** Oh, yes. I _____ traveled to most countries in South America and many countries in Europe. I _____ also been to Japan a few times.
>
> **G** Interesting. Why _____ you go to Japan?
>
> **H** It _____ for my job. I went there to interview some Japanese business leaders.

T 7.2 Listen and check.

PRACTICE

Biographies

1 Here are some more events from Heather Mann's life. Match a line in **A** with a time expression in **B**.

A	B
1. She was born	for the last five years.
2. She went to school in Bogota	in Colombia in 1973.
3. She studied business and journalism	from 1978 to 1984.
4. She worked in Geneva	at Boston University.
5. She's been to Japan	since she was in Geneva.
6. She's worked for Intertec	yet.
7. She hasn't lived abroad	a few times.
8. She hasn't gotten a job at Worldwatch Americas	for a year before she worked for Intertec.

T 7.3 Listen and check.

2 Make a similar chart for your own life. Ask your partner to match the events and the times to tell the story of your life.

> **WRITING:** Writing a cover letter
> ▶▶ Go to page 116

Talking about you

3 Complete the sentences about you.
1. I haven't learned to … yet. **I haven't learned to swim yet.**
2. I've been at this school since …
3. I've known my best friend for …
4. I've never …
5. My mother/father has never …
6. I started … ago.
7. I've lived in … since …
8. I went to … when I was a child.

Have you ever … ?

4 These verbs are all irregular. What is the Past Simple and Past Participle?

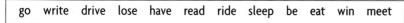

go   write   drive   lose   have   read   ride   sleep   be   eat   win   meet

5 Work with a partner. Choose from the list below and have conversations.
  A Have you ever been to California?
  B Yes, I have. / No, I haven't. I've never been there.
  A When did you go there?
  B Two years ago. I went there on vacation with my family.

- be/to California?
- win/an award?
- have/a serious accident?
- drive/a truck?
- meet/anyone famous?
- ride/a motorcycle?
- be/on TV?
- have/an operation?
- read/a book in English?

Tell the class about your partner.

IT'S IN THE NEWS
Present Perfect active and passive

1 Read the newspaper headlines on page 53. Check any new words.

2 **T 7.4** Read and listen to the TV news headlines of the same stories. Fill in the blanks with the words you hear.

Here are today's news headlines.

1. Convicted murderer Dwayne Locke **has escaped** from the Greenville Correctional Facility in Texas.

2. Two Spanish novelists _____ the Nobel Prize in literature.

3. Hurricane Jeffrey _____ the Caribbean, causing widespread damage in Puerto Rico.

4. Two thousand hotel workers in Anaheim, California _____ due to a slowdown in tourism.

5. Desmond Lewis _____ in the fifth round of his heavyweight championship fight in Las Vegas.

> ### GRAMMAR SPOT
>
> **1** Which of these questions can you answer? Which can't you answer? Why?
>
> Who has escaped from jail?
> Who has given the novelists the Nobel Prize?
> What has hit the Caribbean?
> Who has laid off the hotel workers?
> Who knocked out Desmond Lewis?
>
> **2** Which sentences in Exercise 2 are active? Which are passive?
>
> ▶▶ **Grammar Reference 7.2 p. 145**

NOVELISTS AWARDED NOBEL PRIZE

Hurricane Hits Caribbean

Lewis Knocked Out in 5th Round

Dangerous Prisoner Escapes

HOTEL WORKERS LAID OFF

PRACTICE

Writing news stories

1 Here are some more headlines from newspapers. Make them into TV news headlines. Use the Present Perfect tense.

1. Dangerous Prisoner Recaptured
   The murderer Dwayne Locke has been recaptured by city police.
2. Cruise Ship Sinks Near Florida
   A Sunny Vacations cruise ship has sunk off the coast of Florida, near Miami.
3. Famous Movie Star Leaves $3 Million to Her Pet Cat
4. Priceless Painting Stolen from New York Art Museum
5. Typhoon Kills 20, Leaves 13,000 Homeless
6. 18-Year-Old College Student Elected Mayor
7. Senator Forced to Resign
8. Runner Fails Drug Test

T 7.5 Listen and compare your answers.

2 What's in the news today? What national or international stories do you know?

Discussing grammar

3 Work with a partner and decide which is the correct verb form.
1. The president *has resigned* / *has been resigned* and a new president *has elected* / *has been elected*.
2. His resignation *announced* / *was announced* yesterday on television.
3. "Where *did you go* / *have you gone* on your last vacation?" "To Peru. It was fabulous."
4. "*Did* John ever *go* / *Has* John ever *been* to Paris?" "Oh, yes. Five times."
5. The plane *took off* / *has taken off* a few minutes ago.
6. A huge snowstorm *has hit* / *has been hit* Toronto, where over 50 cm of snow *fell* / *has fallen* in one hour. Residents *have advised* / *have been advised* to stay home.

READING AND SPEAKING
Dream jobs

1 What is your dream job? Close your eyes and think about it. Then answer these questions.

  1. Does the job require a lot of training or experience?
  2. Is it well-paid?
  3. Does it involve working with other people?
  4. Is it indoors or outdoors?
  5. Do you need to be physically strong to do it?
  6. Is it dangerous?
  7. Does it involve travel?

Work with a partner. Ask and answer the questions to guess each other's dream jobs.

2 Here are the stories of three people who believe they have found their dream job.

Divide into three groups.

Group A Read about Stanley Karras, the hurricane hunter.

Group B Read about Linda Spelman, the trapeze artist.

Group C Read about Michael Doyle, the cowboy in the sky.

Answer the questions in Exercise 1 about your person.

What do you think?

3 Find a partner from the other two groups and compare information.

• Which of the jobs do you find most interesting?

• Would you like to do any of them?

4 Read the other two articles quickly. Answer the questions.

  1. Who <u>gets along well</u> with coworkers?
  2. Who <u>took up</u> gymnastics?
  3. Who hasn't <u>come up with</u> an experiment for space yet?
  4. Whose job <u>was handed down</u> from father to son?
  5. Who is <u>cut off from</u> his/her family?
  6. Who finds it exciting <u>to end up</u> in different cities and countries?
  7. Who wants to <u>carry on</u> working until at least 50?
  8. Who often <u>takes off</u> at a moment's notice?
  9. Who <u>came across</u> an ad?

Language work

The <u>underlined</u> words in Exercise 4 are all phrasal verbs. Match them with a verb or expression from the box below.

start doing (a hobby)	separated
leave the ground and fly	pass down
find yourself somewhere unexpectedly	devise/think of
have a good relationship with	find by chance
continue	

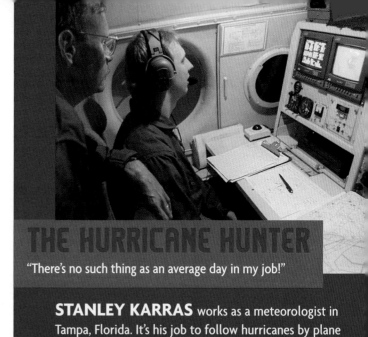

THE HURRICANE HUNTER

"There's no such thing as an average day in my job!"

STANLEY KARRAS works as a meteorologist in Tampa, Florida. It's his job to follow hurricanes by plane and provide information about them to scientists.

How did you get the job? I was working for the National Weather Service in Michigan in the fall of 1995, and I saw a movie with my family called *Storm Chasers*. It was about hurricane hunters and I thought, "Wow, that's an interesting job!" As it happened, two months later I came across an ad for a meteorologist to work with the same people who had made the movie. I applied, was interviewed, and started work here in Tampa in May 1996.

What do you like most about it? I love the travel. I've been all over the world chasing hurricanes. It's exciting to end up in different cities and different countries day after day. If you're a meteorologist, you have to love flying. I also love working with top scientists. I've learned so much from them. For me, it's like a classroom in the sky.

What's an average day like? There's no such thing as an average day in my job! It all depends on the weather, and things are constantly changing. We often take off at a moment's notice to chase storms. I'm the one who decides whether we fly low through a storm. I don't want to take us into a hurricane that could be too strong for us.

Have you made any sacrifices to do this job? Yes, one big one. I'm away from my family. They all live in Pennsylvania. My wife's with me, of course, but her family comes from the Midwest, so we're pretty cut off from them.

What would you like to do next? I'd like to join a space program and be the first meteorologist in space, but I haven't come up with an experiment to do in space yet. There aren't any hurricanes!

What advice would you give to someone who wanted to do your job? Study math and science and get a degree in meteorology. I've taken the hurricane hunter path, but you could be a weather forecaster or do research. It's a fascinating subject and the pay's pretty good.

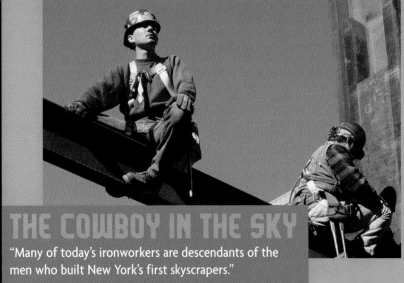

THE TRAPEZE ARTIST

"You only live once, so why stay in a boring job?"

LINDA SPELMAN was a lawyer who found a new career in a circus. She now works as a trapeze artist, traveling with circuses throughout Canada, Europe, and East Asia.

How did you get the job? That's quite a long story. My father's a lawyer, so I thought I'd become one, too. Law school was really, really hard, so I took up gymnastics in the evenings to help me relax. When I finally passed my exams, I thought, "I need a break. I want to travel and learn a language." I'd heard of the Ecole Nationale du Cirque in Montreal, so I thought, "I'll join the circus." I went to Canada and took a trapeze class and, amazingly, I was good at it.

What do you like most about it? The excitement and the travel. I always wanted to travel and learn languages and I've done all of that. Also, I get along really well with circus people. They're all nationalities. I've learned so much about life from them.

What's an average day like? Everyone has to help in the circus, so you begin the day in a new town handing out flyers. In the afternoon, you work in the box office and rehearse. Then you do the act in the evening. At the end of a week, I'm so tired I spend a day in bed. Last month I twisted my shoulder and couldn't work for a week.

Have you made any sacrifices to do this job? No, I haven't, not really. I quit doing something that I hated and I'm doing something that I love. I do miss my family sometimes, but that's all. And of course I earn a lot less than a lawyer.

What would you like to do next? I'm 34 now. I'd like to carry on doing this until I'm at least 50. There are Russian trapeze artists still going strong in their fifties.

What advice would you give to someone who wanted to do your job? You need to be in good shape and strong and have a good head for heights. But generally, I'd say to anyone with a dream, "Go for it! You only live once, so why stay in a boring job?"

THE COWBOY IN THE SKY

"Many of today's ironworkers are descendants of the men who built New York's first skyscrapers."

MICHAEL DOYLE is an ironworker in New York City. He's one of 100 or so ironworkers currently erecting the steel frame of a new 40-story building in Times Square. These ironworkers are known as "cowboys in the sky."

How did you get the job? Ironwork is a trade that is still handed down from father to son. Many of today's ironworkers are descendants of the men who built New York's first skyscrapers. My great-grandfather came over from Ireland in 1930 to work on the construction of the Empire State Building. My father and grandfather were also ironworkers.

What do you like most about it? To me, ironworkers are the kings of construction. We make the skeleton that the other workers build on. We have real pride in our work—you look at the New York skyline and think "I helped build that." Also, we work hard, we play hard. We get along well together. We ironworkers depend on each other for our lives. Oh, and the pay is good!

What's an average day like? You never stop in this job. Eight hours a day, from seven in the morning until three in the afternoon. You're moving all the time. The crane lifts the iron girders and you have to move them into place. There's always danger. It's a fact of life for us.

Have you made any sacrifices to do this job? Yes, one big one—physical health. The wear and tear to the body is enormous. I've fallen three times. My father fell two stories, lost a finger, and broke his ankles.

What would you like to do next? I'd like to work on something real important like my great-grandfather did. Or like my father did, who helped build the World Trade Center. It's weird—he helped build it and I helped take it away.

What advice would you give to someone who wanted to do your job? You need to be strong, really strong. You have to be OK with height. It usually takes about a year to get used to it. You can't work and hold on with one hand all the time. Many guys try it once, then back off and say, "This is not for me."

Role play

Work with a partner. Go to page 103.

Student A You are a journalist.
Student B You have your dream job from Exercise 1.

VOCABULARY
Phrasal verbs

> ❶ **1** There are many examples of phrasal verbs in the reading texts on pages 54–55.
>   I **came across** an ad …
>   It's exciting to **end up** in different cities …
>   Find more examples.
>
> **2** Some phrasal verbs are literal and some are idiomatic.
>   Literal: She **looked out** the window at the sunset.
>   Idiomatic: **Look out!** That dog's going to bite!
>
> ▶▶ **Grammar Reference 7.4 p. 146**

looking forward to
GONE OUT
get out of
back off
run out of
take off
END UP **look out!**
come up with
Cut off
put up with
came get across along
looked out

1 In these pairs of sentences, one meaning of the phrasal verb is literal and the other is idiomatic. Say which is which.

1. a. The plane has just *taken off*. **idiomatic**
   b. Please *take off* your coat and sit down. **literal**

2. a. Oh, no! The lights have *gone out* again.
   b. If you *go out*, take an umbrella. It's going to rain.

3. a. (On the phone) Hello? Hello? I can't hear you. I think we've been *cut off*.
   b. She *cut off* a big piece of meat and gave it to the dog.

4. a. She *looked up* and smiled.
   b. I *looked up* the word in the dictionary.

5. a. Can you *pick up* my pen for me? It's under your chair.
   b. I *picked up* some Italian when I was working in Rome.

2 Replace the word in *italics* with the pronoun.

1. He turned on *the light*. **He turned it on.**
2. I came across *the ad*. **I came across it.**
3. She's taken off *her boots*.
4. He took up *golf* when he retired.
5. I get along well with *my parents*.
6. I'm looking for *my glasses*.
7. I looked up *the words* in my dictionary.
8. The waiter took away *the dirty plates*.

3 Complete each pair of sentences below with one of the phrasal verbs from the box.

| get along with   put up with   run out of |
| looking forward to   come up with |

1. How do you manage to | the noise from your neighbors?
   Some parents have to | bad behavior from their kids.

2. I'm broke. I have to | an idea for making money.
   We need to | a solution to this problem.

3. Has the photocopier | paper again?
   The children always | school as soon as the bell rings.

4. How well do you | your colleagues?
   I really don't | my teacher. She's too strict.

5. She's | going on vacation.
   We're | meeting you very much.

In which pairs of sentences above is the meaning different?

56   Unit 7 · The world of work

LISTENING AND SPEAKING
The busy life of a retired man

1 Work in groups and discuss the questions.
- Is anyone in your family retired? Who?
- What job did they do before retiring?
- How old were they when they retired? How long have they been retired?
- What do they do now?

2 **T 7.6** Look at the photograph of Lou Norris and his granddaughter, Patti. Lou used to be an engineer for Siemco Engineering in Indiana. Now he is retired. Listen to them talking.

Who do you think is happier, Lou or Patti? Why?

3 Underline the verbs. Then answer the questions.
1. How long *was he / has he been* retired?
2. How long *did he work / has he worked* for Siemco Engineering?
3. How long *was he married / has he been married*?
4. Who *did he go / has he gone* to Florida with?

4 Answer the questions.
1. Why does he like playing golf?
2. Which places has he visited since he retired? Where did he go last month?
3. Who are these people?
   - Bobby
   - Eric
   - Ted
   - Jessica
   - Marjorie
   - Miriam
4. What are the two sad events that Lou mentions?
5. What does Patti complain about?

What do you think?
- What is the usual retirement age for men and women in your country?
- What do you think is the best age to retire?
- When would you like to retire?
- What would you like to do when you retire?

EVERYDAY ENGLISH
Leaving a phone message

1 Complete the conversations with phrases from the box.

Let me give you my number	I'll call back later
I'm just returning his call	He's in a meeting
She's away from her desk	He's on another line

1. **A** Hello. May I speak to Arthur Lee, please?
   B I'm sorry. ___He's in a meeting___ right now. Can I take a message?
   A Yes. This is Pam Haddon. Mr. Lee called me earlier and left a message. _____ . Can you please tell him that I'm back in my office now?

2. **A** Hello. This is Ray Gervin. May I speak to Janet Wolf, please?
   B I'm sorry, Mr. Gervin. _____ at the moment. Would you like Ms. Wolf to call you when she gets back?
   A Yes. If you don't mind. _____ . It's 619-555-3153.

3. **A** Hello. May I speak to Douglas Ryan, please?
   B One moment, please. ... I'm sorry, but _____ . Do you want to hold?
   A No. That's OK. _____ .

2 **T 7.7** Listen and check. Practice the conversations with a partner.

8 Just imagine!

Conditionals · Time clauses · Base and strong adjectives · Making suggestions

1 Match a line in **A** with a line in **B**.

If I had $5 million, I'd quit my job and travel around the world.

A	B
1. If I had $5 million,	I'll tell her the news.
2. If you're going to the post office,	I'd quit my job and travel around the world.
3. If I see Anna,	you have to work hard.
4. If you want to do well in life,	go to bed and rest.
5. If you don't feel well,	could you mail this letter for me?

2 What verb forms are used in the two parts of each sentence?

JIM GOES BACKPACKING
First conditional and time clauses

1 **T 8.1** Jim is going to backpack around Europe with his friend, Frank. Jim's mother is very worried. Listen and complete the conversation with the verbs from the box.

will you do	won't get	'll be (x2)	'll get
'll ask	won't do	get (x2)	

Mom Oh, dear, I hope everything will be all right. You've never been out of the country before.

Jim Don't worry, Mom. I _'ll be_ OK. I can take care of myself. Anyway, I _____ with Frank. We _____ anything stupid.

Mom But what _____ if you run out of money?

Jim We _____ jobs, of course!

Mom Oh? What if you _____ lost?

Jim Mom! If we _____ lost, we _____ someone for directions, but we _____ lost because we know where we're going!

Mom Well, OK. … But what if you … ?

Practice the conversation in pairs.

2 Have more conversations between Jim and his mother.
What will you do if you … ?

- get food poisoning
- lose your passport
- get sunburned
- get homesick
- get mugged
- don't like the food
- don't understand the language
- don't get along with Frank
- fall in love with some girl

What will you do if you get food poisoning?

Don't worry, Mom. I'll …

58 Unit 8 · Just imagine!

3 **T 8.2** Listen to the next part of their conversation and put the verb into the correct tense.

Mom But how will we know if you're all right?

Jim When we ____get____ (get) to a city, I _____ (send) you an e-mail.

Mom But, Jim, it's such a long flight to Madrid!

Jim Look, as soon as we _____ (arrive) in Spain, I _____ (call) you.

Mom I _____ (be) worried until I _____ (hear) from you.

Jim I'll be OK. Really!

GRAMMAR SPOT

1 Which sentence expresses a future certainty, and which a future possibility?

   If we run out of money, we'll get jobs.
   When we get to a city, I'll send you an e-mail.

2 <u>Underline</u> the time expressions in the following sentences:

   When we get to a city, we'll send you an e-mail.
   As soon as we arrive, we'll call you.
   I'll be worried until I hear from you.

▶▶ **Grammar Reference 8.1 and 8.2 p. 147**

PRACTICE

The interview

1 Put *if*, *as soon as*, or *before* into each box. Put the verb into the correct tense.

Joe Bye, Honey! Good luck with the interview!

Sue Thanks. I'll need it. I hope the trains are running on time. ☐**If**☐ I __'m__ (be) late for the interview, I _____ (be) furious with myself!

Joe Just stay calm! Call me when you can.

Sue I will. I _____ (call) you on my cell phone ☐_____☐ I _____ (get) out of the interview.

Joe When _____ you _____ (know) ☐_____☐ you have the job?

Sue They _____ (tell) me in the next few days. ☐_____☐ they _____ (offer) me the job, I _____ (accept) it. You know that, don't you?

Joe Sure. But we'll worry about that later.

Sue OK. Are you going to work now?

Joe Well, I _____ (take) the kids to school ☐_____☐ I _____ (go) to work.

Sue Don't forget to pick them up ☐_____☐ you _____ (come) home.

Joe Don't worry, I won't forget. You'd better get going. ☐_____☐ you _____ (not hurry), you _____ (miss) the train.

Sue OK. I _____ (see) you this evening. Bye!

T 8.3 Listen and check. Practice the conversation with a partner.

2 In pairs, ask and answer questions about the conversation with a partner.

  • How/Sue/feel/if/late for the interview?

> *How will Sue feel if she's late for the interview?*

> *She'll be furious with herself.*

  • When/call/Joe?
  • When/know/if/she has the job?
  • What/she/do/if/they/offer her the job?
  • What/Joe/do/before/go to work?
  • When/pick up the kids?

WINNING THE LOTTERY
Second conditional

1 **T 8.4** Listen to five people saying what they would do if they won $5 million in the lottery. Who says what? Write a number, *1–5*.

a

c

d

b

e

2 Complete the sentences from the interviews.

1. I **'d give** a load of money to charity.
   I _____ my own island in the Caribbean.
2. I _____ it all on myself. Every last cent!
3. I _____ lots of land, so I _____ peace and quiet.
4. I _____ a space tourist and fly to Mars on the space shuttle.
5. I _____ my job and travel. But it _____ me.

Practice the sentences.

GRAMMAR SPOT

1 Look at the conditional sentences.

> If **I have** time, **I'll do** some shopping.
> If **I had** $5 million, **I'd buy** an island.

Which sentence expresses a possible situation? Which sentence expresses an unlikely situation, a dream?

2 We use the past tense and *would* to show unreality. The situation is contrary to facts.

> If I had a lot of money, I'd travel around the world. (But I don't have a lot of money.)

▶▶ **Grammar Reference 8.3 and 8.4 p. 147**

PRACTICE

Group discussion

1 Work in groups to complete the questions.
What would *you* do with $5 million?
Ask and answer questions.

- What ... buy? **What would you buy?**
- How much ... give away? Who ... give it to?
- ... travel? Where ... to?
- What about your job? ... keep on working or
  ... quit your job?
- ... go on a spending spree, or ... invest the
  money?
- ... be happier than you are now?

Conversations with *will* and *would*

2 Look at the situations. Decide if they are
possible or unlikely.
1. There's a good movie on TV tonight.
   Possible
2. You find a burglar in your home.
   Unlikely
3. You see a ghost.
4. Your friend isn't doing anything this
   weekend.
5. You are president of your country.
6. You don't have any homework tonight.
7. You can speak perfect English.

3 Ask and answer questions about what you
will do or would do.

*What will you do if there's a good
movie on TV tonight?*

I'll watch it.

*What would you do if you found a
burglar in your home?*

I'd call the police.

Conditional forms

4 Match a line in **A** with a line in **B** and a sentence in **C**.

A	B	C
1. If Tony calls,	don't wait for me.	It would be really useful for work.
2. If you've finished your work,	I might take an evening class.	He can reach me there.
3. If I'm not back by 8 P.M.,	you have to have a visa.	Keep warm and drink plenty of fluids.
4. If you have the flu,	please let me know.	I'd love to show you around.
5. If you're ever in Vancouver,	tell him I'm at Alex's.	Just be back in 15 minutes.
6. If you go to Brazil,	you can take a break.	I'd love to learn more about photography.
7. I'd buy a computer	if I could afford it.	You can get one at the embassy.
8. If I had more time,	you should go to bed.	Go without me and I'll meet you at the party.

T 8.5 Listen and check. Practice the sentences.

5 Look at these three questions.
- What do you do if you can't get to sleep at night?
- What will you do if the weather's nice this weekend?
- What would you do if you found a wallet with a lot of money in it?

In groups, discuss how you would answer these questions.

READING AND SPEAKING
Who wants to be a millionaire?

1 [T 8.6] Listen to the song "Who Wants to Be a Millionaire?"
- What don't the singers want to do?
- What do the singers want to do?

The tapescript is on page 129. Listen again and check.

2 Look at the chart below. Do you think these are good (✔) or bad (✗) suggestions for people who win a lot of money? Add your opinions to the chart.

If you win a lot of money, ...	Your opinion	The article's opinion
1. you should quit your job.	☐	☐
2. you should buy a new house.	☐	☐
3. you shouldn't tell anyone.	☐	☐
4. you should give money to everyone who asks for it.	☐	☐
5. you should go on a spending spree.	☐	☐
6. you should give away lots of it.	☐	☐

3 Read the article. What does it say about the six suggestions in Exercise 2? Put (✔) or (✗) in the chart.

4 These phrases have been taken out of the text. Where do they go?
- a. his unluckiest bet
- b. to move to a bigger house
- c. we feel at home
- d. among all the members of his family
- e. what the money would do to us
- f. as soon as possible
- g. most of their money will be spent
- h. nothing but misery

5 Answer the questions.
1. According to the article, is it a good thing or a bad thing to win a lot of money?
2. How does winning a large amount of money affect our work? Our home? Our friends? Our relatives?
3. In what way is our life like a jigsaw? How does a windfall smash the jigsaw?
4. How can money be wasted?
5. What are the two bad luck stories?
6. What made Jim Calhoun happy?
7. How has Michael Kovaleski survived?

What do you think?

- How would you answer the questions in the last paragraph of the reading?
- What advice would you give to someone who has won a lot of money?

All over the world, lotteries create new millionaires every week. But what is it actually like to wake up one day with more money than you can imagine?

Nearly all of us have fantasized about winning the big prize in a lottery. We dream about what we would do with the money, but we rarely stop to think about (1) _____ *e* _____ !

For most of us, our way of life is closely linked to our economic circumstances. The different parts of our lives fit together like a jigsaw—work, home, friends, hobbies, and sports make up our world. This is where we belong and where (2) _____ . A sudden huge windfall would dramatically change it all and smash the jigsaw.

For example, most people like the idea of not having to work, but winners have found that without work there is no purpose to their day and no reason to get up in the morning. It is tempting (3) _____ in a wealthy neighborhood, but in so doing, you leave old friends and routines behind.

Winners are usually advised not to publicize their address and phone number, but charity requests and begging letters still arrive. If they are not careful, (4) _____ on lawyers' fees to protect them from demanding relatives, guards to protect their homes and swimming pools, and psychiatrists to protect their sanity!

Winners who lost it all

There are many stories about people who couldn't learn how to be rich. In 1999 **Abby Wilson** from Lake City, Minnesota, won $14 million on Powerball, and it brought her (5) _____ . She immediately went on a spending spree that lasted for four years and five marriages. She is now broke and alone. "I'm a miserable

Who wants to be a millionaire? We do.

person," she says. "Winning that money was the most awful thing that happened to me."

Then there is the story of **William Church,** 37, a cafeteria cook from Boston. He won the Massachusetts lottery, but it turned out to be (6) _____ . Three weeks after winning, he dropped dead of a heart attack, brought on by ceaseless hounding from the press, the public, and relatives, after his $3.6 million win was made public.

Winners who survived

For some people, the easiest thing is to get rid of the money (7) _____ . **Jim Calhoun,** a seaman from Canada, won $2 million, and blew the money in 77 days. He withdrew thousands of dollars a day from the bank and handed it to former shipmates and strangers in the street. On one occasion, he handed out $150,000 to homeless people in a Toronto park. Later he said he had no regrets about his wasted fortune.

Michael Kovaleski was the biggest lottery winner at the time when he won $40 million in the Illinois lottery. It has taken him years to get used to the changes in his life. "I couldn't have done it without my family," he says. "There were so many lies about me in the press. They said I had dumped my girlfriend, bought an island in the Caribbean, and become a drug addict. All wrong." His fortune has been divided (8) _____ .

A final thought

When you next buy a lottery ticket, just stop for a minute and ask yourself why you're doing it. Do you actually *want* to win? Or are you doing it for the excitement of *thinking about* winning?

Language work

The words in **A** are from the text. Match them with their definitions in **B**.

A	B
1. begging	dreamed
2. linked	took out
3. fantasized	connected
4. smash	an unexpected sum of money you receive
5. tempting	break violently
6. withdrew	attractive, inviting
7. broke	asking for something very strongly
8. windfall	having no money

VOCABULARY AND SPEAKING
Base adjectives and strong adjectives

1 Some adjectives have the idea of *very*. Look at these examples from the article on page 62.

> a huge windfall = a very big windfall
> a miserable person = a very unhappy person

2 Put a base adjective from the box next to a strong adjective below.

good   bad   frightened   dirty   funny   tasty   hungry
tired   pretty/attractive   happy   surprised   angry

Base adjective	Strong adjective
good	great, wonderful, fantastic, superb
_____	exhausted
_____	delicious
_____	filthy
_____	terrified
_____	starving
_____	horrible, awful, terrible, disgusting
_____	thrilled, delighted
_____	astonished, amazed
_____	hilarious
_____	beautiful, gorgeous
_____	furious

> **!**
> **1** We can make adjectives more extreme with adverbs such as *very* and *absolutely*.
>   Their house is **very** big.
>   Their backyard is **absolutely** enormous.
> **2** We can use *very* only with base adjectives.
>   very tired   NOT ~~very exhausted~~
> **3** We can use *absolutely* only with strong adjectives.
>   absolutely wonderful   NOT ~~absolutely good~~
> **4** We can use *really* with both base and strong adjectives.
>   really tired   really exhausted

3 **T 8.7** Listen to the conversations and write down the adjectives and adverbs you hear. What do they refer to?

1. ___*good, absolutely superb*___ ___*movie*___
2. _____ _____
3. _____ _____
4. _____ _____
5. _____ _____
6. _____ _____

LISTENING
Charity appeals

1 Work with a partner. Look at the list of charities and charitable causes below. Pick three of the charities and discuss why you think people should donate to them. Compare your answers with other pairs.

- a charity that helps elderly people with food and housing
- a hospice for people who are dying of an incurable disease
- an organization that provides emergency supplies and medicine for disaster victims
- a charity that helps homeless people
- cancer research
- a charity that helps people with AIDS
- animal shelters

2 **T 8.8** Listen to information about three charities and complete the chart.

• Who or what does the charity try to help?
• How does the charity help?

	Who or what the charity tries to help	How the charity helps
1		
2		
3		

What do you think?

Imagine that you have $10,000 that you want to give to charity. Who would you give the money to? How would you divide it?

Think about what you would do, and then discuss your ideas with a partner.

If I had $10,000 to give away, I'd give it to three charities …

WRITING: Words that join ideas
▶▶ Go to page 117

EVERYDAY ENGLISH
Making suggestions

1 Maria is bored and Paul is broke. Look at the suggestions made by their friends. Are they talking to Maria or Paul? Write **M** or **P**.

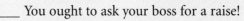
I'm bored!
I'm broke!

__M__ Let's go shopping!
____ If I were you, I'd get a better job.
____ Why don't you ask your parents?
____ You ought to ask your boss for a raise!
____ Why don't we go for a walk?
____ I don't think you should spend so much.
____ How about watching TV?
____ You'd better get a loan from the bank.

Which suggestions include the speaker?

2 **T 8.9** Listen to Maria and Paul and their friends. How can we make suggestions in English?

3 Listen again and read the tapescript on page 130. Notice how we accept and reject suggestions.

Work in pairs. Practice the conversations. Take turns covering the page.

Role play

4 Work in pairs. Make conversations for the situations, using different ways of making suggestions.

• You have a terrible cold.

A My head is killing me! And my nose is running!
B I think you should go to bed with a hot drink.
A That's a good idea. I'll go right now.
B How about a hot lemon drink? I'll make it for you.
A Oh, that would be great!

• You both have the evening free, and there's nothing good on TV.
• Your best friend is having a birthday party next week. You don't know what to give your friend as a gift.
• Your neighbor leaves his dog home alone every night while he's at work. The dog barks all the time when there's nobody home, and the noise is keeping you awake.
• Your apartment is a mess, the carpets and drapes are ragged, and the furniture is ancient. Suddenly, you inherit some money!
• You've been invited to a "potluck dinner" at an American friend's home. Each guest brings a dish of food to contribute, and you are supposed to bring a main dish.

9 Relationships

Modal verbs 2 — probability · Character adjectives · *So do I! Neither do I!*

TEST YOUR GRAMMAR

1 Read each pair of sentences. If the sentence is a fact, put (✓). If the sentence is only a possibility, put (*?*).

1. ☑ I'm in love!

   [?] I must be in love!

2. ☐ She could be taking a shower.

   ☐ She's taking a shower.

3. ☐ That isn't your bag.

   ☐ That can't be your bag.

4. ☐ You must have met my brother.

   ☐ You've met my brother.

5. ☐ They haven't met the president.

   ☐ They can't have met the president.

6. ☐ Shakespeare might have lived there.

   ☐ Shakespeare lived there.

> *Shakespeare might have lived there.*

2 Which sentences talk about the present? Which talk about the past?

I NEED HELP!

must be, could be, might be, can't be

1 Do you ever read advice columns in magazines or newspapers? What kind of problems do people often write about?

2 Lucy and Pam have problems. They wrote about them to "Debbie's Problem Page" in *Metro Magazine*. Read Debbie's advice.

Debbie's
Problem Page

Lucy's problem:

"I think about him night and day!"

Debbie replies:

Hi Lucy,

Everyone has daydreams and there's nothing wrong with that. It's only a problem when you forget where dreams end and the real world begins. Don't write to him anymore. You know in reality that a relationship with him is impossible, and that running away to Hollywood is a crazy idea. You need to find other interests and friends your own age to talk to. Sitting at home watching him on TV won't help you. Your parents are clearly too busy to notice or listen. Your future is in your hands, so get a life, study hard, and good luck!

Yours,

Debbie

3 Look at Debbie's replies. Say who *he, she,* or *they* refer to in these sentences.

1. She must be exhausted. **Pam**
2. She must be in love with a movie star.
3. She could be a doctor or a nurse.
4. She can't be very old.
5. He must be unemployed.
6. She can't have many friends.
7. He might be a problem gambler.
8. They can't have much money.

4 Give reasons for each statement. Discuss with the class.
Pam must be exhausted because she works hard and she does all the housework.

5 Read Lucy and Pam's letters to Debbie on page 104 to find out if your ideas are correct.

GRAMMAR SPOT

1 The following sentences all express *It's possible that she's in love.* Which sentence is the most sure? Which sentences are less sure?

> She **must be** in love.
> She **might be** in love.
> She **could be** in love.

2 How do we express *I **don't** think it's possible that she's in love?*

▶▶ **Grammar Reference 9.1 p. 148**

Pam's problem:

"We don't communicate anymore!"

Debbie replies:

Hi Pam,

   You're not helping your marriage by saying nothing to him. He doesn't seem to notice how you feel. I know he's worried about his mother, but it's unfair that he's always at her house and leaves you to do all the housework. You have a tiring and stressful job, caring for sick people all day. You must make him understand this and ask him about the hundreds of lottery tickets you found. Encourage him to look for work—he'd feel better about himself if he had a job. In the meantime, don't hide your feelings; otherwise your anger and resentment will grow.

Yours,

Debbie

PRACTICE

Grammar and speaking

1 Respond to the statements or questions using the words in parentheses.

1. I haven't eaten anything since breakfast. (must, hungry)
   You must be hungry.
2. Bob works three jobs. (can't, much free time)
3. The phone's ringing. (might, Jane)
4. Paula's umbrella is soaking wet! (must, raining)
5. Listen to all those fire engines! (must, somewhere)
6. I don't know where Sam is. (could, his bedroom)
7. Marta isn't in the kitchen. (can't, cooking dinner)
8. Whose coat is this? (might, John's)

T 9.1 Listen and check. Practice the sentences with a partner.

What are they talking about?

2 **T 9.2** Listen to five short conversations and guess the answers to the questions below. Work with a partner.

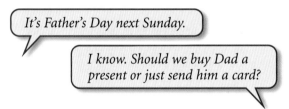

> *It's Father's Day next Sunday.*

> *I know. Should we buy Dad a present or just send him a card?*

Conversation 1:
Who do you think they are? Friends? Brother and sister? Husband and wife?

They can't be just friends. They could be brother and sister. They might be husband and wife.

Conversation 2:
Where do you think the people are? At home? In a hotel? In a restaurant?

Conversation 3:
What do you think his job is? A truck driver? A taxi driver? An actor?

Conversation 4:
What do you think she's talking about? Taking a test? Adopting a baby? A job interview?

Conversation 5:
Who or what do you think they are talking about? A cat? A dog? A baby?

Who's who in the family?

Work in small groups. Go to page 105.

A VACATION WITH FRIENDS
must have been / can't have been

1 **T 9.3** Andy is calling Carl. In pairs, read and listen to Andy's side of the conversation. What do you think they are talking about?

- Hi! Carl? It's Andy. How are you? Doing better?

- Really? Still on crutches, eh? So you're not back at work yet?

- Another week! Is that when the cast comes off?

- I'm fine. We're both fine. Julie sends her love, by the way.

- Yes, yes, we have. Julie picked them up today. They're good. I didn't realize we'd taken so many of us all.

- Yes, the sunset? It's beautiful. All of us together on Bob and Marcia's balcony, with the mountains and the snow in the background. It brings back memories.

- Yes, I know. I'm sorry. But at least it happened at the end; it could have been the first day. You only missed the last two days.

- Yeah, and it was noisy too! We didn't have any views of the mountains from our room. Yeah, we've written. We e-mailed the manager yesterday, but I don't know if we'll get any money back.

- Yeah. The airline found it and put it on the next flight. Marcia was very relieved.

- Absolutely. It was a *great* vacation. Some ups and downs, but we all had fun. Should we go again next year?

- Great! It's a date. Next time go around the trees! I'll call you again soon, Carl. Take care!

- Bye.

2 Read the questions. Put (✓) next to the sentence you think is possible. Put (✗) next to the one you think is not possible.

1. What is the relationship between Andy and Carl?
   - ✓ They must be friends.
   - ✗ They could be business colleagues.

2. Where have they been?
   - ☐ They could have been on a skiing vacation.
   - ☐ They can't have been on a skiing vacation.

3. What happened to Carl?
   - ☐ He must have broken his leg.
   - ☐ He might have broken his arm.

4. How many people went on vacation?
   - ☐ There must have been four.
   - ☐ There might have been five or more.

5. Where did they stay?
   - ☐ They could have stayed with friends.
   - ☐ They must have stayed at a hotel.

6. What did they do on vacation?
   - ☐ They must have taken a lot of photos.
   - ☐ They can't have taken any photos.

7. Why did Andy and Julie send an e-mail to the manager?
   - ☐ They could have written to thank him.
   - ☐ They might have written to complain about their room.

8. What did Marcia lose?
   - ☐ It might have been her skis.
   - ☐ It could have been her suitcase.

3 Use some of the ideas in sentences 1–8 to say what you think happened to Andy and Carl.

Andy and Carl must be friends and they could have been on ...

4 **T 9.4** Listen to the full conversation between Andy and Carl. Which of your ideas were correct?

GRAMMAR SPOT

1 What is the past tense of these sentences?

She	must can't could might	be on vacation.

2 What is the past tense of these sentences?
- I must buy some sunglasses.
- I have to go home early.
- I can see the mountains from my room.

▶▶ **Grammar Reference 9.2 p. 148**

PRACTICE

Grammar and speaking

1 Respond to the statements or questions using the words in parentheses.

1. I can't find my ticket. (must, drop)
   You must have dropped it.
2. Mark didn't come to school last week. (must, sick)
3. Why is Isabel late for class? (might, oversleep)
4. I can't find my homework. (must, forget)
5. The teacher's checking Maria's work.
   (can't, finish already)
6. How did Bob get such a good grade on that test?
   (must, cheat)

T 9.5 Listen and check. Practice the sentences with a partner.

Discussing grammar

2 Here is a list of modal auxiliary verbs. How many can you fit naturally into each blank? Discuss as a class the differences in meaning.

can	can't	could	must	might	should

1. He _____ have been born during World War II.
2. _____ you help me with the dishes, please?
3. You _____ see the doctor immediately.
4. It _____ be raining.
5. _____ we go out for dinner tonight?
6. I _____ stop smoking.
7. It _____ have been Bill that you met at the party.
8. I _____ learn to speak English.

READING AND SPEAKING
A father and daughter

1 Talk about these questions with a partner and then with the class.
- Who do you look more like, your mother or your father?
- Who are you more like in character, your mother or your father?
- Do you want to raise your children in the same way you were raised?

2 In the magazine article on the right, two different members of the same family describe their relationship with each other.

Divide into two groups.

Group A Read what Oliver Darrow says about his daughter, Carmen.

Group B Read what Carmen Darrow says about her father, Oliver.

3 Discuss in your groups the answers to the questions about your person.
1. Which two sentences best describe their relationship?
   a. It was closer when Carmen was a child.
   b. They get along well and have similar interests.
   c. They don't have much in common.
2. Which two sentences best describe Oliver?
   a. He's done a lot for his daughter.
   b. He isn't very sensitive to how she feels.
   c. He's more interested in himself than his family.
3. Which two sentences best describe Carmen?
   a. She is selfish and spoiled.
   b. She tried to please her father.
   c. She was never really happy until she married George.
4. How did Oliver behave in front of Carmen's friends?
5. Why did she leave school?
6. Is she happily married? How do you know?
7. What does Carmen think of her father's career?
8. Why don't they see each other very much?

FAMILY MATTERS

Two points of view on a family relationship

OLIVER DARROW, actor, talks about his daughter, Carmen.

"My first wife and I only had one child. It might have been nice to have more. I would have liked a son, but we just had Carmen.

I see her as my best friend. I think she always comes to me first if she has a problem. We have the same sense of humor and share many interests, except that she's crazy about animals, obsessed with them—she has always had dogs, cats, and horses in her life.

We were closest when she was about four, which I think is a wonderful age for a child. That's when they need their parents most. But as soon as Carmen went to school, she seemed to grow up and grow apart from her family, and any father finds it difficult with a teenage daughter. She was very moody and had an odd group of friends. There was an endless stream of strange young men coming to our house. I remember I once got annoyed with her in front of her friends and she didn't talk to me for days.

> *"I see her as my best friend."*

I've always wanted the best for her. We sent her to a good school, but she wasn't happy there. She left because she wanted to become an actress, so with my connections I got her into drama school, but she didn't like that either. She worked for a while doing small roles in movies, but she must have found it boring because she gave it up, though she never really said why. She got married a few years ago; her husband's a veterinarian. They must be happy because they work together, and she loves animals.

We have the same tastes in books and music. When she was younger, I used to take her to the opera—that's my passion—but she can't have liked it very much because she hasn't come with me for years. I don't think she goes to the movies or watches TV much. She might watch my movies, but I don't know. It's not the kind of thing she talks to me about.

I'm very pleased to have Carmen. She's a good daughter, but I don't think she likes my new wife very much because she doesn't visit very often. I'm looking forward to being a grandfather someday. I hope she'll have a son."

CARMEN DARROW, an assistant vet in Vermont, talks about her father, Oliver.

"I don't really know my father. He isn't easy to get along with. I've always found him difficult to talk to. He's kind of reserved, but he loves to be recognized and asked for his autograph. I think people see his movies and think he's very easygoing, but he really isn't. He's won some awards for his movies, and he's really proud of them. He used to show them to my friends when they came to the house and that really embarrassed me.

He can't have been home much when I was a small child because I don't remember much about him. He mostly stayed away from family life. His work always came first, and he was often away from home making movies. I wasn't surprised when he and my mother split up.

He must have wanted the best for me, but the best was always what *he* wanted. He chose my school and I hated it. I had no friends there, I was miserable and didn't do well, so I was asked to leave. He must have been very disappointed, but he said nothing to me. He wanted me to be an actor like him but I'm not at all like him. I tried it for a while, but I was miserable until I met my husband. He's a veterinarian and I'm his assistant. I'm now doing what I always wanted to do, work with animals.

My father and I have always been so different. I love animals and he loves books and music, and above all opera, which I hate. If he

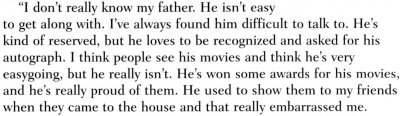

"He's like a stranger."

comes to see us (we live on a farm), he always wears the totally wrong clothes, but we don't see much of each other these days. It's because he really didn't want me to marry George. He wanted me to marry a famous movie star or something, but of course I didn't. George and I don't want children, we have our animals, but my father would love to have a grandson. Maybe his new wife will give him the son he wants, but probably not. She cares too much about being slim and beautiful.

I occasionally see one of his movies on TV. I find it hard to believe he's my father. He's like a stranger."

4 Find a partner from the other group and compare your answers. Then read the other text.

What do you think?

Who has the more realistic view of the relationship? Oliver or Carmen? Why?

Language work

Rewrite these sentences about Oliver and Carmen. Use the modal verb in parentheses in either the present or past and complete the sentence.

1. I'm sure Carmen likes animals a lot because … (must)
   She must like animals because she enjoys working with them.
2. I don't think Oliver is a very famous actor because … (can't)
3. I think maybe he has won an Academy Award® because … (might)
4. I'm sure she had a lot of friends when she was a teenager because … (must)
5. I don't think she worked hard in school because … (can't)

VOCABULARY AND SPEAKING
Character adjectives

1 Take the personality quiz to discover what type of person you are. Use a dictionary to check any new words. Write **Y** for *Yes*, **N** for *No*, and **S** for *Sometimes*.

What type of person are YOU?

1 Are you usually smiling and happy? ☐
2 Do you enjoy the company of other people? ☐
3 Do you find it difficult to meet new people? ☐
4 Do you have definite plans for your future career? ☐
5 Does your mood change often and suddenly for no reason? ☐
6 Do you notice other people's feelings? ☐
7 Do you think the future will be good? ☐
8 Can your friends depend on you? ☐

9 Is your room often a mess? ☐
10 Do you get annoyed if you have to wait for anyone or anything? ☐
11 Do you put off until tomorrow what you could do today? ☐
12 Do you work hard? ☐
13 Do you keep your feelings and ideas to yourself? ☐
14 Do you often give presents? ☐
15 Do you talk a lot? ☐
16 Are you usually calm and not worried by things? ☐

2 Work with a partner. Ask your partner to take the quiz about *you*. Compare your ideas and your partner's ideas about you. Are they the same or different?

3 Match these adjectives with the questions in the quiz.

a.	reliable	_8_	i.	lazy _____
b.	optimistic _____		j.	generous _____
c.	sociable _____		k.	moody _____
d.	talkative _____		l.	hardworking _____
e.	reserved _____		m.	easygoing _____
f.	shy _____		n.	messy _____
g.	impatient _____		o.	cheerful _____
h.	ambitious _____		p.	sensitive _____

4 Which are positive qualities and which are negative? Which could be both?

Positive	Negative	Both
reliable		

5 What is the opposite of each of the 16 adjectives in Exercise 3? Remember that the prefixes *in-* and *un-* can sometimes be used to make negatives. Which of the adjectives in Exercise 3 can use these?

unreliable

6 Describe someone in the class to your partner, but don't say who it is. Can your partner guess who it is?

LISTENING AND SPEAKING
Brothers and sisters

1 Do a class survey.
   1. Find out who has any brothers and/or sisters.
   2. Who has the most? How many? Do they like having lots of brothers and sisters?
   3. Does anyone have a twin brother or sister? Do they like being a twin?
   4. Is anyone in the class an only child? Do they like being an only child?

2 **T 9.6** Listen to two people talking about their families. Complete the chart.

	Luisa	Rose
1. How many brothers and sisters does she have?		
2. Was she happy as a child? Why or why not?		
3. Is she happy now? Why or why not?		
4. What do you learn about other members of her family?		

What do you think?

Discuss these questions.
   • How many children do you have? / would you like to have?
   • What size is the perfect family?
   • Would you like to have twins?

> **WRITING:** Beginning and ending letters
> ▶▶ Go to page 118

EVERYDAY ENGLISH
So do I! Neither do I!

1 **T 9.7** Listen to Sue. She is at a party and her friends are talking about themselves. Put a ✓ if Sue agrees with them and an ✗ if she disagrees.

Sue's friends	Sue	Sue's words
1. I want to travel the world.	✓	*So do I.*
2. I don't want to have lots of children.		
3. I can speak four languages.		
4. I can't drive.		
5. I'm not going to get married until I'm 35.		
6. I went to London last year.		
7. I've never been to Australia.		
8. I don't like politicians.		
9. I'm bored with Hollywood actors.		
10. I love going to parties.		

2 **T 9.7** Listen again and write the exact words Sue uses. Choose from the lists below.

So am I.	Neither am I.	I am.	I'm not.
So do I.	Neither do I.	I do.	I don't.
So can I.	Neither can I.	I can.	I can't.
So did I.	Neither did I.	I did.	I didn't.
So have I.	Neither have I.	I have.	I haven't.

Listen again and check your answers.

What does Sue say when it is the same for her?

What does she say when it is different?

▶▶ **Grammar Reference 9.3 and 9.4 p. 148**

3 Work in pairs. Read aloud the statements in Exercise 1 to each other and give the true response for you.

4 Go around the class. Everyone must make a statement about themselves or give an opinion about something. The others in the class must respond.

I love chocolate!

So do I. / Me too.

I don't!

I didn't do my homework.

Neither did I. / Me neither.

I did!

TEST YOUR GRAMMAR

1 For each pair, match a line in **A** with a line or picture in **B**.

A	**B**
1. What do you do What are you doing	these days? for a living?
2. He speaks He's speaking	three languages. to the teacher.
3. She has She's having	a baby next month. a sister and a brother.
4. What have you done What have you been doing	with my pen? I can't find it. since I last saw you?

5. Who drank my soda?

Who's been drinking my soda?

6. I read that book. I was reading that book	It was really good. when you called.

2 Look at the second verbs in each pair of sentences. What do they have in common?

TRY, TRY AGAIN
Present Perfect Continuous

1 Read the newspaper article. Answer the questions.
1. Why is Father Dan celebrating?
2. How long has he been learning to drive?
3. Was it easy?
4. How many lessons has he had?

Finally He Passes!

PRIEST PASSES DRIVING TEST AFTER 632 LESSONS OVER 17 YEARS

Father Daniel Hernandez is celebrating. He has finally passed his driving test. He has been learning to drive for the past 17 years, and he has had a total of 632 driving lessons.

Father Dan, 34, has spent over $15,000 on driving lessons, he has had 8 different instructors, and he has crashed his car 5 times. Then last week he finally managed to pass.

Father Dan, a parish priest in San Antonio, Texas, began driving at the age of 17. "My instructors have been telling me for years that I would never pass, but I was determined to prove them wrong."

Father Dan's luck changed when he took his test for the 56th time. He said, "When I was told that I'd passed, I got down on my knees and thanked God."

So how has he been celebrating? "I've been visiting all my friends and relatives and people who live in the small towns around here. I haven't seen some of them for years, because I haven't been able to get to them. Now I can go everywhere!"

2 Here are the answers to some questions. Write the questions using *he*.

1. Seventeen years. (*How long … ?*)
   How long has he been learning to drive?
2. Six hundred thirty-two.
   (*How many … ?*)
3. Over $15,000. (*How much … ?*)
4. Eight. (*How many … ?*)
5. Five times. (*How many times … ?*)
6. When he was 17. (*When … ?*)
7. Fifty-six times. (*How many … ?*)
8. By visiting all his friends and relatives.
   (*How … ?*)

T 10.1 Listen and check.

GRAMMAR SPOT

1 Find examples of the Present Perfect
Simple and the Present Perfect
Continuous in the text.

2 Look at the questions below. Which one
asks about an activity? Which one asks
about a quantity?

> How long have you been learning
> English?
> How many teachers have you had?

▶▶ **Grammar Reference 10.1–10.2 p. 149**

PRACTICE

Conversations

1 Write a question with *How long … ?* Use either the Present Perfect Simple or the Present Perfect Continuous. (If both are possible, use the Continuous.)

1. I live in the country. How long <u>have you been living in the country</u> ?
2. I play tennis. How long _____ ?
3. I know Jack well. How long _____ ?
4. I work in Hong Kong. How long _____ ?
5. I have a Japanese car. How long _____ ?

2 Make sentences with the same verbs about yourself. In pairs, ask and answer questions with *How long … ?*

3 For each of the sentences in Exercise 1, write another question in the Past Simple.

1. When ___<u>did you</u>___ move there?
2. How old _____ when _____ started _____ ?
3. Where _____ meet _____ ?
4. Why _____ decide _____ ?
5. How much _____ pay _____ ?

4 **T 10.2** Read and listen to the conversation.

A You look tired. What have you been doing?
B I'm exhausted! I've been getting ready to go on vacation.
A Have you done everything?
B Well, I've packed the suitcases, but I haven't been to the bank yet.

Work in pairs. Make similar conversations.

1. A covered in paint/what/doing?
   B redecorating the bathroom.
   A finished yet?
   B painted the door/haven't put up the wallpaper yet.
2. A hands dirty/what/doing?
   B filthy/working in the garden.
   A finished yet?
   B cut the grass/haven't watered the flowers yet.
3. A your eyes are red/what/doing?
   B exhausted/studying for my final exams.
   A finished yet?
   B finished my chemistry and history/haven't started English yet.

T 10.3 Listen and check. Practice the conversations again.

Discussing grammar

5 Why are these sentences strange? What would be better?

1. Ouch! I've been cutting my finger.
2. "Why is your hair wet?" "I've swum."
3. You've got tears in your eyes. Why have you cried?
4. I'm really sorry, but I've been crashing into the back of your car.
5. I've written my autobiography this afternoon.

A WRITER'S LIFE
Time expressions

1 Ellen McDonald is a writer. Look at the chart of events in her life. Answer the questions.

  1. Ellen has had an interesting life so far. What are some of the things she has done?
  2. How long has she been writing?
  3. What kinds of things has she written?
  4. How many novels has she written?
  5. Has she won any prizes for her writing?
  6. How long has she been married to Jack?
  7. How many times has she been married?
  8. How long has she been writing her autobiography?

Age	Life Event
0	Born on April 10, 1960, in Boston
6	Wrote short stories about animals
8	Collection of poems published in April 1968; visit to Ireland
11	September 16, 1971, mother died; visit to France and Spain
18–22	Went to Columbia University and majored in English literature
19	Met her first husband
21	Got married in spring 1981
22	Graduated with honors in June 1982 First novel, *Chains*, published in fall 1982
23	Daughter born June 14, 1983
25	Novel *Strangers in the Night*, 1985, won the National Book Award for best fiction
29	Divorced; visit to Vietnam, China, Japan
31	Bought a house in Greenwich, Connecticut
33	Novel *The Cry at Dawn* published
35–37	Wrote scripts for a TV series; met Jack, a TV producer
38	Got married on August 3, 1998, to Jack; moved to her current address in southern California
40	Won the Library Association Award for literary merit
42	Began her autobiography in 2002
Now	Still writing her autobiography

2 Complete the sentences with words from the box.

while she was in college	at the age of six
since she married Jack	two years after she got married
after the publication	until she married Jack
while she was working	between 1978 and 1982

  1. She wrote her first stories __at the age of six__ .
  2. _____ of a collection of poems in 1968, she went to Ireland.
  3. She was at Columbia University _____ .
  4. She met her first husband _____ .
  5. Her daughter was born _____ .
  6. She met Jack _____ on a TV series.
  7. She lived in Greenwich, Connecticut, _____ .
  8. She has been living in southern California _____ .

▶▶ **Grammar Reference 10.3 p. 149**

WRITING: Sentence combination
▶▶ Go to page 119

PRACTICE

Questions and answers

1 Ask and answer the questions about Ellen McDonald.

1. When … born?

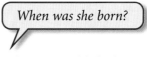

When was she born?

In 1960.

2. When … collection of poems published?
3. When … get married for the first time?
4. What … major in at Columbia?
5. Which countries … been to?
6. How long … first marriage last?
7. When … for the second time?
8. How long … in southern California?

T 10.4 Listen and check.

2 Make a similar chart of the events of your life or the life of someone you know well. In pairs, ask and answer questions.

3 Ellen is on a two-week tour of England and Scotland. Look at her schedule.

	Week 1	Week 2
Sunday	London	Birmingham
Monday	London	Manchester
Tuesday	London	Manchester
Wednesday	London	Edinburgh
Thursday	Oxford	Edinburgh
Friday	Oxford	Edinburgh
Saturday	Birmingham	Fly home

4 It is Monday of the second week, and Ellen is at a press conference. How does she answer these questions?

1. How long are you here in Britain for? **Just two weeks.**
2. How long have you been in Britain? **Eight days.**
3. When do you go back to California?
4. Where were you the day before yesterday?
5. Where were you this time last week?
6. Where will you be the day after tomorrow?

T 10.5 Listen and check.

Discussing grammar

5 Correct the mistakes in the questions.

1. What time did you go to bed at last night?
2. What have you done last weekend?
3. What are you doing this night?
4. Are you going to study English the next month?
5. Have you been studying English since three years?
6. How long you live in this town?
7. When is your mother born?
8. How long have you been knowing your teacher?

6 Work with a partner. Ask and answer the questions in Exercise 5.

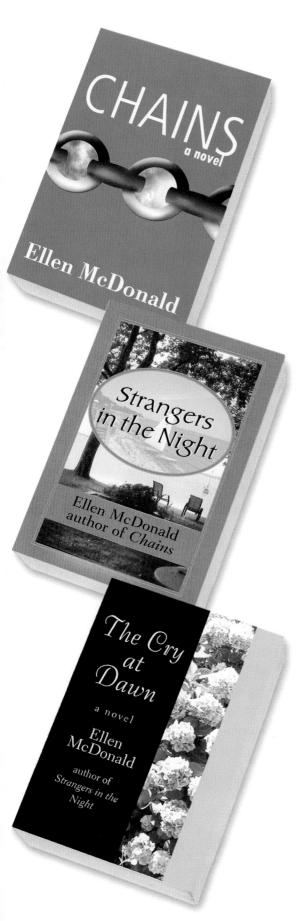

READING AND SPEAKING
A big name in Hollywood

1 Discuss the questions about your favorite movie actor or actress.

- What movies has he/she been in?
- What kind of movies does he/she act in? Action? Romance? Comedy?
- What is the best role he/she has ever played?
- What do you think he/she is like as a person? What does he/she look like?
- Where does he/she live?
- What do you know about his/her family?
- What is he/she most famous for? Looks? Acting ability? Behavior off-screen?

2 Match a line in **A** with a line in **B**.

A	B
1. She won	as the bad guy.
2. I was once	She has real talent.
3. In movies he is always cast	the big time.
4. She auditioned	a fake painting.
5. He's going to make	an award.
6. She was turned down	for the part of Mary. (x2)
7. Give her a break!	an extra in a movie.
8. I was sold	

3 Read the magazine article about Dennis Woodruff. Then answer the questions in Exercise 1 about Dennis.

4 Answer the questions.

1. Who will you probably not see if you go to Hollywood?
2. How does Dennis try to sell himself?
3. Is he famous?
4. Will he make the big time?
5. Where does he audition? How do people react?
6. Why is he tired?
7. How did he get the idea of promoting himself?
8. Is Dennis optimistic?

Famous for

F YOU GO to Hollywood and look around the trendy coffee shops and restaurants, it is unlikely that you will meet your favorite movie star. However, it is almost certain that you will meet Dennis Woodruff.

Dennis is a movie star—well, sort of. You learn this quickly because he tells everyone he meets. He wears a T-shirt that says "Dennis Woodruff, world-famous actor." On his modified Chevrolet convertible he has five Oscars® (fake, unfortunately) and other awards that he has won. He also hands out videotapes of his movies in exchange for a modest $10.

If fame is a matter of being known by influential people, then Dennis Woodruff is certainly famous. He describes himself as Hollywood's best known out-of-work actor. He has been looking for work for 25 years. It is true that he has been on television over 300 times and done work in about 45 motion pictures, but invariably as an extra.

But mostly he is known as the hippie guy with the long blond ponytail, who is trapped in the only role he has been able to play with any success—playing Dennis. Everything about Dennis has to do with selling himself. He talks

not being famous

Dennis Woodruff, Hollywood movie star—sort of

constantly about his life, his talent, his artistic abilities, his ambitions. His never-ending search for work in the movie industry no longer has any realistic chance of success, so now he acts out the role of an actor looking for work. "Cast me!" shouts the writing on his car. "Buy my movie!"

"Actually," says Dennis, "I am a movie star. It's just that no one has realized it yet." His movies, titled *Dennis Woodruff the Movie, Parts I and II* and *Double Feature, starring Dennis Woodruff* are heavily autobiographical—more documentaries of his life than anything else. You can watch him auditioning for parts in front of the security cameras at local restaurants. People recognize him and then, sadly, ignore him.

He has rugged, unconventional good looks, though he seems tired. "I've been making another movie about me. It's called *Life Is Art*. I want to show everyone how my life is like a work of art."

One of the most miserable tales he tells is about how he nearly made the big time. The famous actor John Wayne was going to give him a break, but unfortunately he died. Legendary producer Otto Preminger wanted to make him a star. He also died.

Now nearly 50, Dennis first had the idea of promoting himself over 20 years ago when he asked a casting director why he had been turned down for a part. "Because you're not a big name in Hollywood," came the answer. Dennis immediately wrote his name in huge letters on the top of his car. It didn't get him any work, but it did get him noticed.

He's been living in a mobile home in East Hollywood for 30 years, and to his credit, he manages to earn a living. He has set up a production company with his brother, and he has sold 15,000 copies of his video. True success, he feels, is just around the corner. Now there's optimism for you.

Language work

5 Here are the answers to some questions. Write the questions.

1. A <u>How many fake Oscars®</u>
   <u>does he have?</u>
   B Five.
2. A _____ ?
   B For 25 years.
3. A _____ ?
   B Over 300 times.
4. A _____ ?
   B For 30 years.
5. A _____ ?
   B 15,000.

6 The words in **A** are in the text. Match them with similar meanings in **B**.

A	B
1. trendy	improbable
2. unlikely	not real
3. fake	caught so you can't move
4. trapped	pay no attention
5. ignore	different from what is considered usual
6. unconventional	stories
7. tales	enormous
8. huge	fashionable

VOCABULARY
Compound nouns

1 Nouns can be combined to make a new word or phrase. These are called compound nouns. They are written in different ways. Look at these words from the article about Dennis Woodruff.

One word	Two words
ponytail	coffee shop
videotape	movie star

2 Put one word in each box to form three compound nouns.

1
dining
bath _____room_____
waiting

2
_____ ache
_____ brush
_____ paste

3
phone
fax _____
credit card

4
_____ director
_____ theater
_____ review

5
_____ place
_____ engine
_____ works

6
credit
birthday _____
business

7
_____ brush
_____ stylist
_____ cut

8
_____ mail
_____ conditioning
_____ port

9
_____ cup
_____ shop
_____ pot

10
_____ set
_____ glasses
_____ tan

11
wrapping
writing _____
toilet

12
_____ mall
_____ cart
_____ list

3 Here are definitions of some compound words from Exercise 2. What are the words?
   1. A pain in your tooth or teeth
      toothache
   2. A place where airplanes take off and land
   3. A newspaper article that gives an opinion about a new movie
   4. A person whose job is to cut and style people's hair
   5. The time when the sun goes down and night begins
   6. A large building or buildings with many stores, restaurants, etc.

4 Write similar definitions of other words from Exercise 2 and test your classmates.

LISTENING AND SPEAKING
Collectors

1 Discuss these questions as a class.
   • What kinds of things do people often collect?
   • Do you collect anything? Did you used to collect things when you were younger?
   • Why do people collect things?

2 You are going to listen to two people who are both passionate collectors. Divide into two groups.

Group A `T 10.6` Listen to Andrea Levitt who collects dolls.

Group B `T 10.7` Listen to Jeff Parker who collects *Star Wars* memorabilia.

Look at the pictures of your person. What can you see? What does he/she collect? What questions would you like to ask him/her?

3 Answer the questions.
   1. Where does he/she live? Who with?
   2. What does he/she do for a living?
   3. How long has he/she been collecting?
   4. How many items has he/she collected?
   5. How many rooms of the house are taken up with the collection?
   6. What's his/her favorite item?
   7. Where do the items come from?
   8. Is he/she in touch with other people who share the same hobby?

4 Find a partner from the other group. Compare and exchange information.

Andrea Levitt and her doll collection

Jeff Parker and his *Star Wars* collection

Expressing quantity

1 Choose a word or words from the box to complete the sentences. Some are used more than once.

too much	a few	any	How many
as much as	some	How much	too many
	as many as	enough	a little

1. **A** _____ coffee do you drink?

   B At least six cups a day.

   A That's _____ . You shouldn't drink _____ that.

2. **A** Do we have _____ sugar?

   B Yes, but not _____ . We need _____ more.

3. **A** _____ do you earn?

   B Not _____ to pay all my bills!

4. **A** _____ people are there in your class?

   B Forty.

   A I think that's _____ .

5. **A** _____ aspirins do you usually take when you have a headache?

   B About four or five.

   A That's _____ . You shouldn't take _____ that!

6. **A** How old are you?

   B Seventeen. I'm old _____ to get married, but not old _____ to vote!

7. **A** When did you last go to the movies?

   B Pretty recently. Just _____ days ago.

8. **A** Do you take milk in your coffee?

   B Just _____ .

T 10.8 Listen and check. Practice the conversations with a partner.

2 In pairs, ask and answer the questions in Exercise 1.

11 Tell me about it!

Indirect questions · Question tags · The body · Informal language

1 All of these sentences are correct. Why is there no *does* in sentences 2 and 3?

   1. Where does she live?
   2. I know where she lives.
   3. Can you tell me where she lives?

2 Choose the correct question tag.

It's a beautiful day, isn't it?

   1. It's a beautiful day,   did he?
   2. You like learning English,   isn't it?
   3. You've been to Australia,   don't you?
   4. Henry didn't say that,   haven't you?

THE FIRST DAY OF VACATION
Indirect questions

1 **T 11.1** Flavia has just checked into her hotel in Toronto. Look at the information she wants, then listen to the conversation. Complete her sentences.

What Flavia wants to know	What Flavia says
1. Could you help me?	I wonder if _____ help me.
2. Are we near the CN Tower?	I'm not sure _____ near the CN Tower.
3. Are there any good restaurants nearby?	Can you tell me if _____ ?
4. When do the banks open?	I don't know when _____ .
5. Which restaurant did you suggest?	I'm sorry, but I can't remember which restaurant _____ .

2 Read the tapescript on page 133 and practice the conversation. Then close your books and do it again.

3 Here is some more information that Flavia wants to know. Use the prompts to ask indirect questions.

1. When was Toronto founded?
   (I wonder when …)
   I wonder when Toronto was founded.
2. What's the population of the city?
   (Do you know … ?)
3. Where can I exchange some money?
   (I'd like to know …)
4. What's the exchange rate today?
   (Do you happen to know … ?)
5. Is there a post office near here?
   (Could you tell me … ?)
6. Where is there a good place to buy souvenirs?
   (Do you have any idea … ?)

4 In pairs, ask and answer similar indirect questions about the city or town where you are now.

PRACTICE

Asking polite questions

1 Match a word in **A** with a line in **B** and a line in **C**.

A	B	C
What How Which	newspaper sports long far kind of many much	times have you been on a plane? do you follow? music do you like? do you read? is it to the station from here? time do you spend watching TV? does it take you to get ready in the morning?

2 In pairs, ask and answer indirect questions using the ideas in Exercise 1.

> *Could you tell me which sports you follow?*

> *Would you mind telling me which newspaper you read?*

Who was Walt Disney?

3 What do you know about Walt Disney?

> *He made cartoons and animated movies.*

> *He built Disneyland.*

4 Make sentences about Walt Disney using these beginnings and the prompts in 1–8 below.

I wonder … I'd like to know …	I have no idea … Does anybody know …

1. when … born

> *I wonder when he was born.*

2. where … live as a child
3. how old … when … start … draw
4. if … any children
5. when the first Mickey Mouse movie … come out
6. if … won any Oscars®
7. when … the first Disneyland park … open
8. if … still alive

5 Work with a partner. You each have different information about Walt Disney. Ask and answer questions to complete the information.

Student A Go to page 106.
Student B Go to page 108.

WE LIKE ANIMALS, DON'T WE?
Question tags

1 **T 11.2** Listen to Gabriella, age 4, talking to her mother, Karen.

G Mommy?
K Yes, Gabby?
G I have ten fingers, don't I?
K Yes, that's right, Sweetie. Ten pretty little fingers.
G And Daddy didn't go to work this morning, did he?
K No, it's Saturday. He's working in the yard today.
G And we like animals, don't we, Mommy?
K Yes, we do. Especially our cats, Sammy and Teddy.
G Can I have a cookie now, Mommy?

2 **T 11.2** Listen again. Does Gabriella's intonation go up or down at the end of the sentences?

> ### GRAMMAR SPOT
>
> **1** Gabriella knows that she has ten fingers, and she knows that her father didn't go to work. Is Gabriella asking for information or just making conversation?
>
> **2** How do we form question tags?
>
> ▶▶ **Grammar Reference 11.2 p. 150**

3 Look at the conversation between Karen and her assistant. Fill in the blanks with a question tag from the box.

didn't I?	isn't it?	am I?	don't I?

K Now, what's happening today? I have a meeting this afternoon, _____ ?
A Yes, that's right. With Henry and Tom.
K And the meeting's here, _____ ?
A No, it isn't. It's in Tom's office at 3 P.M.
K Oh! I'm not having lunch with anyone, _____ ?
A No, you're free for lunch.
K Phew! And I signed all my letters, _____ ?
A No, you didn't, actually. They're on your desk, waiting for you.
K OK. I'll do them now. Thanks a lot.

T 11.3 Listen and check. Practice the conversation with a partner.

> ### GRAMMAR SPOT
>
> **1** Did the intonation of Karen's question tags go up or down?
>
> **2** Which speaker, Karen or Gabriella, uses question tags to mean "I'm not sure, so I'm checking"?
>
> Which speaker, Karen or Gabriella, uses question tags to mean "Talk to me"?
>
> ▶▶ **Grammar Reference 11.2 p. 150**

PRACTICE

Question tags and intonation

1 Look at the sentences in the box and complete the question tags.

a.	It isn't very warm today, ___*is it?*___	⬎
b.	You can cook, _____	
c.	You have a CD player, _____	
d.	Mary's very smart, _____	
e.	There are a lot of people here, _____	
f.	The movie wasn't very good, _____	
g.	I'm next in line, _____	
h.	You aren't going out dressed like that, _____	

2 **T 11.4** Listen and check. Write ⬏ if the questions tag rises and ⬎ if it falls.

3 Match a response with a sentence in Exercise 1.

___d___ 1. Yes. She's extremely bright.

_____ 2. Believe it or not, I don't. I have a cassette player, though.

_____ 3. Why? What's wrong with my clothes? I thought I looked really cool.

_____ 4. No, it's freezing.

_____ 5. Yes, you are. You'll be called next.

_____ 6. Me? No! I can't even boil an egg.

_____ 7. I know! It's absolutely packed! I can't move!

_____ 8. It was terrible! The worst I've seen in ages.

T 11.5 Listen and check. Practice the conversations with a partner.

Conversations

3 Add three question tags to the conversation below. Do they rise or fall?

A It's so romantic.
B What is?
A Well, they're really in love.
B Who?
A Paul and Mary.
B Paul and Mary aren't in love.
A Oh, yes, they are. They're crazy about each other.

T 11.6 Listen and compare your answers.

4 Choose one of the conversations on page 107 and add question tags. Learn it by heart, and act it out for the rest of the class.

5 **T 11.7** Listen and check. Are your ideas the same?

READING AND SPEAKING
How well do you know your world?

1 Do you know the answers to these questions?

○ Do animals have feelings?

● What are the Earth's oldest living things?

● What is the most terrible natural disaster to have hit the Earth?

● Why isn't there a row 13 on airplanes?

○ Why do women live longer than men?

● What man-made things can be seen from space?

○ Was Uncle Sam a real person?

2 Put one of these lines before each question in Exercise 1. What is true for you?

> I think ... I think I know ... I'm not sure ...
> I don't know ... I have no idea ... I wonder ...

I think animals have feelings.

I have no idea what the Earth's oldest living things are.

Discuss your ideas as a class. Which question interests you the most?

3 Read the questions and answers from a science magazine. Here are the last lines of the seven texts. Which text do they go with?

  a. The country with the highest life expectancy is Japan—84 years for women and 77 for men.

  b. Less than 24 hours after the meal, Christ was crucified.

  c. It is very likely that this explosion wiped out all the dinosaurs.

  d. Fear is instinctive and requires no conscious thought.

  e. You can also see fires burning in the tropical rainforest.

  f. There are other pine trees nearby, one of which is nearly 5,000 years old.

  g. Over the years, various cartoonists gave him his characteristic appearance.

4 Here are seven questions, one for each text. What do the <u>underlined</u> words refer to?

  1. Where is the oldest <u>one</u> in the world?
     tree
  2. Why is <u>this</u> difficult to see from space?
  3. Do <u>they</u> have the full range of emotions?
  4. How did <u>they</u> become extinct?
  5. What did <u>he</u> say "US" stood for?
  6. Do <u>they</u> have a thirteenth floor?
  7. Why are <u>they</u> more likely to have accidents?

  Answer questions 1–7.

5 These numbers are from the texts. What do they refer to?

84	1815	1766	14	5,000
6	1906	200	83	15

Producing a class poster

6 What else would you like to know about the world? Work in groups and write some questions. Think of:

  • places (countries, cities, buildings)
  • people (customs, languages, superstitions, famous people)
  • things (machines, gadgets, transportation, etc.)
  • plants and animals

7 Choose two questions from Exercise 6 and research the answers. You could use the Internet, an encyclopedia, or other reference books from the library.

  Make them into a poster for your classroom wall.

You ask ...

1

Q Do animals have feelings?

A All pet owners would say "Yes." Molly the dog and Whiskers the cat can feel angry, depressed, neglected, happy, even jealous and guilty.

  Many scientists, however, are skeptical about giving animals the full range of emotions that humans can feel. Part of the problem is that it is impossible to prove that even a human being is feeling happy or sad. It is only because we can observe body language and facial expression that we can deduce it. And of course humans can express the emotion with language.

  However, most researchers do agree that many creatures experience fear. Some scientists define this as a primary emotion. ___*d*___

2

Q What are the Earth's oldest living things?

A Trees! Two National Parks in California are home to our oldest living things. In the Giant Forest you'll find the largest sequoias /sɪˈkwɔɪyəz/ in the world, standing as tall as a 26-story building. Among them is a tree called General Sherman, which is 83 m tall and 31 m in circumference. This is the world's largest living thing. However, it isn't the oldest by any means. _____

3

Q What man-made things on Earth can be seen from space?

A "When humans first flew in space, they were amazed to discover that the only man-made object visible from orbit was the Great Wall of China." This is a nice idea, but it's not true. The Great Wall is mostly gray stone in a gray landscape and, in fact, is very difficult to see even from an airplane flying at a mere 15 kilometers above. What can be seen when orbiting the earth (from about 200 kilometers up) are the lights of the world's large metropolitan areas. _____

we answer!

4

Q What is the most terrible natural disaster to have hit the Earth?

A Earthquakes, volcanic eruptions, and hurricanes are responsible for the deaths of thousands of people every year.

One of the most violent earthquakes ever recorded was in Ecuador in 1906. It was the equivalent of 100 H-bombs, but it was nothing compared to a volcanic eruption in Tambora, Indonesia in 1815. This was the equivalent of 10,000 H-bombs. But, even these are nothing compared to many tropical hurricanes: they regularly have the energy of an amazing 100,000 H-bombs.

However, there is one natural disaster that beats all of these by a very long way. A meteor that hit the Earth 65 million years ago and caused an explosion the equivalent of 10 million H-bombs. _____

6

Q Why do women live longer than men?

A Women generally live about 6 years longer than men. Evidence suggests that boys are the weaker sex at birth, which means that more die in infancy. Men also have a greater risk of heart disease than women, and they have heart attacks earlier in life. Men smoke and drink more than women, and their behavior is generally more aggressive, particularly when driving, so they are more likely to die in accidents. Also, men are more often in dangerous occupations, such as construction work.

Historically, women died in childbirth and men in wars. So nuns and philosophers often lived to great ages. Now childbearing is less risky and there are fewer wars. _____

5

Q Why isn't there a row 13 on airplanes?

A In many countries, the number 13 is considered to be very unlucky. In France, there is never a house with the number 13. In the United States, modern high-rise buildings label the floor that follows 12 as 14.

Where did this fear of a number come from? The idea goes back at least to Norse mythology in pre-Christian times. There was a banquet with 12 gods. Loki, the spirit of evil, decided to join without being invited. In the fight that followed, Balder, the favorite of the gods, was killed.

In Christianity, this theme was repeated at the Last Supper. Jesus Christ and his apostles numbered 13 people at the table. _____

7

Q Was Uncle Sam a real person?

A Yes, he was! This symbol of the United States with a long white beard, wearing striped pants and top hat, was a meat packer from New York state.

Uncle Sam was Samuel Wilson, born in Arlington, Massachusetts in 1766. At age eight, he was a drummer boy in the American Revolution. Later in life he moved to New York and opened a meat-packing company. He was a good and caring employer and became affectionately known as Uncle Sam.

Sam Wilson sold meat to the army, and he wrote the letters US on the crates. This meant "United States," but this abbreviation was not yet common. One day a company worker was asked what the letters US stood for. He wasn't sure, and said that perhaps the letters stood for his employer, Uncle Sam. This mistake continued. Soon soldiers started referring to all military goods as coming from Uncle Sam. They even saw themselves as Uncle Sam's men. _____

VOCABULARY AND IDIOMS
What can your body do?

1 As a class, write all the parts of the body that you know on the board.

2 Work in pairs. Say which parts of the body you use to do these things.

kick	bite	hit	hold	hug	kiss	lick	point
climb	think	chew	whistle	stare	drop		

3 Which verbs go with which nouns and phrases? Match a word in **A** with a line in **B**.

A	B	A	B
whistle	a ladder	kiss	into an apple
lick	litter on the ground	point	me on the cheek
climb	into the distance	hit	about the meaning of life
drop	a tune	think	a soccer ball
hug	your grandmother	bite	a gun
stare	gum	kick	a nail with a hammer
chew	an ice-cream cone	hold	me in your arms

4 Look at these idioms formed with some of the verbs. Can you guess their meaning?

hold your breath	kick the habit	think twice (about something)
kiss something good-bye	hit the roof	drop someone a line

Fill in the blanks with the idioms above. If necessary, change the form of the verb. The first letter of each missing word is given.

1. The best way to stop hiccups is to h_____ your b_____ and count to ten.
2. My parents h_____ the r_____ when I said I'd been to an all-night party.
3. I've tried so many times to stop biting my nails, but I just can't k_____ the h_____ .
4. I almost bought a new sports car, but then I t_____ t_____ about it and realized it wasn't such a great idea.
5. **A** I lost my purse with $200 in it.
   B Well, you can k_____ that money g_____ !
6. D_____ me a l_____ when you know what time you're coming, and I'll meet you at the station.

LISTENING AND SPEAKING
The forgetful generation

1 **T 11.8** Listen to the introduction to a radio program called "What's Your Problem?" and answer the questions.
   1. What problem are they talking about?
   2. What do they think is causing it?

2 Discuss these questions.
   - Does your lifestyle mean that you have a lot to remember to do each day?
   - Do you think modern society is busier and more stressful than 100 years ago?
   - How do you remember all the things that you have to do each day?

3 **T 11.9** Listen to the stories of LeeAnn, Jerry, and Keiko, and take notes about them in the chart.

What did they forget?	What did they do?
LeeAnn	
Jerry	
Keiko	

4 **T 11.10** Listen to the rest of the radio program and answer the questions.

1. What is Professor Alan Buchan's job?
2. What is it about some modern day working practices that causes forgetfulness?
3. Why did the lady think that she was going insane?
4. What was the lady's problem?
5. What helped the lady feel more relaxed?
6. Does Professor Buchan advise using a personal computer to help remember things?
7. What does he advise? Why does he advise this?
8. How does the presenter try to be funny at the end of the interview?

What do you think?

Do you think Professor Buchan's explanation for forgetfulness is true? Do you know any stories of forgetfulness, either your own or somebody else's?

WRITING: For and against
▶▶ Go to page 120

EVERYDAY ENGLISH
Informal English

1 When we speak, we use a lot of informal language, depending on who we're speaking to!

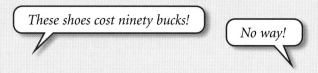

These shoes cost ninety bucks!

No way!

In the conversations, choose the words that fit best.

1. **A** What do you say we take a break for lunch?
   B ☐ Great idea. | We can grab a sandwich at the deli.
   ☐ I get it.

2. **A** ☐ How are you doing?
   ☐ What are you up to?
   B Nothing much. Just sitting around watching TV all weekend.
   A You're such a couch potato.
   B Hey, give me a break! I work hard all week. I like to chill out in front of the TV.

3. **A** Quick! Give me your homework so I can copy it.
   B ☐ Look out! | Do your own homework!
   ☐ No way.

4. **A** Did you fix the TV?
   B ☐ Kind of. | The picture's OK, but the sound isn't quite right.
   ☐ All right.
   A What's on tonight?
   B ☐ Beats me. | Did you look in the paper?
   ☐ What's up?

5. **A** What do you call that stuff that you use to clean between your teeth?
   B What do you mean?
   A ☐ You see! | It's like string. White.
   ☐ You know!
   B ☐ Wow! | You mean dental floss.
   ☐ Oh!
   A Yeah. That's it!

T 11.11 Listen and check. Practice the conversations with a partner.

2 There are lots of other examples of informal language in the conversations. How do we say them more formally? Be careful if you try to use them!

12 Life's great events!

Reported speech · Reporting verbs · Birth, marriage, and death · Saying sorry

TEST YOUR GRAMMAR

1 Read the story of Joel and Tara in **A** and complete their actual conversation in **B**.

THE MARRIAGE PROPOSAL

A Joel greeted Tara and asked how she was.

She told him she was fine.

He said it was great to see her again.

She said they hadn't seen each other for a while.

Joel said there was something he wanted to ask her. He told Tara that he loved her and asked if she would marry him.

She said that she would and that she loved him too.

B **Joel** "Hi, Tara. How <u>are you</u> ?"

Tara "I'm _____ , thanks."

Joel "It's _____ to see you again."

Tara "You too. We _____ seen each other for a while."

Joel "Yes. You know, there _____ something I _____ to ask you. ... I _____ you. _____ you _____ me?"

Tara "Oh, yes! Yes, I _____ . I _____ you, too."

2 Which is direct speech and which is reported speech?

THE WEDDING
Reported statements and questions

1 Elliot and Martha are guests at Joel and Tara's wedding in Atlanta. Match a line in **A** with a line in **B** to complete their conversation.

A	Elliot	B	Martha
1.	How do you know Joel and Tara?		Yes, we do.
2.	Are you married?		Sure. I'll introduce you to my husband.
3.	Where did you meet your husband?		We're staying at the Four Seasons Hotel.
4.	Have you traveled far to get here?		I studied at UCLA with Tara.
5.	Do you live in Orlando?		Yes, I am. That's my husband over there.
6.	So, where are you staying in Atlanta?		Actually, I met him at a wedding.
7.	So am I. Can we meet there later for coffee?		No, we haven't. We just got here yesterday. We flew in from Orlando.

2 **T 12.1** Listen and check.

3 Martha is telling her husband, Ron, about the conversation with Elliot. Read what she says.

*"I just met this really nice guy named Elliot. He was very friendly. Do you know what he said? First, he asked me how I **knew** Joel and Tara. I told him that I **had studied** with Tara at UCLA. Then he asked if I **was** married. Of course I said that I **was**! And next ..."*

GRAMMAR SPOT

1 Complete the reported speech.

Direct speech	Reported speech
"**Are** you married?" he asked.	He asked if I <u>was</u> married.
"We**'re** married," she said.	She said that they <u>were</u> married.
"How **do** you **know** Joel and Tara?" he asked.	He asked me how I ____ Joel and Tara.
"I **studied** with Tara," she told him.	She told him that she ____ with Tara.

2 What happens to tenses in reported speech?

3 What is the difference in the way *say* and *tell* are used?

4 When is *if* used?

▶▶ **Grammar Reference 12.1–12.3 p. 151**

PRACTICE

What did Elliot say?

1 Continue reporting Martha's conversation with Elliot. Work with a partner.

"*... next he asked where we'd met and I told him that we ...*"

2 [T 12.2] Listen to Martha reporting the conversation to her husband.

He's a liar!

3 Martha and Ron are talking about Elliot. Complete Martha's lines in the conversation.

1. **R** Elliot lives in Detroit.
   M But he told me he <u>lived in New York.</u> (New York)
2. **R** He doesn't like his new job.
   M But he said that he _____ it! (love)
3. **R** He's moving to Iowa.
   M But he told me _____ ! (Florida)
4. **R** He stayed home on his last vacation.
   M But he told me _____ ! (Paris)
5. **R** He'll be 40 next week.
   M But he told me _____ ! (30)
6. **R** He's been married three times.
   M But he told me _____ ! (never/married)
   R You see! I told you he was a liar!

4 [T 12.3] Listen and check. Pay particular attention to the stress and intonation. Practice the conversation with a partner.

Discussing grammar

5 Work with a partner. What's the difference in meaning in the following pairs of sentences? When does 'd = had? When does 'd = would?

1. He asked them how they'd traveled to Acapulco.
   He asked them how they'd travel to Acapulco.
2. She told her mother that she loved Joel.
   She told her mother that she'd love Joel.
3. She said they lived in Orlando.
   She said they'd lived in Orlando.

What did the people actually say in direct speech?

6 Change the direct speech into reported speech.

1. "I'm tired!" he said.   **He said that he was tired.**
2. "Are you leaving on Friday?" she asked me.
3. "We haven't seen Jack for a long time," they said.
4. "We flew to Tokyo," they said.
5. "Which airport did you fly from?" I asked them.
6. "The flight has been canceled," the announcement said.
7. "I'll call you later," he said.
8. "We can't do the exercise," they told the teacher.

GO TO JAIL!
Reported commands and requests

1 Read the newspaper article. Name the people in the photos.

"A Marriage Made in Hell!"

This is how Judge Margaret Kramer described the marriage of Kenny and Kathleen Brady as she ordered them to spend 14 days in jail.

T HE COUPLE married only six months ago, and already they are famous for their fights. Neighbors complained that they could hear them shouting from across the street. Ann West, who lives next door, said, "First I asked them nicely to stop because my baby couldn't get to sleep, but they didn't. Then my husband knocked on their door and told them to stop, but they refused to listen. They threw a chair out the window at him. It just missed him! So that was it! We called the police and asked them to come right away."

Mr. and Mrs. Brady admitted they had been arguing. Mrs. Brady said that she had accused Mr. Brady of wasting their money on drinking and gambling. However, they denied throwing the chair.

The judge clearly did not believe them. She reminded them that they had already had two previous warnings from the police. She advised them to talk to a marriage counselor after they'd served 14 days in jail.

Mr. and Mrs. West and their baby are looking forward to some sleep!

2 Who is speaking? Find the lines in the text that report the following sentences.

1. "You have to go to jail for 14 days."
   Judge Kramer ordered them to spend 14 days in jail.
2. "It's terrible. We can hear them shouting from across the street."
3. "Please, will you stop making noise? My baby can't get to sleep."
4. "Stop making that noise!"
5. "Please, can you come right away?"
6. "OK. OK. It's true. We were arguing."
7. "You've been wasting our money on drinking and gambling again!"
8. "We didn't throw the chair."
9. "Remember that you have already had two warnings from the police."
10. "I think you should see a marriage counselor after you've served 14 days in jail."

GRAMMAR SPOT

1 Which sentence is a reported statement? Which is a reported command?
  He **told them to stop** making noise.
  He **told them that she lived** on the next block.

2 Which sentence is a reported question? Which is a reported request?
  I **asked them to stop** making noise.
  She **asked me if I had met** them before.

3 *Say, tell,* and *ask* are all used in reported speech. Underline other verbs in the article that can be used to report conversations. *She <u>ordered</u> them.*

▶▶ **Grammar Reference 12.4 p. 151**

PRACTICE

Other reporting verbs

1 Match the verbs with the direct speech.

a. ask	e. remind
b. tell	f. advise
c. order	g. beg
d. invite	h. refuse

1. "Sign on the dotted line," the mail carrier said to me. __b__
2. "Please, can you translate this sentence for me?" Maria said to Mark. _____
3. "Don't forget to send Aunt Judy a birthday card," Mary said to her son.
   _____
4. "Please, please, please marry me. I can't live without you," Joel said to Tara. _____
5. "Please come to our wedding," Joel said to his boss. _____
6. "I won't go to bed!" Tommy said.
   _____
7. "You should talk to your lawyer," Ben said to Bill. _____
8. "Take that gum out of your mouth right now!" the teacher said to Joanna.
   _____

2 Put the sentences in Exercise 1 into reported speech using the verbs 1–8.

The mail carrier told me to sign on the dotted line.

T 12.4 Listen and check.

Listening and note-taking

1 You are police officers taking statements. Divide into two groups.

T 12.5 **Group A** Listen to Kathleen Brady and take notes.

T 12.6 **Group B** Listen to Ann West and take notes.

2 Find a partner from the other group and report what you heard. Find the differences. Begin like this.

A Kathleen admitted that they sometimes argued. She said that …

B Ann complained that they argued every night. She said that …

3 Write the reports for the police records. You can use the verbs below.

admit apologize complain offer order promise refuse say tell

There is a list of verb patterns on page 153.

COMPLETE THIS FORM ON DELIVERY

A. Signature
X..........................
B. Received by (Printed Name)   C. Del_____ ___ate

D. Service Type
☐ Certified Mail   ☐ Express ___ _l
☐ Registered Mail   ☐ Retur ___ eceipt
☐ Insured Mail   ☐ Cos___ Delivery

E. Tracking Number (on label)

VOCABULARY AND SPEAKING
Birth, marriage, and death

1 Use your dictionary to sort the following words and phrases into the categories in the chart.

> wedding funeral get engaged have a baby bouquet
> wreath pregnant reception bury groom midwife widow
> crib mourners honeymoon diaper get divorced   coffin

BIRTH	MARRIAGE	DEATH
have a baby		

2 Here are the opening and closing lines of a short story of a long life.

VICTOR PARROT was born one cold, stormy night in …

He died, aged ninety-five, with a smile on his face. Over five hundred mourners came to his funeral …

Work with a partner. Write the story of the main events of Victor's life. Use as many of the words from Exercise 1 as possible. Read your story aloud to the class.

3 What happens at births, weddings, and funerals in your country?

LISTENING AND SPEAKING
A birth

1 Work in small groups.

Obviously you can't remember anything about the day you were born, but what have you been told about it? Who told you? What did they say?

Tell any interesting stories to the whole class.

2 **T 12.7** Lenora Switt's family comes from Prince Edward Island, Canada. Listen to her telling the story of her Great Aunt Dodi's birth and complete the sentences.

1. My aunt was born on Prince Edward Island on January __16__ , _____ .
2. She was the _____ of _____ children.
3. The _____ only just managed to get there in time.
4. She said, "I'm afraid the child isn't _____ ."
5. My great-grandmother _____ the baby and ran downstairs.
6. She opened the door of the wood stove and put the _____ into the oven.
7. A few minutes later, a great _____ _____ came from the oven.
8. My Great Aunt Dodi is still _____ . She has _____ grandchildren and _____ great-grandchildren.

Role play

3 Work with a partner.

Student A Imagine you are Great Aunt Dodi. Tell the story of your birth to one of your grandchildren.
Student B You are one of Great Aunt Dodi's grandchildren. She is telling you again the story of her birth. Remind her that you've heard it many times before.

A Have I ever told you the story of when I was born? It was January …
B Yes, I know, and it was very cold …

READING AND SPEAKING
A death

1 You are going to read and listen to a poem by W.H. Auden (1907–1973). The poem is called "Funeral Blues." What does the title tell you about the poem?

2 **T 12.8** Close your books and close your eyes and listen to the poem. Don't try to understand every word.
   1. What has happened?
   2. How does the writer feel about the world now?
   3. What words or lines can you remember?

   Share what you can remember with the rest of the class.

3 Read the poem and answer the questions. Use your dictionary to check new words.
   1. A loved one has died. What, in general, does the poet want the rest of the world to do? Why does the poet feel like this?
   2. Which lines describe things that could possibly happen? Which lines describe impossible things?
   3. Which verse describes the closeness of the relationship?
   4. When you fall in love it is said that you see the world through "rose-colored glasses." What does this mean? In what ways is the poem the opposite of this?

Learning by heart

4 Divide into four groups.
   1. Each group should choose one verse and learn it by heart.
   2. Recite the poem around the class.

FUNERAL BLUES

Stop all the clocks, cut off the telephone,
   Prevent the dog from barking with a juicy bone,
Silence the pianos and with muffled drum
   Bring out the coffin, let the mourners come.

Let airplanes circle moaning overhead
   Scribbling on the sky the message *He Is Dead*,
Put crepe bows round the white necks of the public doves,
   Let the traffic policemen wear black cotton gloves.

He was my North, my South, my East and West,
   My working week and my Sunday rest,
My noon, my midnight, my talk, my song;
   I thought that love would last forever: I was wrong.

The stars are not wanted now; put out every one;
   Pack up the moon and dismantle the sun;
Pour away the ocean and sweep up the wood;
   For nothing now can ever come to any good.

W. H. Auden (1907–1973)

LISTENING AND SPEAKING

My Way

1 **T 12.9** Listen to the song called "My Way" made famous by Frank Sinatra.
- What is the message about life in this song?
- At what stage in his life is the singer?

2 Work with a partner. Discuss which words on the right best complete the lines.

Frank Sinatra

3 **T 12.9** Listen again and check. Sing along if you can!

WRITING: Correcting mistakes

▶▶ Go to page 121

My Way

And now, the end is near
And so I ___(1)___ the final curtain
My friend, I'll say it clear
I'll ___(2)___ my case, of which I'm certain
I've lived a life that's full
I've ___(3)___ each and every highway
And more, much more than this,
I did it my way ...

Regrets, I've had ___(4)___
But then again, too few to mention
I did what I ___(5)___ to do
and saw it through without exemption,
I planned each charted course,
each careful ___(6)___ along the byway
And more, much more than this,
I did it my way ...

Yes, there were ___(7)___,
I'm sure you knew,
When I bit off
more than I could ___(8)___
But through it all,
when there was doubt
I ate it up and spit it out
I faced it all and I stood ___(9)___
and did it my way ...

I've loved, I've ___(10)___ and cried
I've had my fill, my share of losing
And now, as tears subside,
I find it all so ___(11)___
To think I did all that
And may I say, not in a ___(12)___ way,
"Oh, no, oh, no, not me, I did it my way."
For what is a man, what has he got?
If not himself, then he has ___(13)___.
To say the things he truly ___(14)___
and not the words of one who kneels,
The record shows I took the ___(15)___
and did it my way ...
Yes, it was my way ...

1. meet	face
2. state	say
3. traveled	ridden
4. a lot	a few
5. had	wanted
6. step	stop
7. days	times
8. chew	eat
9. tall	up
10. joked	laughed
11. exciting	amusing
12. sad	shy
13. nothing	naught
14. feels	knows
15. blows	time

EVERYDAY ENGLISH
Saying sorry

1 Read the conversations and fill in the blanks with the correct expressions from the box.

| (I'm) sorry   I'm so sorry   Pardon me   Excuse me   What |

1. **A** _____ , what's that creature called?
   B It's a Tyrannosaurus.
   A _____ ?
   B A Tyrannosaurus. Tyrannosaurus Rex.
   A Thank you very much.

2. **A** Ouch! That's my foot!
   B _____ . I wasn't looking where I was going.

3. **A** Excuse me, can you tell me where the post office is?
   B _____ , I'm a stranger here myself.

4. **A** I failed my driving test for the sixth time!
   B _____ .

5. **A** _____ ! We need to get past. My little boy isn't feeling well.

6. **A** Do you want your hearing aid, Grandma?
   B _____ ?
   A I said: Do you want your hearing aid?
   B _____ ?
   A DO YOU WANT YOUR HEARING AID?!
   B _____ , I can't hear you. I need my hearing aid.

2 [T 12.10] Listen and check. Practice the conversations with a partner.

3 What exactly would you say in the following situations?
Use about two to four sentences in your response.

1. You were cut off in the middle of an important phone call to a business colleague. You call your colleague back.

2. You want the attention of the waiter in a very crowded restaurant. You want another large bottle of mineral water for your table.

3. A friend tells you that she can't meet you for lunch as planned next Thursday because she suddenly has to go to an aunt's funeral.

4. You thought you had bought a medium-size sweater, but when you get home you see it is the wrong size. You take it back to the store.

5. You want to get off a very crowded train at the next stop. You have a large suitcase.

6. Your dinner guest reminds you that he is a vegetarian. You have just put a huge steak on his plate.

> *Hello? I think we must have been cut off. I'm sorry about that.*

Getting Information

PRACTICE
Getting information

Ask and answer questions to complete the information about Kaori Sato.
Write in the replies your partner gives you.

Student A Where was Kaori Sato born?
Student B In Osaka.
How many movies has she made?
Student A Over 40.
How long … ?

KAORI SATO—United Nations Goodwill Ambassador

Kaori Sato was born in <u>Osaka, Japan</u> *(Where?)*, in 1956. She is a famous movie star and has made over 40 movies.

She has been a UN Goodwill Ambassador for _____ *(How long?)*. Her special interest is children's health and education. She goes to Africa _____ *(How often?)*, and she visits schools and hospitals. She has raised _____ *(How much money?)* from people in Japan. As a Goodwill Ambassador, she is paid just $1 a year.

Her father was a famous _____ *(What/do?)*. Kaori went to college in Tokyo, then studied _____ *(What?)* at the Tokyo School of Drama. She has also written seven best-selling books.

She is married, and has _____ *(How many?)* children. They are both in college, studying languages.

PRACTICE

An amazing thing happened!

Ask and answer questions to fill in the blanks in your text. Write in the replies
your partner gives you.

Student A Where did Wanda and Roy go on vacation?
Student B They went to Florida.
            What did they do every day?
Student A They went swimming and lay in the sun.
            Where … ?

THE TALE OF TWO WAVES (A true story)

Last summer, Wanda and Roy went _____**on vacation to Florida**_____ (Where?).
Every day, they went swimming and lay in the sun.

One morning, they were _____ (Where?) when a
huge wave knocked Wanda's expensive Italian sunglasses into the water. Wanda
was very upset because _____ (Why?).

The next day, they were sunbathing on a different beach and Wanda was
wearing _____ (What?), when suddenly there was
another huge wave, which totally covered Wanda. She was
_____ (How/feel?), but then she looked down
and to her amazement she saw the expensive sunglasses that she
had lost the day before.

PRACTICE
Getting Information

Ask and answer questions to complete the information about Kaori Sato.
Write in the replies your partner gives you.

Student A	Where was Kaori Sato born?
Student B	In Osaka.
	How many movies has she made?
Student A	Over 40.
	How long … ?

KAORI SATO—United Nations Goodwill Ambassador

Kaori Sato was born in Osaka, Japan, in 1956. She is a famous
movie star and has made ___over 40___ *(How many?)* movies.

She has been a UN Goodwill Ambassador for 20 years. Her special
interest is _____ *(What?)*. She goes to Africa every year, and
she visits _____ *(Where?)*. She has raised $25 million from
people in Japan. As a Goodwill Ambassador, she is paid
_____ *(How much?)*.

Her father was a famous painter. Kaori went to college in
_____ *(Where?)*, then studied theater at the Tokyo School
of Drama. She has also written _____ *(How many?)* best-selling
books.

She is married, and has two children. They are both in college,
studying _____ *(What?)*.

PRACTICE

An amazing thing happened!

Ask and answer questions to fill in the blanks in your text. Write in the replies your partner gives you.

Student A Where did Wanda and Roy go on vacation?
Student B They went to Florida.
What did they do every day?
Student A They went swimming and lay in the sun.
Where … ?

THE TALE OF TWO WAVES *(A true story)*

Last summer, Wanda and Roy went on vacation to Florida. Every day, they
__went swimming and lay in the sun____ *(What/do?).*

One morning, they were on the beach near their hotel when a huge wave
_____ *(What/do?).* Wanda was very upset because
Roy had given her the sunglasses for her birthday.

The next day, they were sunbathing _____ *(Where?)*
and Wanda was wearing a new, cheap pair of sunglasses, when suddenly there
was another huge wave, which _____ *(What/do?).* She
was furious, but then she looked down and to her amazement she saw
_____ *(What?).*

VOCABULARY AND PRONUNCIATION
Talking about you

1 Work with a partner. List the following information.
- the name of a restaurant where you had a memorable meal
- the name of a city, town, or village that you have visited and that you would like to visit again
- the name of a relative, friend, or colleague who is important to you

Choose names of people and places that your partner does not know.

2 Exchange lists with your partner. Ask and answer questions to find out about the places and people your partner listed.

3 Report back to the class about one of the names your partner wrote.

READING AND SPEAKING
Role play

1 Work with a partner.

Student A Imagine that you are a journalist. Interview your partner about his/her dream job from Exercise 1 on page 54. Ask these questions.

- What do you do?
- How did you get the job?
- What do you like most about it?
- What's an average day like?
- Have you made any sacrifices to do this job?
- What would you like to do next?
- What advice would you give to someone who wanted to do your job?

Student B Imagine that you actually do your dream job from Exercise 1 on page 54. Your partner is a journalist. Answer his/her questions.

2 Switch roles.

Student A Imagine that you actually do your dream job.
Student B Imagine that you are a journalist. Interview Student A.

I NEED HELP!
Lucy and Pam's letters

Here are Lucy and Pam's letters to "Debbie's Problem Page."

Dear Debbie,

I am 16 years old and totally depressed. I'm in love with Leon Rossi, the movie star. I think of him night and day. I just sit in my room and watch videos of his movies over and over. I've written hundreds of letters to him and sent e-mails to his fan club, but all I get back are autographed photos. I dream that someday I'll meet him and that he'll feel the same way about me. My friends think I'm crazy, so I don't see them anymore. I can't concentrate on my homework, and I have final exams next month. I've tried to talk to my Mom and Dad, but they're both lawyers and much too busy to listen to me.

Please, please help me! I'm desperate. I'm thinking of running away to Hollywood to meet him.

Yours in misery,

Lucy

Dear Debbie,

I'm almost too tired to write, but I have no one to turn to. I've been married for three years and everything was just fine until a year ago when Brian, my husband, lost his job. He became depressed, and because he has nothing to do, he just goes over to his mother's house on the next block and spends all day with her. He says he's worried about her because she lives alone.

I'm a nurse at a hospital. I'm exhausted after work, but when I get home I have to cook and clean the house. Brian refuses to cook or do housework—he says it's boring and gets angry with me if I ask him to do anything around the house. His whole personality has changed—we just don't communicate anymore. Also, I'm worried that he's becoming a problem gambler. I found hundreds of lottery tickets in a drawer yesterday, but I haven't said anything about it.

What can I do? I still love him. We were hoping to start a family soon, but now I'm not so sure this is a good idea.

Sincerely,

Pam

PRACTICE
Who's who in the family?

1 Work in small groups. Look at the photos. They are all of Jeff and his family. In each photo, which one do you think is Jeff?

Who do you think the others are?
Why?

2 Check your guesses. Go to page 109.

> *This must be Jeff because …*

> *But this could be Jeff …*

PRACTICE
Information gap

Ask and answer questions to complete the information about Walt Disney. Write in the replies your partner gives you.

Student A When was Walt Disney born?
Student B On December 5, 1901.
            Where did he live?
Student A On his parents' farm in Missouri.
            What jobs … ?

WALT DISNEY

Walt Disney was born <u>on December 5, 1901</u> *(When?)*, and lived on his parents' farm in Missouri. His family was poor and Walt had a difficult childhood. He had to work many different jobs to earn extra money— _____ *(What jobs?)*. He became interested in drawing when he was about seven, but his father thought it was a waste of time.

The Disney family moved to _____ *(Where to?)* when Walt was 12. He started going to art classes where he learned to draw cartoons. Then the United States entered World War I in _____ *(When?)*. Walt was only 16, but he forged his parents' signatures and went to France to become an ambulance driver for the Red Cross. His ambulance was covered with _____ *(What?)*.

After the war, Walt worked as a commercial artist. He produced a series of short films called _____ *(What called?)*. He was paid $1,500 for each film. This was his first break. Walt met and married one of his employees, _____ *(Who?)*, when he was 24, and the marriage lasted until his death 41 years later.

One of Walt's early creations was Mickey Mouse, and Walt provided Mickey's voice. Mickey's first animated movie was called _____ *(What?)*, which came out in 1928. It was a huge success. He went on to win _____ *(How many?)* Academy Awards® for his animated movies, and in 1955 he opened the first Disneyland park in _____ *(Where?)*. He died in 1966.

PRACTICE
Conversations

1 Work with a partner. Choose one of the conversations below and add question tags.

Conversation 1

  A You broke that vase.
  B Yes, I did. I dropped it. I'm sorry.
  A You'll replace it.
  B Yes, of course I will. How much did it cost?
  A $300.
  B $300?! It *wasn't* that much.
  A Yes, it *was.*

Conversation 2

  A Did you pay the electric bill?
  B No, *you* paid it.
  A No, I didn't pay it. I thought you paid it.
  B Me? You *always* pay it.
  A No, I don't. I always pay the phone bill.
  B Oh, that's right.

Conversation 3

  A We love each other.
  B Um, I think so.
  A We don't ever want to be apart.
  B Well …
  A And we'll get married and have lots of children.
  B What? You didn't buy me a ring.
  A Yes, I did. Diamonds are forever.
  B Oh, no!

Conversation 4

  A Helen didn't win the lottery.
  B Yes, she did. She won $4 million!
  A She isn't going to give it all to charity.
  B As a matter of fact, she is.
  A Wow. Not many people would do that.
  B Well, *I* certainly wouldn't.

Conversation 5

  A I think we're lost. Let's look at the map.
  B Uh-oh.
  A What do you mean, "Uh-oh"? You didn't forget the map?
  B Sorry.
  A How are we going to get back to the campground without a map?
  B Well, we could ask a police officer.
  A There aren't many police officers on this mountain!

2 Act out your conversation for the class.

PRACTICE

Information gap

Ask and answer questions to complete the information about Walt Disney. Write in the replies your partner gives you.

Student A When was Walt Disney born?
Student B On December 5, 1901.
              Where did he live?
Student A On his parents' farm in Missouri.
              What jobs … ?

WALT DISNEY

Walt Disney was born on December 5, 1901, and lived _on his parents' farm_ *(Where?)* in Missouri. His family was poor and Walt had a difficult childhood. He had to work many different jobs to earn extra money—delivering papers, picking apples, and helping on the farm. He became interested in drawing when he was _____ *(How old?)*, but his father thought it was a waste of time.

The Disney family moved to Chicago when Walt was 12. He started going to art classes where he learned to _____ *(What?)*. Then the United States entered World War I in 1917. Walt was only 16, but he forged his parents' signatures and went to France to _____ *(Why?)*. His ambulance was covered with Disney cartoons.

After the war, Walt worked as a _____ *(What?)*. He produced a series of short films called *Alice in Cartoonland*. He was paid _____ *(How much?)* for each film. This was his first break. Walt met and married one of his employees, Lillian Bounds, when he was 24, and the marriage lasted _____ *(How long?)*.

One of Walt's early creations was Mickey Mouse, and Walt provided Mickey's voice. Mickey's first animated movie was called *Steamboat Willie*, which came out _____ *(When?)*. It was a huge success. He went on to win 32 Academy Awards® for his animated movies, and in _____ *(When?)* he opened the first Disneyland park in Anaheim, California. He died in 1966.

PRACTICE
Who's who in the family?

Picture 1 *(back row, left to right)* grandmother, grandfather
          (front row, left to right) brother, Jeff

Picture 2 *(left to right)* father, wife, Jeff, mother, brother

Picture 3 *(back row, left to right)* Jeff, wife, mother, brother, sister-in-law
          (middle row, left to right) son, niece, niece
          (front row, left to right) son, nephew

Picture 4 *(left to right)* son, Jeff, daughter, son, wife

Writing

UNIT 1

WRITING
Correcting mistakes

T	Tense	WW	Wrong Word
P	Punctuation	Gr	Grammar
WO	Word Order	∧	Word missing
Prep	Preposition	Sp	Spelling

1 It is important to try to correct your own mistakes when you write. Look at the letter that a student has written to her friend. Her teacher has used symbols to show her the kind of mistakes she has made. Read the letter and correct the mistakes.

18 Greencroft Street
Chicago, IL 60657
Tuesday, May 10

Dear Stephanie,

How are you? I'm very well. I came <u>in</u> [Prep] the United States two weeks ago <u>for to</u> [Gr]

study at a language school. I want ∧ [P] learn English because ∧ is a very important

language. I'm <u>stay</u> [Gr] with <u>a</u> [Gr] American family. They have two <u>son</u> [Gr] and a daughter.

Mr. Kendall is ∧ teacher and Mrs. Kendall <u>work</u> [Gr] in a hospital. Americans <u>is</u> [Gr]

very kind, but they speak very quickly!

I study in the morning. My <u>teachers</u> [P] name is Ann. She <u>said</u> [WW] me my English is

OK, but I <u>do</u> [WW] a lot of mistakes. Ann <u>don't</u> [Gr] give us too much homework, so in the

afternoons I <u>go always</u> [WO] sightseeing. Chicago is much <u>more big</u> [Gr] than my town.

I like <u>very much painting</u> [WO] and I'm very <u>interesting</u> [Gr] <u>for</u> [Prep] modern art, so I visit

galleries and museums. I met a girl named Martina. She <u>came</u> [T] from Spain

and <u>go</u> [T] to Northwestern University. Last night we <u>go</u> [T] to the movies, but the film

wasn't very <u>exiting</u> [Sp].

<u>Do</u> [WW] you like to visit me? Why don't you come for a weekend? I'd love to see you.

Write to me soon.

Love,

Katia

2 Imagine that you are a student in another town. Write a similar letter to a friend giving some of your own news.

WRITING
Describing a person

1 Think of someone in your family. Answer the following questions about him/her.

1. What is his/her name?

_____

2. How is this person related to you?

_____

3. What is he/she like?

_____

4. What does he/she look like?

_____

5. What does he/she like to do?

_____

Read your sentences aloud to the rest of the class.

2 Which relative did you choose? Why did you choose that person?

3 Read the description of Martha Ferris and underline like this:

_ _ _ _ _ the parts that describe her physical appearance

_____ the parts that describe her character

.... the parts that describe her habits

4 *She's not very tolerant* in paragraph 2 of the text is a polite way of saying *She is intolerant*. Make polite forms of the words below.

1. rude __not very polite__   4. ugly _____

2. boring _____   5. cruel _____

3. cheap _____   6. stupid _____

5 Use your sentences from Exercise 1 to write a similar description of someone in your family. Be sure to include the following information:

- your opinion of the person
- physical description
- his/her character, habits, likes, and dislikes

MARTHA FERRIS, MY AUNT ❧

Of all my relatives, I like my Aunt Martha the best. She's my mother's youngest sister. She has never married, and she lives alone in a town outside Boston. She's in her late fifties, but she's still quite young in spirit. She has thick gray hair which she wears in a bun, and deep blue eyes. She has a kind face, and when you meet her, the first thing you notice about her is her warm, friendly smile. Her face is a little wrinkled now, but I think she is still pretty attractive. She is the kind of person you can always go to if you have a problem.

Aunt Martha likes reading and gardening, and she likes to take her dog, Buster, for walks in the park. She's a very active person. Either she's making something or fixing something or doing something to help others. She does the shopping for some of the older people in the town. She's extremely generous, but not very tolerant with people who don't agree with her. I hope that I am as happy and contented as she is when I'm her age.

WRITING
Telling tales

1 Complete the sentences with a linking word from the box.

before	as soon as	while	when	during
but	however	so	who	

1. There was once an old emperor __who__ lived in a palace.
2. He had three young daughters, _____ no sons.
3. He wanted his daughters to marry _____ he died.
4. He found three rich princes. _____ , his daughters didn't like them.
5. They refused to marry the princes, _____ the emperor became very angry.
6. He said that they had to marry the princes _____ they were 16 years old.
7. The three daughters ran away _____ the night and found work on a farm.
8. They fell in love with the farmer's sons _____ they were working there.
9. They married the sons _____ they were 16.

2 Complete the story with the linking words from Exercise 1.

The Farmer and His Sons

There was once an old farmer (1) __who__ had worked hard in his vineyard all his life. (2) _____ he died he wanted to teach his three sons how to be good farmers. (3) _____ he called them to his bed and said, "My boys, I have an important secret to tell you. There is a great treasure buried in our vineyard. Promise me that (4) _____ I am dead you will look for it." The sons promised.

(5) _____ the night their father died and the next morning they began looking for the treasure. They worked very hard in the hot sun and (6) _____ they were working they wondered about the treasure. They pictured gold coins, diamond necklaces, and other such things. Soon they had dug up every part of the vineyard, (7) _____ they didn't find a single penny. They were very upset. They thought that all their hard work had been for nothing. (8) _____ , when the grapes started to appear on the vines they saw that their grapes were the biggest and best in the neighborhood. They sold them for a lot of money and became rich men.

Now they understood what their father had meant (9) _____ he had talked of a great treasure. They worked hard and lived happily ever after.

The moral of the story is: Hard work brings its own reward.

3 Write a folktale that you know. Write about 200 words. Include the following parts:
- **Beginning:** *There was once …*
  or *Once upon a time there …*
- **Ending:** *… and they lived happily ever after.*
- **Moral:** If your story has a moral, give it at the end.

WRITING
Filling out a form

1 What occasions can you think of for when you have to fill out a form? What kind of information do you have to provide?

2 Match the expressions with the questions.

A	B
1. First name 2. Last name 3. Date of birth 4. Place of birth 5. Permanent address 6. Current address 7. Marital status 8. Occupation 9. Annual income	Where do you live? What do you do? Where are you living now? Are you married or single? What's your first name? How much do you earn a year? When were you born? What's your last name? Where were you born?

3 Do these things. Write about you.

Write your name in capital letters. _____

Sign your name. _____

Delete where not applicable. *I am a student / an employee / an employer.*

Check (✓) the appropriate box. Are you male ☐ or female ☐?

4 Complete the form.

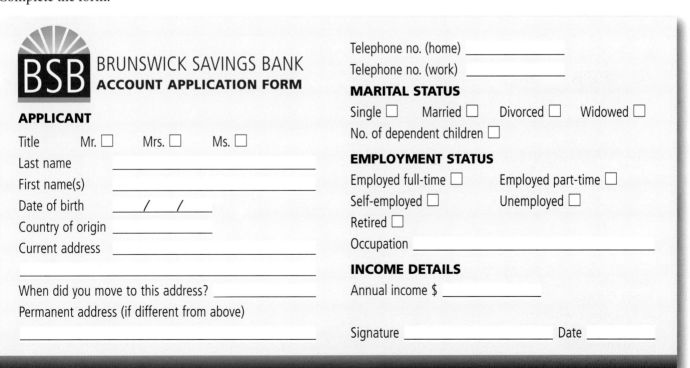

BSB BRUNSWICK SAVINGS BANK
ACCOUNT APPLICATION FORM

APPLICANT

Title   Mr. ☐   Mrs. ☐   Ms. ☐

Last name   _____

First name(s)   _____

Date of birth   ____ / ____ / ____

Country of origin   _____

Current address   _____

_____

When did you move to this address?   _____

Permanent address (if different from above)

_____

Telephone no. (home)   _____

Telephone no. (work)   _____

MARITAL STATUS

Single ☐   Married ☐   Divorced ☐   Widowed ☐

No. of dependent children ☐

EMPLOYMENT STATUS

Employed full-time ☐   Employed part-time ☐

Self-employed ☐   Unemployed ☐

Retired ☐

Occupation _____

INCOME DETAILS

Annual income $ _____

Signature _____   Date _____

WRITING

Making a reservation

1 Tracy Cooper wants to go on vacation to Florida with her family. Put the words in the correct order and add them to Tracy's e-mail below.

1. two / rooms / hotel / I / to / would / like / reserve / at / your
2. December 27 / We / on / are / arriving
3. six / hope / stay / to / We / for / nights / departing / January 2 / on
4. and / husband / like / room / I / My / double / balcony / a / would / with / preferably / a
5. also / reserve / like / two / to / I / a / room / for / would / teenage / our / daughters
6. should / non-smoking / rooms / be / Both
7. ocean / the / possible / Is / have / it / rooms / to / facing / ?
8. available / for / you / Do / have / dates / these / rooms / ?
9. also / me / you / Could / tell / room / each / price / the / of / ?
10. from / I / forward / look / you / to / hearing

2 Write a reply from the hotel. Include the following information:
- Thank her for her inquiry.
- Say you are pleased to confirm her reservation for the rooms she wants and for the dates she wants.
- Tell her that all the rooms come with cable TV and an ocean view.
- Each room is $85 per night.
- End the letter saying that you look forward to welcoming her and her family to the hotel.

PALM TREE HOTEL

Get away from the cold and the snow! Escape to a world of luxury and warm sunshine!

For reservations and inquiries:
PHONE: (888) 555-4264
FAX: (800) 555-8448

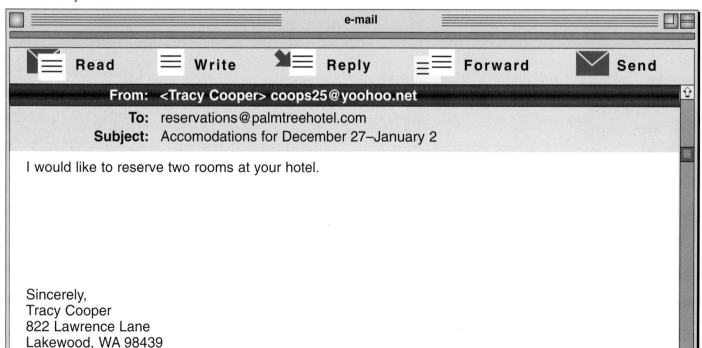

Read   Write   Reply   Forward   Send

From: <Tracy Cooper> coops25@yoohoo.net
To: reservations@palmtreehotel.com
Subject: Accomodations for December 27–January 2

I would like to reserve two rooms at your hotel.

Sincerely,
Tracy Cooper
822 Lawrence Lane
Lakewood, WA 98439
(235) 555-6739

WRITING
Describing a room

1 Think of your favorite room. Draw a picture of it on a piece of paper. Why do you like it? Write some adjectives to describe it.

My favorite room is ...
I like it because it is ...

Show a partner your drawing and talk about why you like the room.

2 Look at the picture. Then read the description of someone's favorite room. There are four mistakes in the picture. What are they?

My Favorite Room

My favorite room is our kitchen. Perhaps the kitchen is the most important room in many houses, but it is particularly so in our house because it's not only where we cook and eat, but it's also the main meeting place for family and friends. I have so many happy memories of times spent there. Whenever we have a party, people gravitate to the kitchen. It always ends up the fullest and noisiest room in the house.

So what does this special room look like? It's big, but not huge. It's big enough to have a good-sized rectangular table in the center which is the focal point of the room. There is a large window above the sink, which looks out onto the backyard. The oven is at one end, and above it are some pots and pans. At the other end is a wall with a large bulletin board, which tells the story of our lives—past, present, and future—in words and pictures. There are drawings by our children, pictures of our summer vacation, a postcard from my brother, a menu from a Chinese restaurant, and a wedding invitation for next Saturday. All our world is there for everyone to read!

The front door is seldom used in our house, only by strangers. All our friends use the back door, which means they come straight into the kitchen and join in whatever is happening there. Without a doubt, some of the happiest times of my life have been spent in our kitchen.

3 The relative pronouns *which* and *where* are used in the text. Find them and <u>underline</u> them. What does each one mean?

►► **Grammar Reference 6.5 p. 144**

4 Link the following sentences with the correct relative pronoun—*who, which, that, where,* or *whose*.

1. There's the hospital. My sister works there.
   There's the hospital where my sister works.
2. My sister is the blonde woman. She works in the bank.
3. The postcard is from São Paulo. My aunt lives there.
4. I got good grades in school. This made my father very proud.
5. Did you meet the girl? Her mother teaches Japanese.

5 Write a similar description of your favorite room in about 250 words. Describe it and give reasons why you like it.

WRITING
Writing a cover letter

1 Complete Heather Mann's cover letter to Worldwatch Americas with the words from the box.

> qualifications   advertisement
> studied   to   interested   fluent
> traveled   for   have

2 Write a cover letter for the following job advertisement.

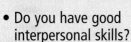

TRANS-GLOBE TOURS

Tour Guides
Europe –
East Asia –
South America

- Do you have good interpersonal skills?
- Can you speak two or more languages?
- Do you want to see the world?

Please apply with resume to:
Human Resources
Trans-Globe Tours
144 E. 42nd Street
New York, NY 10017

HEATHER W. MANN
3421 Irish Road · Berwyn, PA 19312 · (610) 555-3762

January 17, 2003

George Butler
Worldwatch Americas
7950 Merritts Avenue
Overland Park, IL 51551

Dear Mr. Butler:

I saw your **advertisement** for a Business Journalist in today's *Chicago Tribune*. I am very _____ in the job and I think that I have many of the necessary _____ .

I _____ journalism and modern languages at Boston University. I am _____ in Spanish and Portuguese. I have _____ widely in Europe and South America, and I _____ worked as a journalist for Intertec Publishing _____ the last five years.

Enclosed is a copy of my resume. I look forward _____ hearing from you soon. Please let me know if you need more information.

Sincerely,

Heather Mann

Heather Mann

WRITING
Words that join ideas

1 Some words and expressions are used to make a comment on what is being expressed.

In fact = I'm going to give you some more detailed information.
Peter doesn't like carrots. **In fact,** he hates them!

Of course = I'm going to tell you something you expect to hear.
Of course, having a baby has changed our life a lot.

Actually = I'm going to give you some information you didn't know.
Actually, Jane knows a lot about food. Her parents own a restaurant.

Unfortunately = I'm going to give you some news that is bad.
Unfortunately, there was nothing we could do to help.

Nevertheless = The result or effect of something is not what you would expect.
The accident wasn't her fault. **Nevertheless,** she felt bad.

Anyway = Let's change the subject and talk about something else.
What an awful trip you had! You must be exhausted!
Anyway, you're here now so let's not worry anymore.

2 Some words are used to join ideas and sentences.

George was rich. He wasn't a happy man.
Although George was rich, he wasn't a happy man.
George was rich. **However,** he wasn't a happy man.
George was rich, **but** he wasn't a happy man.

Carol called me. She couldn't find her passport.
Carol called me **because** she couldn't find her passport.
Carol couldn't find her passport, **so** she called me.

Read the e-mail and write the word or words that fit best.

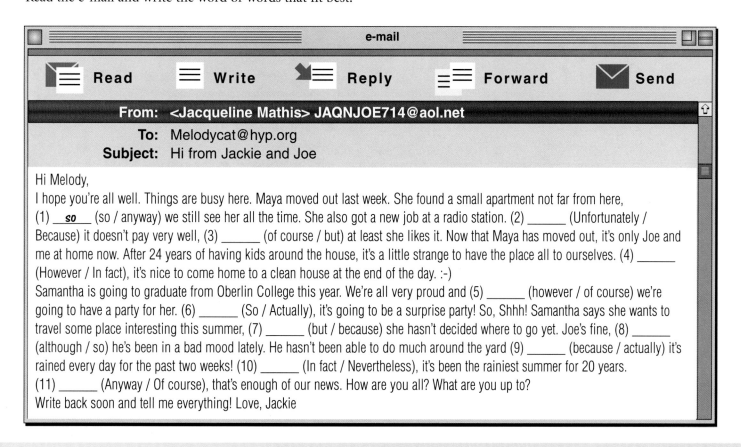

From: <Jacqueline Mathis> JAQNJOE714@aol.net
To: Melodycat@hyp.org
Subject: Hi from Jackie and Joe

Hi Melody,
I hope you're all well. Things are busy here. Maya moved out last week. She found a small apartment not far from here, (1) __so__ (so / anyway) we still see her all the time. She also got a new job at a radio station. (2) _____ (Unfortunately / Because) it doesn't pay very well, (3) _____ (of course / but) at least she likes it. Now that Maya has moved out, it's only Joe and me at home now. After 24 years of having kids around the house, it's a little strange to have the place all to ourselves. (4) _____ (However / In fact), it's nice to come home to a clean house at the end of the day. :-)
Samantha is going to graduate from Oberlin College this year. We're all very proud and (5) _____ (however / of course) we're going to have a party for her. (6) _____ (So / Actually), it's going to be a surprise party! So, Shhh! Samantha says she wants to travel some place interesting this summer, (7) _____ (but / because) she hasn't decided where to go yet. Joe's fine, (8) _____ (although / so) he's been in a bad mood lately. He hasn't been able to do much around the yard (9) _____ (because / actually) it's rained every day for the past two weeks! (10) _____ (In fact / Nevertheless), it's been the rainiest summer for 20 years.
(11) _____ (Anyway / Of course), that's enough of our news. How are you all? What are you up to?
Write back soon and tell me everything! Love, Jackie

WRITING
Beginning and ending letters

 Notice the following points about formal and informal letters:

1 We can write contractions (*I've, we've, I'll*) in an informal letter, but not in a formal one.

All letters begin with *Dear,*
You can end an informal letter with *Best wishes* or *Love*.

2 Here are some useful phrases for informal letters:

Beginning
- It was great to hear from you. I was happy to hear that ...
- Thank you for your letter. I was sorry to hear that ...
- I'm sorry I haven't written before, but ...
- This is just a note to say ...

Ending
- I'm looking forward to seeing you ...
- I'm looking forward to hearing from you soon ...
- Say hello to Robert ...
- Write to me soon ...
- I hope to hear from you soon ...
- Write and tell me when ...

1 Look at the chart below and match the beginning of each letter to the sentence that follows it. Which letter ...

- asks for information?
- invites people?
- gives news?
- accepts an invitation?
- says that money has been received?

2 Match each ending to one of the letters in Exercise 1.

___3___ Thank you very much. I look forward to hearing from you in the near future.
Sincerely,
James Fox

_____ We will complete your order as soon as we can.
Sincerely,
Silicon Valley Software

_____ It would be great to meet sometime. Please let me know if you ever come to Boston.
Love,
Pat

_____ Write back soon and tell me if you can make it.
Yours,
Peter

_____ We're really looking forward to seeing you again and meeting your friends.
Best wishes,
Mary

3 Write a letter to a friend who you haven't been in touch with for a long time. Include the following parts:

- Tell your friend about what you've been doing recently. Include your future plans.
- Ask your friend about his/her recent activities and future plans.
- Try to arrange to meet somewhere.
- Remember to put your address and the date in the top right-hand corner of your letter.

A	B
1. Dear Mary, This is just a note to ask if you and Dave are free on the evening of July 11.	Could you please send me your brochure and a price list?
2. Dear Jane, Thanks for your letter. It was good to hear from you after such a long time. You asked me what I've been doing. Well, ...	I've changed jobs a few times since I last spoke to you and, as you know, I've moved, too.
3. Dear Sir or Madam, I saw an advertisement in *The Chicago Tribune* for weekend specials at your hotel.	Unfortunately, this amount did not include shipping and handling, which is $7.50.
4. Dear Peter, Thank you so much for inviting Dave and me to your summer party.	Jen and I are having a barbecue with all our friends, and we were wondering if you could come.
5. Dear Mr. Smith, We received your order for the *World Encyclopedia* on CD-ROM, and your check for $75.	We'd love to come. I haven't been to your place for a long time.

WRITING
Sentence combination

1 Read the sentences about Johnny Appleseed and then compare them with the paragraph below. Notice the ways that the sentences are combined.

Johnny Appleseed's real name was John Chapman.
He was born in 1774.
He was born in Massachusetts.
He traveled westward.
At that time, he was 23 years old.
He went to the Ohio River Valley.
He found no apple orchards.
He found no apple trees.
Johnny had a love of nature.
This love gave him an idea.
He planted thousands of seeds.
The seeds were for apples.
The seeds grew into apple trees.
This made the wilderness bloom.
Johnny Appleseed died in 1845.
He spent 50 years traveling and planting seeds.
Some of the trees still bear apples.
He planted those trees 200 years ago.

Johnny Appleseed, whose real name was John Chapman, was born in Massachusetts in 1774. When he was 23 years old, he traveled westward to the Ohio River Valley, where he found no apple orchards or apple trees. Johnny's love of nature gave him an idea. He planted thousands of apple seeds, which grew into apple trees, making the wilderness bloom. Johnny Appleseed died in 1845, after 50 years of traveling and planting seeds. Some of the trees that he planted 200 years ago still bear apples.

2 Rewrite each group of sentences to form a more natural sounding paragraph.

1. **A person**
   Alicia Vargas is a writer.
   She writes mysteries.
   She is famous.
   She comes from Chile.
   She has recently moved to California.
   She has written 25 novels.
   Her novels have been translated into 15 languages.
   A Hollywood studio is going to make a movie of her latest novel.
   The novel is called *A Charmed Life*.
   The movie will star Sunny Shaw.
   Sunny Shaw's last movie was a huge box-office success.
   The movie was called *Hot Night in the Snow*.

2. **A place**

   Philadelphia was founded in 1682.
   It was founded by William Penn.
   It is the largest city in the state of Pennsylvania.
   It is the fifth largest city in the United States.
   Its name comes from the Greek.
   In Greek, it means "city of brotherly love."
   Philadelphia is sometimes called the birthplace of the nation.
   It is where the Declaration of Independence was signed in 1776.
   It is where the Constitution was signed in 1787.
   Philadelphia was the capital of the United States from 1790 to 1800.
   Not everyone knows this.
   Philadelphia is also the home of the Liberty Bell.
   The Liberty Bell is famous.
   It weighs 909 kilograms.
   It is now kept in a special glass pavilion for visitors to view.

3 Write a short profile of a person or a place that is important to you.

WRITING
For and against

1 Do you live or work in a city? Is it very big? Write down five advantages and five disadvantages of living in the city. Compare your ideas with a partner.

2 Write down five advantages and five disadvantages of living in the country. Compare your ideas with your partner.

3 Read the text and add the phrases from the box.

> finally   all in all   one disadvantage is that   especially
> has both advantages and disadvantages   for example
> what's more   in conclusion   one advantage is that

LIVING IN THE CITY

Living in the city (1) __has both advantages and disadvantages__ .
(2) _____ it is often easier to find work, and there is usually good public transportation, so you don't need to own a car. Also, there are a lot of interesting things to do and places to see. (3) _____ , you can eat in good restaurants, visit museums, and go to the theater and to concerts. (4) _____ , when you want to relax, you can usually find a park where you can feed the ducks or just sit on a park bench and read a book. (5) _____ , city life is full of bustle and variety and you need never feel bored.

However, for every plus there is a minus. (6) _____ , you might have a job, but unless it pays very well, you will not be able to afford many of the things that there are to do, because living in a city is often very expensive. It is (7) _____ difficult to find good, cheap housing. What's more, public transportation is sometimes crowded and dirty, particularly during rush hour. Even the parks can become very crowded, especially on Sundays when it seems as if everyone is looking for some open space and green grass. (8) _____ , despite all the crowds, it is still possible to feel lonely in a city.

(9) _____ , I think that city life can be particularly appealing to young people, who like the excitement of the city and don't mind the noise and pollution. However, many people, when they get older, and particularly when they have young children, often prefer the peace and fresh air of the suburbs.

4 There are three paragraphs. What is the purpose of each one?

5 Write three paragraphs entitled "Living in the Country" about the advantages and disadvantages of living in the country. In the conclusion, give your own opinion. Write about 250 words.

WRITING
Correcting mistakes

1 Ana was a student of English in Chicago, where she stayed with the Bennett family. She has now returned home. Read the letter she has written to Mr. and Mrs. Bennett. Her English has improved, but there are still over 25 mistakes. How many can you find?

28 Nuevo Leon
Mexico City
Mexico, D.F.

Friday, June 14

Dear Mr. and Mrs. Bennett,

I am home now since two weeks, but I have to start work immediately, so this is the first time is possible for me to write. How are you all? Are you busy as usual? Does Tim still work hard for his exam next month? I am miss you a lot and also all my friends from my English class. Yesterday I've received a letter from my Greece friend, Christina, and she told about some of the other students. She say that Atsuko and Yuki will write me from Japan. I am lucky because I made so many good friend during I was in Chicago. It was really interesting for me to meet people from so many different countries. I think that we not only improved our English (I hope this!) but we also knew people from all over the world and this is important.

My family are fine. They had a good summer vacation by the lake. We are all very exciting because my brother will get married just before Christmas and we like very much his girlfriend. They have looked for an apartment near the city center but it is no easy to find one. If they won't find one soon, they will have to stay here with us.

Please can you check something for me? I can't find my red scarf. I think maybe I have forgotten it in the closet in my bedroom.

Please write soon. My family send best wishes to you all. I hope I can come back next year. Stay with you was a very wonderful experience for me. Thank you for all things and excuse my mistakes. I already forget so much words.

Love,

Ana

p.s. I hope you like the photo. It's nice, isn't it?

2 Compare the mistakes you have found with a partner. Correct the letter.

3 Write a thank you letter to someone you have stayed with.

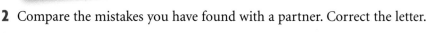

Tapescripts

Unit 1

T 1.1 **General knowledge quiz**

1. The modern Olympic Games started in 1896.
2. It takes eight minutes for the sun's rays to reach Earth.
3. He was walking on the moon.
4. A vegetarian doesn't eat meat.
5. If you are flying over the International Date Line, the Pacific Ocean is below you.
6. VIP stands for Very Important Person.
7. Chinese is spoken by the most people in the world.
8. Glasses were invented in Italy.
9. Brazil has won the World Cup five times.
10. Nelson Mandela didn't become president of South Africa until he was 76 years old because he was in prison for 27 years.
11. Abraham Lincoln was watching a play when he was assassinated.
12. Nintendo has been selling video games since 1978.

T 1.2 **Negatives and pronunciation**

1. The sun doesn't rise in the west! It rises in the east!
2. Cows don't eat meat! They eat grass!
3. Mercedes-Benz cars aren't made in Canada! They're made in Germany!
4. Neil Armstrong didn't land on the moon in 1989! He landed in 1969!
5. Abraham Lincoln wasn't giving a speech when he was assassinated! He was watching a play!
6. The Pyramids weren't built by the Chinese! They were built by the Egyptians!
7. We haven't been in class for one month! We've been in class for one week!
8. We're not studying Japanese! We're studying English!

T 1.3 **Complete the questions**

1. A What did you do last night?
   B I stayed home and watched television.
2. A What kind of books do you like to read?
   B Horror stories and science fiction.
3. A Have you ever been to the United States?
   B Yes, I have. I went there last year.
   A Did you like it?
   B Yes, I really enjoyed it.
4. A What's the teacher doing?
   B He's helping Maria with this exercise.
5. A What does your mother do?
   B She works in a bank.
6. A Did you do your homework last night?
   B No, I didn't. I didn't feel well.
7. A What are you doing next weekend?
   B I'm going to a party.
8. A Do you have a TV in your bedroom?
   B No, I don't. Just a CD player.

T 1.4 *is* **and** *has*

1. My sister's a teacher.
2. She's on vacation right now.
3. She's in France.
4. She's never traveled to Europe before.

5. She's been there for two weeks.
6. She's going back to work next week.
7. Her husband's a builder.
8. He's building a house.

T 1.5 **See p. 4**

T 1.6 **Short answers**

D = Dad P = Pam

D Good morning! Did you have a nice time last night?
P Yes, I did. I went to the movies with Bill.
D Do you want breakfast?
P No, I don't, thanks. I'm not hungry.
D Have you had any coffee?
P Yes, I have. I don't want any more, thanks.
D Is Bill coming over tonight?
P No, he isn't. He's going out with his friends.
D OK. Are you leaving for school soon?
P Yes, I am. I'm going right now. Bye!

T 1.7 **Answer the questions**

1. Is it hot today?
2. Is it raining?
3. Are you wearing sneakers?
4. Do you usually come to school by bus?
5. Are you going out tonight?
6. Did you go out last night?
7. Do you have a dictionary?
8. Do you have any brothers or sisters?

T 1.8 **Listen and check**

1. A Do you like studying English?
   B Yes, I do. It's my favorite subject.
2. A Is it a nice day today?
   B No, it isn't. It's rainy and cold.
3. A Have you seen my pen?
   B No, I haven't. You can borrow mine if you want.
4. A Are you staying home this evening?
   B Yes, I am. Do you want to come over?
5. A Did you take a vacation last year?
   B No, I didn't. I couldn't afford to.

T 1.9 **My wonders**

P = Peter S = Sam K = Kelly

P I was just reading this article about the wonders of the ancient world. A lot of them were buildings. I was thinking, what would your wonders of the *modern* world be? Not necessarily buildings, but things that have changed our way of life.
S Well, to me, air travel is the thing that's really changed my life.
P Yeah.
S Flying is so cheap now that you can travel almost anywhere, in your own country or anyplace in the entire world. For people who love to travel, the airplane gives you freedom and extra time.
K That's true, it's pretty easy get somewhere by plane.
P I suppose so. But what about all those airport delays?
S Well, sure, that's the bad part. With all the people traveling these days, airports are overcrowded and planes get delayed a lot,

even canceled. And all the security precautions can slow things down, too.
P I'll say.
S But overall, it's the safest way to travel.
K For me, well, I was thinking the cell phone is the most wonderful thing.
S Really? I don't even know how to use one.
K Oh, I couldn't live without mine. It's so convenient! I can call my friends anytime and they can always call me. Or if I'm in trouble I can call for help…
P You mean like calling your parents?
K Yeah, like parents … and if I'm running late, I'm able to call a friend if I'm, like, on the bus or something.
S But the problem with cell phones is that people use them too much for every little thing. It's practically glued to their ears.
P Boy, do I hate it when people shout into them in a public place and everyone else has to listen to the conversation. Especially in restaurants.
K And movie theaters!
S Well, good manners aren't a wonder of our world!
P You know, I think the most amazing wonder is e-mail. It's changed the world, and it's totally transformed *my* business. Everybody at work is always on the computer, responding to e-mails, sending e-mails … That's where most of our business is done now, through e-mail. You're sending reports, you get information. But the bad part is that you're glued to the computer and people expect things to be done right away.
K Yeah, people are shocked if you go through a day without checking your e-mail.
S I'm glad I didn't have e-mail when I was working!
P And when you go on vacation and then you come back, there's, like, 200 e-mails waiting for you—all of them urgent.
S I guess it's like any other tool or device. If it's used correctly, it's very useful.

T 1.10 see p. 8

T 1.11 **Social expressions**

1. A Sorry I'm late. I got stuck in traffic.
   B Don't worry about it. You're here now. Come and sit down.
2. A Bye, Mom! I'm going to school now.
   B Take care, Honey. Have a nice day!
3. A Have you heard that Jenny's going out with Pete?
   B Really? I don't know what she sees in him.
4. A How long did it take you to do the homework?
   B Ages! How about you?
5. A I don't know about you, but I'm sick and tired of this weather.
   B So am I. I can't stand all this rain.
6. A Who was that I saw you with last night?
   B None of your business!
7. A I'm tired. I'm taking next week off.
   B That sounds like a good idea. You need a break.

8. **A** Hey! Let's go running in the park!
   B Me? Run? You must be kidding!
9. **A** Can we get together this afternoon at 3:00?
   B I'm sorry. I can't make it then. How about a little later?
10. **A** What a gorgeous coat! Was it expensive?
    B Yes, it cost a fortune!

T 1.12 Social expressions

1. I'm taking this Friday and next Monday off. We're going away for a long weekend.
2. Can we meet at about 7:00?
3. I'm really sorry I'm late. I overslept.
4. John is going to take Sue to the party next week.
5. Tonight for homework, I want you to learn 100 new words.

Unit 2

T 2.1 see p. 11

T 2.2 Listen and check

1. **A** Is he married?
   B Yes, he is.
2. **A** What does he do?
   B He's a lawyer.
3. **A** Where does he live?
   B In a big house in Texas.
4. **A** Does he have any children?
   B Yes, he has two.
5. **A** What does his wife do?
   B She's an interior designer.
6. **A** Which sports does he play?
   B Golf.
7. **A** Where is he working right now?
   B In Mexico.
8. **A** Is he paid very well?
   B Yes, he is.

T 2.3 Jeff Norman

People think it's a joke that a man my age with a college degree is a paperboy! But, hey, it's great. I'm paid good money—$60,000 a year for four hours' work a day. On top of that, I often get $50 a week in tips. Not bad!

My job isn't easy. I get up at 2 A.M. every day, seven days a week. The first newspaper is delivered at 2:30 A.M. I finish 4 hours, 65 miles, and 1,000 newspapers later. I drive a red Chevy Blazer, and the newspapers are packed into the back.

I love the peace and quiet in the early morning. Most of the time, I have the world to myself. Occasionally, I meet a jogger.

I usually get back home by 7 A.M. Then, I have the rest of the day to be with my family and do what I want.

I have two teenage children and my wife works at the University of Iowa. Some days I coach my kids' baseball team, other days I play golf. I'm also studying for my master's degree at the moment. I want to be a marriage counselor eventually, but I'm not in a hurry. I'm enjoying life too much. Some people think it's not much of a job but, hey, when *they're* sitting in an office, *I'm* playing golf! So I ask you—who has the better life?

T 2.4 Listen and check

1. I'm paid good money, $60,000 a year. And I often get $50 a week in tips.
2. I get up at 2 A.M. The first newspaper is delivered at 2:30 A.M.
3. I drive a red Chevy Blazer and the newspapers are packed into the back.
4. I love the peace and quiet.
5. Occasionally, I meet a jogger.
6. I usually get back home by 7 A.M.
7. My wife works at the University of Iowa.
8. Some days I coach my kids' baseball team, other days I play golf.
9. I'm also studying for my master's degree at the moment. I want to be a marriage counselor.
10. Some people think it's not much of a job, but when they're sitting in an office, I'm playing golf.

T 2.5 see p. 13

T 2.6 The clown doctor
I = Interviewer   P = Peggy
1. **I** Do you like your job?
   P Oh, yes, I do. I enjoy my job very much.
2. **I** Why do you like it so much?
   P Because I love working with children and making them laugh.
3. **I** What do you wear to work?
   P I wear crazy clothes. I wear a big red coat, a striped shirt, and tights with big colored dots on them.
4. **I** Who are you working with now? Anyone special?
   P Well, at the moment I'm working with a very sick little girl from Costa Rica. She's had so many operations. She's very special to me.
5. **I** Don't you sometimes feel sad?
   P Yes, I do feel sad sometimes, but it's important not to show it. And then again there are some very special moments.
6. **I** Isn't it tiring?
   P Yes, it is. It's very tiring. I'm always exhausted at the end of the day.
7. **I** What do you do in the evenings? Do you just go home and relax?
   P No, I don't. Sometimes I go out with friends. I love to go out. I love life. I have the best friends and the best job in the world.

T 2.7 Favorite sports
Kurt
I play golf. That's my sport. I love it. I'd play every day if I could, but … well … I usually end up playing about once a week. I play with a group of friends and we usually play on one of the public golf courses in the area. Sometimes we play on a private course, but it's expensive so we don't do it too often! When I play I need to have a full set of golf clubs, golf shoes, and golf gloves. And, of course, I also need golf balls and golf tees. If I play on a private course, then I'll need a golf cart, too. Am I a good golfer? Yeah, I'm pretty good, I guess. But I'd like to be better.

John
I guess I'm not a typical American, because soccer is my favorite sport. I like to watch it and I like to play it. Every Sunday morning my friends and I go down to the park to play. As

long as it's not raining or snowing, we'll be there. We all love soccer and we just play for fun. We don't take it very seriously, which is good because we're all really bad! But we don't care! It's good exercise! I usually wear shorts and a T-shirt when I play. Oh, yeah, and soccer shoes. But I don't wear shin guards. I have a pair, but I never wear them.

Suzanne
I've been skiing all my life. I first went with my father when I was six years old and I've been skiing ever since. I live in Denver, Colorado, so there are plenty of ski resorts in the Rocky Mountains, which are right outside the city. During ski season, I go skiing two or three times a week. It's great. When I go skiing I of course need skis, ski poles, and ski boots. I also like to have a ski suit, because I like to look good. A warm hat, and gloves are important, too. Oh, and I also wear a pair of ski goggles. I'm a good skier and in fact I even give lessons. If you haven't gone skiing yet, you should try it! Hey, I could even give you your first lesson!

T 2.8 see p. 17

T 2.9 see p. 17

T 2.10 Numbers
1. **A** When are you going away on vacation?
   B On the fifteenth.
   A And when do you get back?
   B On the twenty-fourth. I'll give you a call when we get home.
2. And now the business news. The unemployment rate this month has risen slightly. The national unemployment rate is now 6.2%, and in our area, an estimated 15,000 people are out of work.
3. **A** Thank you for calling the Fillmore Concert Hall. This is Heather speaking. How can I help you?
   B Hi. Do you still have seats for tonight's concert?
   A Yes, we do.
   B Great. I'll need two tickets. Can I reserve them by phone?
   A Yes, that's fine. Tickets are $25 each. We take all major credit cards. What type of credit card will you be using?
   B Visa.
   A And your account number, please?
   B It's number 4929 … 7983 … 0621 … 8849.
   A Let me read that back. 4929 … 7983 … 0621 … 8849.
   B That's right.
   A Your name as it appears on the card?
   B It's Young-Ho Park.
   A Could you spell that for me, please?
   B Sure. Y-O-U-N-G … dash … H-O … P-A-R-K.
   A Thank you, Mr. Park. You can pick up your tickets at the box office.
4. **A** Hey, I really like your shoes! Where'd you get them?
   B At the Athlete's Foot.
   A How much were they, if you don't mind my asking?
   B $39.99. They're having a sale all month. Everything's half price.

5. **A** Hello?
   B Hi, Bill, it's Jim.
   A Hey, Jim. What's up?
   B Nothing much, except we're having a party this Saturday, and we were wondering if you'd like to come. It's our tenth wedding anniversary.
   A Congratulations. When is it?
   B The party starts at seven o'clock.
   A Saturday at seven? Sounds good.

Unit 3

T 3.1 **The Tale of Gluskap and the Baby**

Gluskap the warrior was very pleased with himself because he had fought and won so many battles. He boasted to a woman friend: "Nobody can beat me!"

"Really?" said the woman. "I know someone who can beat you. His name is Wasis." Gluskap had never heard of Wasis. He immediately wanted to meet him and fight him. So he was taken to the woman's village. The woman pointed to a baby who was sitting and sucking a piece of sugar on the floor of a teepee.

"There," she said. "That is Wasis. He is little, but he is very strong." Gluskap laughed and walked up to the baby. "I am Gluskap. Fight me!" he shouted. Little Wasis looked at him for a moment, then he opened his mouth. "Waaah! Waaah!" he yelled. Gluskap had never heard such a terrible noise. He danced a war dance and sang some war songs. Wasis screamed louder. "Waaah! Waaah! Waaah!" Gluskap covered his ears and ran out of the teepee. After he had run a few miles, he stopped and listened. The baby was still yelling. Gluskap the fearless was terrified. He ran on and was never seen again in the woman's village.

T 3.2 **Listen and repeat**

laughed
stopped
looked
danced
covered
listened
opened
screamed
wanted
shouted
boasted
pointed

T 3.3 **What was she doing?**

1. At 8 A.M. she was driving to the airport.
2. At 10 A.M. she was flying to Chicago.
3. At 11:30 A.M. she was having a meeting.
4. At 1:30 P.M. she was having lunch.
5. At 3 P.M. she was visiting Dot Com Enterprises.
6. At 6 P.M. she was writing a report on the plane.
7. At 8:30 P.M. she was putting the baby to bed.
8. At 10 P.M. she was relaxing and listening to music.

T 3.4 **Listen and check**

1. **A** I didn't laugh at his joke.
   B Why? Had you heard it before?
2. **A** Were you surprised by the ending of the movie?
   B No, I'd read the book, so I already knew the story.
3. **A** I went to the airport, but I couldn't get on the plane.
   B Why? Had you left your passport at home?
4. **A** I was homesick the whole time I was living in France.
   B That's really sad! Had you ever lived abroad before?
5. **A** The hotel where we stayed on our vacation was awful!
   B That's too bad. Hadn't you stayed there before?
6. **A** I met my girlfriend's parents for the first time last Sunday.
   B Really? I thought you'd met them before.
7. **A** My grandfather had two sons from his first marriage.
   B Really? I didn't know he'd been married before.

T 3.5 **An amazing thing happened!**

L = Lim   W = Wanda

L Hi, Wanda. Did you have a good vacation?
W Oh, yeah, we had a great time. But I have to tell you—the most *amazing* thing happened!
L Really? What was that?
W Well, Roy and I were swimming on the beach near the hotel—it was our first day—and this huge wave came along and knocked my sunglasses into the water. I …
L Why were you swimming in your sunglasses?
W Oh, I don't know. I'd just left them on top of my head. I forgot they were there. Anyway, they were gone. I couldn't find them anywhere. I was really upset. You know Roy had given me those sunglasses for my birthday and they were really expensive.
L I remember—nearly $200.
W Yeah. Anyway, I had to have sunglasses, so I bought a new pair—just a cheap pair this time. The next day, I was lying on the beach, sunbathing. Then, suddenly another huge wave …
L You didn't lose *another* pair of sunglasses?
W No, no. You'll never believe this—but there was another huge wave. It completely covered me. I was so wet and …
L Are you sure this was a good vacation?
W Yeah—but listen! When I looked down there, on the sand, right next to me, were my expensive sunglasses. The ones I had lost the day before! I couldn't believe my eyes!
L You're kidding! Wow, that *is* amazing!

T 3.6 **Books and movies**

M = Mary   S = Sue   K = Kevin   L = Luis

M Hey, I just read a great book.
S A book? Hey, we're impressed! What was it?
M *Harry Potter and the Sorcerer's Stone*, by J.K. Rowling.
K *Harry Potter*? Isn't that a children's book?
M Well, yeah, but … No, guys. It was really good. I was so amazed. Lots of adults read Harry Potter books, they're not just for kids.
L Sure, Mary. Do you like cartoons, too?
M As a matter of fact…

S She's right. I've seen people reading *Harry Potter* on the subway. I'd like to see one of the movies.
L Me too. Say, what's your favorite book, Sue?
S My all-time favorite takes place here in New York.
K What's that?
S It's called *A Tree Grows in Brooklyn* by Betty Smith. It's fantastic!
L Why do you like it?
S Oh, it's just a beautiful story. It's about this girl, Francie Nolan, growing up in Brooklyn at the turn of the century.
K Which century?
S Oh, that's right, the twentieth century. It's set in the early 1900s. Her Dad was kind of a drunk, but she adored him … and he was no good to the family, so the mother had to take care of the kids by herself.
L Hmm. Sounds a little like *Angela's Ashes*. I liked that movie.
K Yeah, yeah and the book by Frank McCourt. It painted a fascinating picture of New York at the time. There were lots of immigrants, and people were really poor, but they still had fun. I really enjoyed it.
L Hey, that reminds me. Do you know *Ragtime*? It's a great novel by E.L. Doctorow about America at the turn of the century … the twentieth century, I mean.
M Wasn't *Ragtime* a movie?
L That's right, and a musical play too, but the book was even better. It's all about America in the early 1900s: immigrants, African Americans, rich and poor people, industrialists and socialists, jazz musicians …
K Say, has anyone read Ernest Hemingway?
M Huh—we had to read that stuff at school and I never …
K Well … We didn't study Hemingway in school and when I read my first—it was *The Old Man and the Sea*—I loved it. …

T 3.7 **Giving opinions**

1. **A** Did you like the movie?
   B It was excellent. Have you seen it yet? It stars Julia Roberts and Antonio Banderas.
2. **A** What did you think of the play?
   B It was really boring! I fell asleep during the first act.
3. **A** Did you like your sandwiches?
   B They were delicious. John had turkey and cheese and I had tuna salad.
4. **A** Do you like Stephen King's novels?
   B I didn't like his last one, but I couldn't put his new one down until the last page.
5. **A** What do you think of their children?
   B I think they spoil them. They always give them whatever they want.
6. **A** What was your vacation like?
   B It was a nice break, but the weather wasn't very good.
7. **A** What did you think of Jennifer Lopez?
   B She's usually good, but I don't think she was right for this part.
8. **A** How was the game?
   B It was really exciting, especially when Michael Jordan scored in the last second.

Unit 4

T 4.1 **Teenagers and parents**

I = Interviewer   S = Sarah   L = Lindsey

I Tell me, what are some good things about being a teenager and not an adult?

S Um … well, for one thing, you don't have to go to work.

L Yeah. And you don't have to pay bills.

I OK …

L And you can go out with your friends, and you can go shopping, and you can go to the movies, and …

S Come on, Lindsey. Adults can do all that, too! But what's different is how much freedom teenagers have.

L Don't have, you mean.

S Right. How much freedom we don't have. I mean I always have to tell my Mom and Dad where I'm going and what time I'm coming home.

L Mhmm.

I And what time do you have to get back home?

S We have to be home by 10 P.M. on weeknights, maybe 11 or 12 on weekends.

L But it doesn't matter because you never have enough money anyway!

S Definitely. You get *some* money from your parents, but it's never enough. And you aren't allowed to buy whatever you want.

I What do you think it's like being an adult? Lindsey?

L Well, adults have to worry about paying the bills and taking care of their family. They can't do what they want when they want.

I They have responsibilities, you mean?

L Yeah. I feel more sorry for my Mom. She doesn't have to work full-time, but she still has loads of different things to do in a day, like shopping and cooking and taking me to dance classes and soccer practice.

I So, do you think your Dad has an easier life?

L Well, I don't know. He has to drive over 500 miles a week.

I Wow, that is a lot. … Sarah, tell me about school. What are some of the rules at your high school?

S Oh, my gosh! There are so many! Let me see. We can't wear makeup. We're not allowed to chew gum. We're not allowed to bring cell phones to class …

L There are millions of rules—all of them stupid.

S And if you break one of the rules, you have to stay after school!

L Well, speaking of school, I've got to go. I've got to do my homework!

T 4.2 **Listen and check**

1. You don't have to go to work.
2. You don't have to pay bills.
3. You can go out with your friends.
4. I always have to tell my Mom and Dad where I'm going.
5. What time do you have to get back home?
6. You aren't allowed to buy whatever you want.
7. We can't wear makeup.
8. I've got to go. I've got to do my homework.

T 4.3 **Listen and check**

1. Where's my briefcase? I have to go to work.
2. Look at those dirty plates! We have to do the dishes.
3. Pam and Chuck don't have any food in their house. They have to go shopping.
4. John needs to get an alarm clock. He has to get up early.
5. I don't have any clean socks. I have to do the laundry.
6. My mother comes home late from work, so I have to do the cooking.

T 4.4 **Planning a trip**

B = Brad   G = George

B I'm so excited. I can't stop thinking about this trip.

G Me too. I spend all my time just looking at maps.

B What do you think? Should we take cash or traveler's checks?

G I think we should take traveler's checks. It'll be safer.

B Yeah, I think you're right.

G When should we go to Thailand?

B Well, I don't think we should go during the rainy season. I'd rather go in February or March, when it's drier.

G Sounds like a good idea to me. I can't wait to get going!

T 4.5 **A new job**

D = Dave   M = Manager

D So, uh … what time do I have to start?

M Eleven in the morning or four in the afternoon.

D And do I have to wear a uniform?

M You bet. You have to wear the same uniform as everyone else—a short-sleeved white shirt, black pants, and a red hat. And a name tag.

D So … what do I do exactly?

M You serve the customers. Remember—you must always be polite. You say "Good morning" or whatever the time of day, and then "Can I help you?" When they tell you what they want, you have to enter it into the computer, and when they're finished, you should read back what they ordered. Then you take their money, and you put together their order. That's it.

D OK. When can I start?

M You start at 4:00 tomorrow afternoon.

D Cool.

M Here's your hat. And your name tag. You're all set. Welcome to Burger Heaven, Dave.

T 4.6 **Nationality words**

the United States	American
Japan	Japanese
China	Chinese
Mexico	Mexican
Korea	Korean
Greece	Greek
Thailand	Thai
Brazil	Brazilian

T 4.7 **Come over to my place!**

Aya

My name is Aya. I come from Nagano, Japan. In my country, we usually invite guests home on the weekend for dinner, at about 7 o'clock in the evening. Before they come, we must clean the front garden and the entry way. Then we must spray it all with water to show that we welcome our guests with cleanliness. The guests usually bring a gift, and when they give you the gift they say, "I'm sorry this is such a small gift," but in fact, they have chosen the gift very carefully.

When the meal is ready the hostess says, "We have nothing special for you today, but you are welcome to come this way." You can see that in Japan you should try to be modest and you should not show off too much. If you don't understand our culture, you may think this is very strange. When we have foreign guests, we try to serve traditional Japanese meals like sushi, tempura, or sukiyaki, but when we have Japanese guests, we serve all kinds of food such as spaghetti, Chinese food, or steaks.

When guests leave, the host and hostess see them out of the house and wait until their car turns the corner of the street; they wait until they can't see them anymore.

Mary

My name is Mary and I'm from Columbus, Ohio. We like to have people over for dinner, and we usually have them come at around seven in the evening. We have regular dinners for our guests but sometimes, when we invite a lot of people over, we have what's called a "pot luck supper."

A pot luck is an informal occasion, so people dress casually. If the weather is nice, we'll have it outside in the backyard. What makes a pot luck fun is that everyone who comes is asked to bring a dish of food. They're given a choice: appetizer, main course, salad or vegetable, or dessert. As the host, I'll know how many of each kind of dish the guests will bring, but not exactly what the foods will be. That's why it's called "pot luck"—it's a surprise, having a dinner party and not knowing what you're going to feed the guests!

As the guests arrive, they put their dish on the table. The meal is then served buffet-style, and drinks are provided, although some guests might bring a bottle of wine as a gift. It's a fun, relaxed way of getting together with friends.

Lucas

My name is Lucas and I'm from Porto Alegre, which is in the southern part of Brazil. We like to invite our friends over on weekends, on a Friday or a Saturday night for a *churrasco*, or Brazilian barbecue. These are very popular in this part of Brazil. A *churrasco* is different in different parts of Brazil, but here's how we do it at our house.

People come at about 8 P.M. and stay till midnight or even later—sometimes until two in the morning, when someone gets sleepy. People stay a long time; there is no set time for dinner to end. We'll sit around and play cards or just talk. It's very informal. If people want to bring something, I'll tell them to bring something for the meal like a bottle of wine or something for dessert.

Ah, but what about the food? At a *churrasco*, we cook different kinds of meat on long metal skewers over an open flame. We make all kinds of meat: beef, pork, and maybe Brazilian sausage. Sometimes chicken, too. Then we cut off slices of meat from the skewers to serve the guests. It's really delicious. We usually have potato salad or rice as side dishes. After the meal, we drink coffee or espresso.

T 4.8 Requests and offers

1. A Could we have the check, please?
   B Yes, sir. I'll bring it right away.
2. A Could you fill it up, please?
   B Sure. Should I check the oil, too?
3. A Can I help you?
   B Just looking, thanks.
4. A Two large sodas, please.
   B Diet or regular?
5. A Can you tell me the city code for Seoul, please?
   B One moment. I'll look it up.
6. A Can I give you a ride?
   B That would be great! Could you drop me off at the library?
7. A Would you mind opening the window?
   B No problem. It's stuffy in here.
8. A Could I have extension 238, please?
   B That line's busy. Would you like to hold?

T 4.9 Requests and offers

1. A So, anyway, there I was, sitting in my boss's office. All of a sudden, the phone rings and my boss says …
   B Sorry to interrupt, Honey, but I think the baby's crying. … Could you go and check on her? And maybe give her her bottle? Oh, and check her diaper!
2. A May I help you?
   B Yes, I bought these shoes here two days ago, and the heel on this one is already broken. Can I exchange them for a new pair?
   A Of course. Let me see if we have another pair.
3. A Will you turn down that awful music?
   B What?
   A Will you turn down that awful music? Or better still, turn it off!
   B Oh, all right.
4. A Hi, Bob. Where are you going?
   B I have a meeting with the web designer and the programmer about our new web page this afternoon.
   A Could you do me a favor? Would you mind asking the programmer to call me? I have a question for him about the budget.
   B Sure. No problem.

Unit 5

T 5.1 Bill's list

B = Bill   A = Alice

B I'm going shopping. Do we need anything?
A I don't think so. … Oh, wait. We don't have any sugar.
B It's OK, it's on my list. I'm going to buy some.
A What about bread?
B Good idea! I'll pick up a loaf.
A What time will you be back?
B I don't know. I might stop at Nick's. It depends on how much time I have.
A Don't forget, we're playing tennis with David and Pam this afternoon.
B Don't worry. I won't forget. I'll be back before then.
A OK. See you later, Honey.

T 5.2 Going on vacation

M = Mike   C = Cindy

M Do you have the plane tickets?
C Yes. They're with the passports and traveler's checks.
M What time is the taxi coming?
C In about half an hour. Do you have the address of the hotel we're staying at?
M No, just the name. The Grand Hotel. Do we need the address?
C No. I suppose the airport bus will drop us off.
M Did you remember your swimsuit this year?
C Yes! It's packed. What about the tennis rackets?
M I put them in my suitcase, with the 15 books.
C Well … we both like to read on vacation …
M I guess so. Now let's try and close these suitcases … if we can.

T 5.3 What do you think will happen?

1. I think Jerry will win the tennis match. He's been playing really well lately.
2. I think it'll be a nice day tomorrow. The forecast is for warm and dry weather.
3. I think I'll pass my test on Friday. I've been studying for weeks.
4. I think you'll like the movie. It's a wonderful story, and the acting is excellent.
5. I think we'll get to the airport in time. But we'd better get going.
6. I think you'll get the job. You have the right qualifications and plenty of experience.

T 5.4 What do you think will happen?

1. I don't think Jerry will win the tennis match. He hasn't practiced for weeks.
2. I don't think it'll be a nice day tomorrow. The forecast said rainy and windy.
3. I don't think I'll pass my test on Friday. I haven't studied at all.
4. I don't think you'll like the movie. It's kind of boring.
5. I don't think we'll get to the airport in time. There's too much traffic.
6. I don't think you'll get the job. They're looking for someone with more experience.

T 5.5 Arranging to meet

H = Han   L = Liz

H Hello?
L Hi, Han! It's Liz.
H Oh, hi, Liz. How are you?
L Pretty good. Listen, I'm calling because we need to meet sometime this weekend to talk about our project.
H OK. What are you doing today?
L Well, this afternoon I have a dance class, but I'm not doing anything this evening. What about you?
H I'm going shopping this afternoon, and this evening I'm going to the movies. What about tomorrow?
L Well, I'm having my hair cut tomorrow afternoon, so that'll take a while.
H What time will you be finished at the hairstylist's?
L About 4:00 in the afternoon. What are you doing around then?
H I'm painting the kitchen tomorrow, but I might be done by 4:00.

L OK. Why don't we meet at the Internet Cafe at about 5:00? We can have coffee and do our work.
H Sounds good to me. Are you going out in the evening?
L Yes. I'm going out for dinner with a couple of friends. Do you want to join us?
H That would be great! I'd love to.
L OK. So we'll meet tomorrow at 5:00 at the Internet Cafe.
H Cool.

T 5.6 A weather forecast

Good morning. Here's a brief look at the weather for today in cities across the United States.

Expect heavy snow in Chicago today with up to five inches expected to fall. The high temperature today will only be 25 degrees.

In the New York area, and throughout the northeast, it looks like rain, rain, and more rain. Heavy rain is expected with temperatures only getting up to about 37 degrees.

In the south, the weather continues to be simply fantastic. If you live in Atlanta, you're going to have a beautiful day today—warm and sunny with plenty of blue skies. Temperatures today will get up to a warm 65 degrees.

In Seattle, you can expect cloudy and cool weather for today with a high temperature of 52 degrees.

But if you really want to find hot weather, the southwest is where it's at, with hot, dry weather expected to continue for the rest of the week. In Las Vegas today it will be sunny and very warm with a high of 83.

T 5.7 Traveling around

1. A Do you think it'll be a rough crossing?
   B Well, the forecast is good, so it should be pretty smooth.
2. A Excuse me, I think those seats facing the front are ours.
   B Oh, I'm sorry. We didn't know they were reserved.
3. A We're going to Market Street. Could you tell us when it's our stop?
   B Just sit up front and I'll call it out.
4. A Can you take us to the airport?
   B Sure. Hop in!
5. A Can I take these bags on with me?
   B I'm sorry. Only one carry-on item per passenger.
6. A Here you go. Keep the change.
   B Thank you, sir. Can I help you with those bags?
7. A Excuse me, are we landing on time?
   B Yes. We're beginning our descent soon.
8. A No, no! He said turn left at the light, not right!
   B Look! *You* drive and *I'll* navigate from now on!
9. A Which line goes to Yankee Stadium?
   B Go downstairs and follow the signs for the number 4 train going uptown.

Unit 6

T 6.1 A student visitor

S = Sandy   N = Nina

S Our student from Seoul arrived on Monday.
N What's her name?
S Soon-hee.
N That's a pretty name! What's she like?
S She's really nice. I'm sure we'll get along well. We seem to have a lot in common.
N How do you know that already? What does she like doing?
S Well, she likes dancing, and so do I. And we both like listening to the same kind of music.
N What does she look like?
S She's really pretty. She has big, brown eyes and long, dark hair.
N Why don't we do something with Soon-hee this weekend? What should we do? Get a pizza? Go to the movies? What would she like to do?
S I'll ask her tonight. She was kind of homesick at first, so I'm pretty sure she'll want to go out and make some friends.
N How is she now?
S Oh, she's OK now. She called her folks back home and she felt much better after she spoke to them.
N Oh, that's good. I can't wait to meet her.

T 6.2 What are the questions?

1. Thai food? It's delicious. It can be spicy, but it doesn't have to be.
2. Oh, she's very nice. You'd really like her. She's the kind of person you can always go to with a problem.
3. Not very well. He still has a fever and a bad cough.
4. Well, she's crazy about horses. I don't think she has any other hobbies. Oh, she plays golf sometimes.
5. It's not very nice at all. It's raining, it's cold, and it's pretty miserable. What about where you are?
6. Mmm … a little like you, as a matter of fact. He's about the same height, tall with blond hair, but your hair's longer and straighter than his. Other than that, you two are pretty similar.
7. It was great. Really relaxing. Lots of sunshine, good food. We did almost nothing but sit next to the pool and read books for the whole two weeks.
8. I like all kinds, but I suppose I like biographies and detective stories best.

T 6.3 A thank you letter

Dear Sandy and family,
   I just wanted to say thank you for having me as your guest in your beautiful home. I had a great time. I really enjoyed meeting your friends. You all made me feel so welcome. You know how much I missed my family at first, but you were so kind that I soon stopped feeling homesick. I can't find the words to tell you how grateful I am. I'd like to call you sometime. What's a good time to call?
   You know that on my way home I stopped to visit my aunt in Canada. Toronto was so cold. It snowed all the time, but I loved it. My aunt wanted me to stay longer, but I wanted to see my

parents and my brother. But my aunt has invited me to go back and I'd love to do that. I'm thinking of going next year.
   Anyway, I'm looking forward to hearing from you very soon. Let me know if you ever want to visit Seoul. My brother and I could take you to a *nore bang* (a singing room). It's kind of like karaoke!
Love to you all,
Soon-hee
P.S. How do you like the picture of my brother and me?

T 6.4 What's the pattern?

1. The teacher told me to do my homework.
2. I promised to do it carefully.
3. I finished painting my bedroom yesterday.
4. Jack helped me paint it.
5. Please don't forget to mail my letter. It's really important.
6. I hate shopping for clothes. They never have my size.
7. I can't stand living so close to the freeway. The noise drives me crazy.
8. Excuse me. I need to go to the bathroom. I'll be back in a minute.
9. She asked us to water her plants while she was on vacation.
10. She finally succeeded in getting a job.

T 6.5 see p. 46

T 6.6 Adjectives for food, towns, and people

1. A Tommy's really quiet and shy. He didn't say a word.
   B Well, he's only three. He is the youngest in the family.
2. A What is Carrie's brother like?
   B Well, he's tall, dark, and handsome, but he's not very polite. In fact, he's even ruder than Carrie!
3. A How was your lunch?
   B Yuck! It was awful. The pizza was disgusting. We were really starving, but we still couldn't eat it!
4. A Mmm! These tomatoes are really delicious. Did you grow them yourselves?
   B Yes, we did. All our vegetables are homegrown.
5. A Did you have a good time in London?
   B We had a great time. There's so much to do. It's a really exciting city. And there are so many people from all over the world. I think it's almost as cosmopolitan as New York.

T 6.7 Living in New York

I = Interviewer   J = Justin   C = Cinda

I How long have you been here in New York?
J Uhh … Nearly three years.
I And are you enjoying it?
J We love it here.
C It's brilliant.
I So what do you like best?
C Oh, the buzz, the atmosphere, the mixture of all kinds of people. The speed of everything— it's exciting …
J I love the architecture, it's so different from London. Walking the streets and looking up at all those skyscrapers.
I And what about the people?

C Well, New Yorkers have a reputation for being rude and unfriendly, but I don't think that's true. New Yorkers are always in a hurry, but they're not unfriendly.
J What I love is the great mix of nationalities and cultures. It's got to be the most cosmopolitan city in the world.
I More than London?
J Uh … I think so, but they're both very mixed.
C Life here seems much faster than in London. Everyone's in such a rush. Everything's done for speed. For example, I don't think people cook at home much—everyone seems to eat out or get food delivered because it's quicker and easier.
I Have you made many friends here?
J I've made friends at work mostly. But it's difficult to make friends outside of work— people are so busy. But mostly I find people pretty friendly.
C Except the taxi drivers! Some of the rudest people I've ever met were New York City taxi drivers!
J And the some of the worst drivers. Every time I sit in a taxi I say a prayer. They drive so fast and suddenly they change lanes. And worst of all, they don't seem to know where anything is.
C Yeah—you spend the entire journey giving directions. Anyway, I like using the subway. It's cheap.
J Yeah, and easy to use and it seems safe to me. We walk a lot as well.
I Do you have a car?
J No, we don't. Not many of our friends do, actually. You don't really need one.
C I'd hate to drive in the city, I'd be terrified. Anyway, you can get everything delivered to your door—not just food.
I Don't you go shopping?
J Oh, yes, of course we do. Not all of us can afford to shop on Fifth Avenue, you know! But it's fun to look.
C Actually, the shops—sorry, the stores—are great. Always open—well nearly always, till 9:00 or 10:00 at night.
J People work much later here. I wasn't expecting to work such long hours! And the holidays—sorry, vacation time—and the public holidays are much shorter. I only get ten days a year. It's difficult for people like us with families in other countries. It's difficult to find time to visit them.
I But generally you're happy?
J Fantastic!
C It's an amazing place, but in a few years I think I'll be exhausted and ready for a quieter life!

T 6.8 Living in London

I = Interviewer   A = Alan

I Alan, how long have you lived in London?
A Fifteen years.
I And do you like it here?
A Sure I like it—but London is one of those cities that you love and hate at the same time.
I So first—what do you hate?
A Oh, the usual big city things—the crowds, the dirt, the traffic, and of course, the Underground—I mean, it's so expensive compared with the subway in New York.
I And what do you like?

A Oh, a lot: fantastic theaters—I'm an actor so that's important for me—great art galleries, museums, I love the the Natural History Museum, concerts, wonderful orchestras. The best of everything comes to London.

I And what's best for you?

A For me? Oh, I just love standing on Waterloo Bridge and looking down the river at the Houses of Parliament. And now, of course, there's the London Eye—I think it's just wonderful. And I like traveling in the black cabs. Taxi drivers here are great, so friendly! They tell you their life stories *and* they know every street in London—not like in New York.

I And what about the people? What do you think of Londoners?

A Ah, well, generally speaking, I, uh, think that they do live up to their reputation—they *are* reserved. It takes a while to get to know people. They won't tell you about themselves. You say to an American "How are you?" and you get "Oh, man, I'm just great. I just got a promotion and I just love working here in Dallas, Denver, Detroit, Delaware, etc., etc." You ask an Englishman "How are you?" and you get "Er … Fine, thank you."

I So the stereotype's true?

A Yeah, they're pretty reserved. They don't like giving personal details, but they complain a lot about life generally. They seem much less positive about life—much more cynical than Americans. They grumble about transportation and politicians and money, how much things cost, their work …

I So, we're a miserable lot then!

A Oh, not really. Leisure time is really important to the British. I think for many Americans, work is the most important thing in their lives. Americans work much longer hours. In Britain, they get more vacation time and time off …

I … and still they grumble!

A Yeah.

I You've been in London 15 years. Has it changed in that time?

A Oh, yeah, a lot—especially the shops, they stay open much longer now. They used to close every Wednesday afternoon. People in the States could never believe that. Oh, and the food!

I Everyone says English food is terrible. Is it?

A Well, when I first came it *was* terrible. It was so hard to get good food. Nowadays, it's not hard at all. London has some great restaurants —my favorite here is the Indian food, it's fantastic. I think we have one of the best right here in our street. Just the best.

I You live in south London. Do you like it there?

A Very much. I love the mix of cultures and nationalities in every street.

I How long do you think you'll stay here?

A Oh, I don't know. Maybe five more years. Maybe forever!

Unit 7

T 7.1 The job interview, part 1

G = George Butler   H = Heather Mann

G Who do you work for now, Heather?

H I work for Intertec Publishing. We publish international business magazines.

G I see. And how long have you worked there?

H I've worked there for five years. Yes, exactly five years.

G And how long have you been in charge of East Asia publications?

H For two years.

G And what did you do before you were at Intertec?

H I worked as an interpreter for the United Nations.

T 7.2 The job interview, part 2

G = George Butler   H = Heather Mann

G As you know, this job is based in Santiago, Chile. Have you ever lived abroad before?

H Oh, yes. Yes, I have.

G And when did you live abroad?

H Well, in fact, I was born in Colombia and I lived there until I was 11. Also, I lived in Geneva for one year when I was working for the UN.

G That's interesting. Have you traveled much?

H Oh, yes. I've traveled to most countries in South America and many countries in Europe. I've also been to Japan a few times.

G Interesting. Why did you go to Japan?

H It was for my job. I went there to interview some Japanese business leaders.

T 7.3 Listen and check

1. She was born in Colombia in 1973.
2. She went to school in Bogota from 1978 to 1984.
3. She studied business and journalism at Boston University.
4. She worked in Geneva for a year before she worked for Intertec.
5. She's been to Japan a few times.
6. She's worked for Intertec for the last five years.
7. She hasn't lived abroad since she was in Geneva
8. She hasn't gotten a job at Worldwatch Americas yet.

T 7.4 It's in the news

Here are today's news headlines. … Convicted murderer Dwayne Locke has escaped from the Greenville Correctional Facility in Texas. … Two Spanish novelists have been awarded the Nobel Prize in literature. … Hurricane Jeffrey has hit the Caribbean, causing widespread damage in Puerto Rico. … Two thousand hotel workers in Anaheim, California have been laid off due to a slowdown in tourism. … Desmond Lewis has been knocked out in the fifth round of his heavyweight championship fight in Las Vegas.

T 7.5 News stories

1. The murderer Dwayne Locke has been recaptured by city police.
2. A Sunny Vacations cruise ship has sunk off the coast of Florida, near Miami.
3. Maria Martin, the famous movie star, has left $3 million to her pet cat, Fluffy.
4. A priceless Van Gogh painting has been stolen from the Museum of Modern Art in New York City.
5. Typhoon Ling-ling has killed at least 20 people and left 13,000 homeless in Vietnam.
6. An 18-year-old college student has been elected mayor of a town in California.
7. Senator Bill Smith has been forced to resign because of a financial scandal.
8. The world-champion runner Ken Quicksilver has failed a drug test at the Olympic Games and is expected to be disqualified.

T 7.6 The busy life of a retired man

P = Patti   L = Lou Norris

P How long have you been retired now, Grandpa?

L Let me see. It's been four years. Yup, I've been retired nearly four years now. But, you know, I worked for Siemco for nearly 40 years. Can you believe that? Forty years.

P One job for 40 years? Awesome! Don't you miss it? Don't you get bored?

L Ah, well, I'm lucky, I'm still healthy, so I can do a lot. I go out a lot. I've taken up golf, you know. It's a wonderful sport for an old guy like me because it's not really a sport at all, at least not the way your Grandpa plays it! It's just a good excuse for a walk, and I need an excuse since Bobby died. I miss good old Bobby, he and I were great pals … but I don't want another dog at my age. I go to the golf club twice a week. I've made some good friends there, you know. Have you met my friends Ted and Marjorie? They're my age. They're a really nice couple.

P No … I don't think I've met them. Didn't you go on vacation with them?

L Yes, I did. We went to Florida together last year. Oh … we had a great time, a real good time. They've been so kind to me since your Grandma died … you know, I really miss your Grandma. Thirty-five years we were married, 35 years. She was a wonderful lady, your Grandma.

P Oh, I know that, Grandpa. We all miss her a lot.

L Anyway, I like to keep busy. I like to travel and visit family and old friends.

P Mom says you went to visit Uncle Eric in Ohio.

L Oh, yeah. Last month. You have a new baby cousin, you know.

P I know, I haven't seen her yet. What's she like?

L She's beautiful. You'll love her. They named her Jessica, after your Grandma, and she looks just like your Grandma. She really does.

P I'd love to see her … But we never go anywhere. Dad's always working.

L Hey, he has a tough job, your dad. It's not his fault.

P Yeah, right. So, have you been anywhere else, Grandpa?

L Oh, well, I did go on a cruise around the Caribbean. My, that was an experience. I enjoyed every minute! When you're older I'll tell you about the widow from California that I met! Her name was Miriam, just 50 years old, but we got along really well together. Yes, indeed.

P Grandpa!

L Oh, sorry, I was just …

P Grandpa, next time you go away, please think of me. Can't I come with you? I'd love to travel. You and I could travel around Europe together. I'd take care of you!

L Patti, you know your Mom and Dad wouldn't let me. Not until you've finished school.

P Well, I think *you* have a lot more fun than I do! All I have to look forward to is years and years of school, and then years and years of work!

L Oh, Patti. Don't wish your life away. Just enjoy it all. You're 16. Sixteen. Ah, yes … Now, I can remember when I was 16, I …

T 7.7 **Leaving a phone message**

1. **A** Hello. May I speak to Arthur Lee, please?
   B I'm sorry. He's in a meeting right now. Can I take a message?
   A Yes. This is Pam Haddon. Mr. Lee called me earlier and left a message. I'm just returning his call. Can you please tell him that I'm back in my office now?

2. **A** Hello. This is Ray Gervin. May I speak to Janet Wolf, please?
   B I'm sorry, Mr. Gervin. She's away from her desk at the moment. Would you like Ms. Wolf to call you when she gets back?
   A Yes. If you don't mind. Let me give you my number. It's 619-555-3153.

3. **A** Hello. May I speak to Douglas Ryan, please?
   B One moment, please. … I'm sorry, but he's on another line. Do you want to hold?
   A No. That's OK. I'll call back later.

Unit 8

T 8.1 **Jim goes backpacking, part 1**

M = Mom   J = Jim

M Oh, dear, I hope everything will be all right. You've never been out of the country before.

J Don't worry, Mom. I'll be OK. I can take care of myself. Anyway, I'll be with Frank. We won't do anything stupid.

M But what will you do if you run out of money?

J We'll get jobs, of course!

M Oh? What if you get lost?

J Mom! If we get lost, we'll ask someone for directions, but we won't get lost because we know where we're going!

M Well, OK. … But what if you … ?

T 8.2 **Jim goes backpacking, part 2**

M = Mom   J = Jim

M But how will we know if you're all right?

J When we get to a city, I'll send you an e-mail.

M But, Jim, it's such a long flight to Madrid!

J Look, as soon as we arrive in Spain, I'll call you.

M I'll be worried until I hear from you.

J I'll be OK. Really!

T 8.3 **The interview**

J = Joe   S = Sue

J Bye, Honey! Good luck with the interview!

S Thanks. I'll need it. I hope the trains are running on time. If I'm late for the interview, I'll be furious with myself!

J Just stay calm! Call me when you can.

S I will. I'll call you on my cell phone as soon as I get out of the interview.

J When will you know if you have the job?

S They'll tell me in the next few days. If they offer me the job, I'm going to accept it. You know that, don't you?

J Sure. But we'll worry about that later.

S OK. Are you going to work now?

J Well, I'm going to take the kids to school before I go to work.

S Don't forget to pick them up before you come home.

J Don't worry, I won't forget. You'd better get going. If you don't hurry, you'll miss the train.

S OK. I'll see you this evening. Bye!

T 8.4 **Winning the lottery**

1. What would I do if I won $5 million? Well, I'd make sure my family had enough money, and my friends, and I'd give a load of money to charity. And then I'd buy my own island in the Caribbean.

2. If I won $5 million, I'd spend it all on myself. Every last cent!

3. What would I do? I'd buy a nice house in the country. I'd make it the best place I could. And I'd have lots of land, so I could have peace and quiet.

4. I'd be a space tourist and fly to Mars on the space shuttle.

5. Oh, that's easy! I'd quit my job and travel. Anywhere. Everywhere. But it wouldn't change me. I'd still live in the same neighborhood because I like it so much.

T 8.5 **Listen and check**

1. If Tony calls, tell him I'm at Alex's. He can reach me there.

2. If you've finished your work, you can take a break. Just be back in 15 minutes.

3. If I'm not back by 8 P.M., don't wait for me. Go without me and I'll meet you at the party.

4. If you have the flu, you should go to bed. Keep warm and drink plenty of fluids.

5. If you're ever in Vancouver, please let me know. I'd love to show you around.

6. If you go to Brazil, you have to have a visa. You can get one at the embassy.

7. I'd buy a computer if I could afford it. It would be really useful for work.

8. If I had more time, I might take an evening class. I'd love to learn more about photography.

T 8.6 **"Who wants to be a millionaire?"**

Who wants to be a millionaire?
I don't.
Have flashy flunkies everywhere.
I don't.
Who wants the bother of a country estate?
A country estate is something I'd hate.

Who wants to wallow in champagne?
I don't.
Who wants a supersonic plane?
I don't.
Who wants a private landing field too?
I don't.
And I don't cuz all I want is you.

Who wants to be a millionaire?
I don't.
Who wants uranium to spare?
I don't.
Who wants to journey on a gigantic yacht?
Do I want a yacht? Oh, how I do not!

Who wants a fancy foreign car?
I don't.
Who wants to tire of caviar?
I don't.
Who wants a marble swimming pool, too?
I don't.
And I don't cuz all I want is you.

T 8.7 **Base and strong adjectives**

1. **A** What did you do last night?
   B We went to the movies.
   A What did you see?
   B *Murder in the Park.*
   A Was it good?
   B It was absolutely superb!

2. **A** Is it true that Liz won the lottery?
   B Yes! She won $2 million!
   A I'll bet she was really happy.
   B Happy? She was absolutely thrilled!

3. **A** When I got home, I told my parents that I'd failed the exam.
   B Oh, no! What did they say?
   A My Mom was OK, but my Dad was really furious.

4. **A** We went out for dinner at that new restaurant last night.
   B Oh! Was it any good?
   A No! It was awful!

5. **A** We had a wonderful skiing trip last weekend.
   B Oh, yeah? Was the weather good?
   A It was absolutely fantastic!

6. **A** How long was your flight?
   B Fourteen hours.
   A Fourteen hours! You must be really tired.
   B Yeah. I'm absolutely exhausted!

T 8.8 **Charity appeals**

Amnesty International

Amnesty International is a Nobel Prize–winning organization that works to support human rights around the world. It is independent of any government or political party and has over a million members in 162 countries around the world. Amnesty International works to free all prisoners of conscience anywhere in the world. These are people who are in prison because of their beliefs, color, ethnic origin, language, or religion. Amnesty International tries to help these prisoners in two ways. First, by publicizing their cases and, second, by putting pressure on governments to practice human rights.

The World Wildlife Fund
The World Wildlife Fund is the largest privately supported international conservation organization in the world. It is dedicated to protecting wild animals around the world and the places where these animals live. The World Wildlife Fund directs its conservation efforts toward three global goals. First, it works to save endangered species like the black rhino or the giant panda. Second, it works to establish and manage national parks and wildlife reserves around the world. Third, it works to address global threats to our environment, such as pollution and climate change.

Save the Children
Millions of children around the world experience lives filled with poverty, disease, war, violence, and discrimination. Save the Children believes that children, wherever they live, have the right to a happy, healthy, and secure start in life, and is committed to turning this ideal into a reality for all children. Save the Children helps children by supporting programs that involve community members in improving their day-to-day lives, such as maternal and child healthcare services, education for all children, and income-earning opportunities for women. Save the Children also uses its global experience and research to help children and families during natural disasters and times of war, as well as to advocate for government policy changes that will benefit all children, including future generations.

T 8.9 **Making suggestions**

M = Maria   A = Anna
M I'm bored!
A Well, it's a beautiful day. Why don't we go for a walk?
M No, I don't feel like it. I'm too tired.
A You need to get out. Let's go shopping!
M Oh, no! I'd rather do anything but that.
A OK … How about watching TV?
M That's a good idea.
A Do you want to watch the news?
M Mmm, I'd rather watch *The Simpsons*.

P = Paul   B = Bill
P I'm broke, and I don't get paid for two weeks. What am I going to do?
B If I were you, I'd get a better job.
P Oh, why didn't I think of that? Thanks, Bill. That's a big help.
B Well, you'd better get a loan from the bank.
P No, I can't. I owe them too much already.
B Why don't you ask your parents? They'd help you out.
P No, I'd rather not. I'd rather work out my problems myself.
B You ought to ask your boss for a raise!
P Good idea, but I've already tried that and it didn't work.
B Oh. Well, I suppose I could lend you some money.
P Really? That would be great! Thanks, Bill. You're a real pal.
B Yeah, well, just one thing: I don't think you should spend so much. That way, you won't be broke all the time.
P Yeah, yeah. I know. You're right.

Unit 9

T 9.1 **Listen and check**
1. A I haven't eaten anything since breakfast.
    B You must be hungry.
2. A Bob works three jobs.
    B He can't have much free time.
3. A The phone's ringing.
    B It might be Jane.
4. A Paula's umbrella is soaking wet!
    B It must be raining.
5. A Listen to all those fire engines!
    B There must be a fire somewhere.
6. A I don't know where Sam is.
    B He could be in his bedroom.
7. A Marta isn't in the kitchen.
    B She can't be cooking dinner.
8. A Whose coat is this?
    B It might be John's.

T 9.2 **What are they talking about?**

Conversation 1
A It's Father's Day next Sunday.
B I know. Should we buy Dad a present or just send him a card?

Conversation 2
A One coffee and a sparkling mineral water, please.
B Would you like lemon with the mineral water?
A Yes. And can we order dinner now?
B Yes, of course.

Conversation 3
I don't work regular hours and I like that. I'd hate one of those nine-to-five office jobs. Also I meet a lot of really interesting people. Of course, every now and then there's a difficult customer, but most times people are really nice. I took that really famous movie star to the airport last week, now what was her name? … Anyway, she was real nice. Gave me a big tip!

Conversation 4
A So, how did it go?
B I'm not sure. I think it went OK.
A Were you nervous?
B Yeah, very, but I tried not to show it.
A Could you answer all their questions?
B Most of them.
A What happens now?
B Well, they said they'd call me in a couple of days and let me know if I got it.

Conversation 5
A We've never had one before.
B Really? We've always had them in our family. We're all crazy about them.
A Well, we are now. The kids love her. And she is so good with them, very good-natured. But it wasn't fair to have one when we lived in an apartment.
B It's OK if they're small and you live near a park, but I know what you mean. What's her name?
A Trudi.

T 9.3 **See p. 68**

T 9.4 **A vacation with friends**

A = Andy   C= Carl
A Hi! Carl? It's Andy. How are you? Doing better?
C Uh … not really. I have to sit down most of the time. It's too tiring—walking with these crutches.
A Really? Still on crutches, eh? So you're not back at work yet?
C No. And I'm really bored. I don't go back to see the doctor for another week.
A Another week! Is that when the cast comes off?
C I hope so. I can't wait to have two legs again! Anyway, how are you? Do you miss the snow and the mountains?
A I'm fine. We're both fine. Julie sends her love, by the way.
C Thanks. I miss you all. By the way, have you gotten any of your photos back yet?
A Yes, yes, we have. Julie picked them up today. They're good. I didn't realize we'd taken so many of us all.
C What about that one with the fantastic sunset behind the hotel?
A Yes, the sunset? It's beautiful. All of us together on Bob and Marcia's balcony, with the mountains and the snow in the background. It brings back memories.
C Yeah. The memory of me skiing into a tree!
A Yes, I know. I'm sorry. But at least it happened at the end; it could have been the first day. You only missed the last two days.
C OK, OK. Oh, Andy, have you written to the hotel yet to complain about your room? That view you had over the parking lot was awful!
A Yeah, and it was noisy, too! We didn't have any views of the mountains from our room. Yeah, we've written. We e-mailed the manager yesterday, but I don't know if we'll get any money back.
C And Marcia's suitcase, did she find it?
A Yeah. The airline found it and put it on the next flight. Marcia was very relieved.
C I'll bet she was! All in all I suppose it was a pretty good vacation, wasn't it?
A Absolutely. It was a *great* vacation. Some ups and downs, but we all had fun. Should we go again next year?
C I'd like to. All six of us again. Lisa wants to go again, too. It was her first time skiing and she loved it, but she says she'll only come if I don't break a leg!
A Great! It's a date. Next time go around the trees! I'll call you again soon, Carl. Take care!
C You too, Andy. Bye now.
A Bye.

T 9.5 **Listen and check**
1. A I can't find my ticket.
    B You must have dropped it.
2. A Mark didn't come to school last week.
    B He must have been sick.
3. A Why is Isabel late for class?
    B She might have overslept.
4. A I can't find my homework.
    B You must have forgotten it.
5. A The teacher's checking Maria's work.
    B She can't have finished already!
6. A How did Bob get such a good grade on that test?
    B He must have cheated!

T 9.6 Brothers and sisters

Luisa

I = Interviewer   L = Luisa

I Luisa, tell me about your family.

L I'm the youngest of seven children. My oldest sister is still alive, age 93, and there are 16 years between us. There were four girls, two boys, and then me.

I Seven children! Wow! How did you all get along?

L Very well. Very well. Being the youngest, my two young brothers and I called our older sisters "the others," because they were either married or working by the time we were born. But the seven of us all got along very well. But it's different now, of course.

I Really? How so?

L Well, when we were small, my older sisters often took care of us. Now my brothers and I are busy taking care of them.

I Tell me about your big sister, Julia. How has your relationship with her changed over the years?

L Julia was the sister who used to … on her vacations … used to take me for walks and so forth. But then she became a nun and went to Brazil for 23 years. We wrote to one another and I was still her little sister. When she came back, it was shortly after my husband died, we became very close and our whole relationship changed and we became great friends.

I What do you see as the main advantage and disadvantage of coming from such a large family?

L Hmm. I think the main advantage was that we learned how to enjoy life without having a lot of money. I think our other relatives, my rich cousins in the city, envied us. We had old bikes, old clothes, but we also had lots of freedom. In the city, they had to wear nice suits and behave correctly.

I Hmm. Disadvantages?

L I think it was very difficult sometimes to have hand-me-down clothes, especially for a little girl like me. And I was sad that we didn't go away on vacation like some other children. But the advantages outweighed the disadvantages enormously, there's no doubt about that.

I Six out of the seven of you are still alive. How closely have you kept in touch over the years?

L Very closely. Of course, we still call each other all the time and see each other whenever we can. And we have a big family reunion every year. My granddaughter just had twins. That means we'll have four generations there this year. How marvelous!

Rose

I = Interviewer   R = Rose

I So, Rose, do you have any brothers or sisters?

R No, I don't. I'm an only child.

I So what was it like growing up as an only child? Were you happy?

R When I was little, I liked it. I had lots of cousins and most of them lived in the same town, so we all played together all the time. And I had a best friend who lived next door to me. She was the same age as me and so she was kind of like a sister, I suppose. But she moved away and that was sad. It was hard when I was a teenager.

I How so?

R Well, you know how it is being a teenager. You're kind of unsure of how to deal with things and how to deal with people, especially parents. It would have been nice to have a brother or sister to talk to.

I Some people who come from large families might envy you, because you had all of your parents' attention.

R Yes, but I think that has its negatives as well as its positives. I think you don't want all your parents' attention, especially as a teenager. It was hard to find myself and my place in the world, I guess.

I What about now that you're an adult?

R Again, I think it's difficult really. Mmm … my father died about ten years ago, so of course I'm the one who's left totally responsible for my mother. I'm the one who has to take care of her if she has a problem and help her if she needs help in any way. There's nobody else to help at all.

I You're married now with two children of your own. Was that a conscious decision to have more than one child?

R Yes, very definitely. And they seem very happy and they get along very well with one another. Usually.

T 9.7 So do I! Neither do I!

A–J = Sue's friends   S = Sue

1. **A** I want to travel the world.
    S So do I.
2. **B** I don't want to have lots of children.
    S Neither do I.
3. **C** I can speak four languages.
    S I can't.
4. **D** I can't drive.
    S Neither can I.
5. **E** I'm not going to get married until I'm 35.
    S Neither am I.
6. **F** I went to London last year.
    S So did I.
7. **G** I've never been to Australia.
    S I have.
8. **H** I don't like politicians.
    S Neither do I.
9. **I** I'm bored with Hollywood actors.
    S So am I.
10. **J** I love going to parties.
    S So do I.

Unit 10

T 10.1 Asking questions

1. How long has he been learning to drive?
2. How many driving lessons has he had?
3. How much money has he spent on driving lessons?
4. How many different instructors has he had?
5. How many times has he crashed his car?
6. When did he start learning to drive?
7. How many times has he taken his driving test?
8. How has he been celebrating?

T 10.2 See p. 75

T 10.3 Listen and check

1. **A** You're covered in paint! What have you been doing?
    B I've been redecorating the bathroom.
    A Have you finished yet?
    B Well, I've painted the door, but I haven't put up the wallpaper yet.
2. **A** Your hands are really dirty. What have you been doing?
    B They're filthy. I've been working in the garden.
    A Have you finished yet?
    B Well, I've cut the grass, but I haven't watered the flowers yet.
3. **A** Your eyes are red! What have you been doing?
    B I'm exhausted. I've been studying for my final exams.
    A Have you finished yet?
    B Well, I've finished chemistry and history, but I haven't started English yet.

T 10.4 Questions and answers

1. **A** When was she born?
    B In 1960.
2. **A** When was her collection of poems published?
    B In April 1968, when she was eight years old.
3. **A** When did she get married for the first time?
    B In the spring of 1981, when she was 21.
4. **A** What did she major in at Columbia?
    B English literature.
5. **A** Which countries has she been to?
    B She's been to Ireland, France, Spain, China, Japan, and Vietnam.
6. **A** How long did her first marriage last?
    B Eight years.
7. **A** When did she get married for the second time?
    B On August 3, 1998.
8. **A** How long has she been living in southern California?
    B Since 1998.

T 10.5 I = Interviewer   E = Ellen

1. **I** How long are you here in Britain for?
   E Just two weeks.
2. **I** How long have you been in Britain?
   E Eight days.
3. **I** When do you go back to California?
   E On Saturday.
5. **I** Where were you the day before yesterday?
   E In Birmingham.
6. **I** Where were you this time last week?
   E In London.
7. **I** Where will you be the day after tomorrow?
   E I'll be in Edinburgh.

T 10.6 The doll collector

I = Interviewer   A = Andrea Levitt

I First of all, just a little bit about you. Are you originally from New York City?
A I'm from Wilmington, Delaware, but I've been living in New York a long time. I came to New York to work in the fashion industry. I still work in the world of fashion. I love it.
I So, how long have you been collecting dolls?
A Hmm … it must be about 25 years. Yeah, 25 years.
I So what led you to having such a love of dolls? Have you always loved them?
A Well, no. I didn't play with dolls much when I was a kid, but these aren't kids' dolls that I collect.
I No?
A No, they're really works of art. When you say the word "doll" people think of a toy for little girls, but these are not. When I opened my business, Dolls-at-Home, one year ago, that was the message I wanted to get across to all art lovers—that dolls are another art form.
I I can see that these are not dolls for little girls. Some of them are really quite amazing. How many dolls do you have in your collection?
A Oooh, I would say … hmm, I think maybe 300.
I Wow! And where are they all?
A Well, I had to buy a new apartment …
I You bought an apartment for the dolls?!
A Yeah, I really did. My son, he's 31 now, he went off to college and I filled his room with dolls in 2 minutes so I realized that I needed a different apartment. I wanted to show off my dolls.
I So, you have what, maybe four or five rooms, all with dolls …
A Actually, there are dolls in *every* room, even the bathroom and the kitchen.
I I was going to ask, is there one room where you don't allow dolls?
A No! Oh, no, they're part of my life. I mean sometimes when people visit there's nowhere to sit. It's a problem.
I Hmm. So, what about keeping them clean? Dusting them?
A That's a problem too. New York is dirty. I suppose they should be under glass, but I don't want them under glass, I want to enjoy them. I dust them occasionally.
I Well, they look immaculate.
A Thanks.
I That's a very unusual doll. Is it valuable?
A No, not really. But that doll over there … It has an elephant mask? That's my favorite.
I Oh, really?

A You see the mask goes up and it's a little boy's face …
I Oh.
A And it goes down and it's an elephant's face. It's made by one of the best doll makers in the US, Akira Blount.
I And how do you find your dolls?
A I travel all over. I go to doll shows, and now that I have a web site and I've started my own business, doll artists find me. As I said, it's been going on for a year now, and I have a mailing list of 900 people.
I Wow! What does your son think of all this?
A You know, he thinks I'm sort of … crazy. He loves this apartment, but he just can't understand …
I Why you fill it with dolls!
A Yeah, but two weeks ago he came to one of my doll shows, it was his first time, and I think he was impressed. Yeah, I think so.
I Do you think you'll ever stop collecting them?
A No, there's always room for another doll. If you're a real collector you always find room.
I Hmm, I'm sure you're right. That's great Andrea. Thank you very much.

T 10.7 The *Star Wars* collector

I = Interviewer   J = Jeff Parker

I First of all, just a little bit about you, Jeff. Are you originally from New York City?
J No, I'm originally from the Philadelphia area. But I moved to New York about five years ago when I got a job working for a bank on Wall Street.
I And do you mind talking about your *Star Wars* collection?
J No, not at all.
I So, how did you get interested in *Star Wars*?
J Well, *Star Wars* was one of the first movies I ever saw. I think I was four years old. My Dad took me to see it and I just loved it. Loved the story, loved the idea of being in space. I think I saw it ten times.
I Wow! You sure did love *Star Wars*!
J Yeah, I guess so. And then all the toys came out, so I started collecting the action figures.
I Action figures?
J They're these little metallic figures. Models of the characters in the movie.
I I see. And which character did you like best?
J Oh, I was a Han Solo fan. I think he was my favorite. You know, I still have that Han Solo action figure. It's worth a lot of money now, but I like it because it was the first *Star Wars* thing I ever owned.
I So, did you just collect the figures?
J Oh, no. I collected the figures first—Darth Vader, Luke, Obi-Wan Kenobi, R2-D2, and of course, Princess Leia.
I Uh-huh.
J Then I just started collecting everything *Star Wars*—spaceships, space stations, posters, videos …
I Well, you seem to have a lot of pieces in your collection. About how many pieces do you have all together?
J I'm not sure because most of my collection is at my parents' house in Philadelphia.
I Ah.
J I don't have room for all of it here in New York … but I'd say I probably have about 700 pieces in all.

I Seven hundred pieces!? How did you get so many?
J Well, you know, I'd ask my Mom for the newest toys—every holiday, every birthday—and the collection just grew and grew. I think they really liked *Star Wars*, too. When I was a kid my Mom gave me *Star Wars* birthday parties, and bought me *Star Wars* cereal for breakfast … I even had *Star Wars* pajamas and *Star Wars* underwear.
I Aha. A real *Star Wars* family then?
J You could say that. We even called our family dog Princess Leia.
I And did you play with other kids who collected *Star Wars* stuff?
J No, not really. I liked to play with all the things by myself. I loved making up all these *Star Wars* stories about the characters …
I And now? Are you in touch with other *Star Wars* collectors?
J No. I don't have the time really.
I So, what are you going to do with your collection?
J I don't know. I'm not sure. Sometimes I think I might sell it. Other times I think I might just keep it and give it to my kids someday.
I That would be something, wouldn't it? Thanks, Jeff.

T 10.8 Expressing quantity

1. **A** How much coffee do you drink?
   B At least six cups a day.
   A That's too much. You shouldn't drink as much as that.
2. **A** Do we have any sugar?
   B Yes, but not enough. We need some more.
3. **A** How much do you earn?
   B Not enough to pay all my bills!
4. **A** How many people are there in your class?
   B Forty.
   A I think that's too many.
5. **A** How many aspirins do you usually take when you have a headache?
   B About four or five.
   A That's too many. You shouldn't take as many as that!
6. **A** How old are you?
   B Seventeen. I'm old enough to get married, but not old enough to vote!
7. **A** When did you last go to the movies?
   B Pretty recently. Just a few days ago.
8. **A** Do you take milk in your coffee?
   B Just a little.

Unit 11

T 11.1 **The first day of vacation**

F = Flavia   C = Hotel concierge

F Hi. I've just checked in and I wonder if you could help me.
C I'll be happy to try.
F Well, first, I'm not sure if we're near the CN Tower.
C The CN Tower? It's very close. It's only about a ten-minute walk.
F Oh, good. Can you tell me if there are any good restaurants nearby?
C Lots. One good one is the Cafe Giovanni. It's casual, but they have very good food and live music in the evenings.
F Sounds wonderful. Oh, and I need to cash some traveler's checks, but I don't know when the banks are open.
C Most banks are open from 8:30 A.M. till 5:30 P.M. on weekdays, but some have extended hours.
F Thank you very much. Oh … I'm sorry, but I can't remember which restaurant you suggested.
C The Cafe Giovanni.
F Cafe Giovanni. Got it. Thanks for your help.
C My pleasure.

T 11.2 see p. 84

T 11.3 **Listen and check**

K=Karen   A = Karen's Assistant

K Now, what's happening today? I have a meeting this afternoon, don't I?
A Yes, that's right. With Henry and Tom.
K And the meeting's here, isn't it?
A No, it isn't. It's in Tom's office at 3:00 P.M.
K Oh! I'm not having lunch with anyone, am I?
A No, you're free for lunch.
K Phew! And I signed all my letters, didn't I?
A No, you didn't, actually. They're on your desk, waiting for you.
K OK. I'll do them now. Thanks a lot.

T 11.4 **Question tags and intonation**

1. It isn't very warm today, is it?
2. You can cook, can't you?
3. You have a CD player, don't you?
4. Mary's very smart, isn't she?
5. There are a lot of people here, aren't there?
6. The movie wasn't very good, was it?
7. I'm next in line, aren't I?
8. You aren't going out dressed like that, are you?

T 11.5 **Listen and check**

1. A It isn't very warm today, is it?
   B No, it's freezing.
2. A You can cook, can't you?
   B Me? No! I can't even boil an egg.
3. A You have a CD player, don't you?
   B Believe it or not, I don't. I have a cassette player, though.
4. A Mary's very smart, isn't she?
   B Yes. She's extremely bright.
5. A There are a lot of people here, aren't there?
   B I know! It's absolutely packed! I can't move!
6. A The movie wasn't very good, was it?
   B It was terrible! The worst I've seen in ages.
7. A I'm next in line, aren't I?
   B Yes, you are. You'll be called next.
8. A You aren't going out dressed like that, are you?
   B Why? What's wrong with my clothes? I thought I looked really cool.

T 11.6 **Add the question tags**

A It's so romantic, isn't it?
B What is?
A Well, they're really in love, aren't they?
B Who?
A Paul and Mary.
B Paul and Mary aren't in love, are they?
A Oh, yes, they are. They're crazy about each other.

T 11.7 **Listen and check**

1. A You broke that vase, didn't you?
   B Yes, I did. I dropped it. I'm sorry.
   A You'll replace it, won't you?
   B Yes, of course I will. How much did it cost?
   A $300.
   B $300?! It *wasn't* that much, was it?
   A Yes, it *was*.
2. A Did you pay the electric bill?
   B No, *you* paid it, didn't you?
   A No, I didn't pay it. I thought you paid it.
   B Me? You *always* pay it, don't you?
   A No, I don't. I always pay the phone bill.
   B Oh, that's right.
3. A We love each other, don't we?
   B Um, I think so.
   A We don't ever want to be apart, do we?
   B Well …
   A And we'll get married and have lots of children, won't we?
   B What? You didn't buy me a ring, did you?
   A Yes, I did. Diamonds are forever.
   B Oh, no!
4. A Helen didn't win the lottery, did she?
   B Yes, she did. She won $4 million!
   A She isn't going to give it all to charity, is she?
   B As a matter of fact, she is.
   A Wow. Not many people would do that, would they?
   B Well, *I* certainly wouldn't.
5. A I think we're lost. Let's look at the map.
   B Uh-oh.
   A What do you mean, "Uh-oh"? You didn't forget the map, did you?
   B Sorry.
   A How are we going to get back to the campground without a map?
   B Well, we could ask a police officer, couldn't we?
   A There aren't many police officers on this mountain!

T 11.8 **The forgetful generation, part 1**

Hi, and welcome to "What's Your Problem?" How's your day been so far? Have you done all the things you planned? Kept all your appointments? Oh—and did you remember to send your mother a birthday card? If so, good for you! If not—well, you're not alone. Many of us in the busy twenty-first century are finding it more and more difficult to remember everything. Once upon a time we just blamed getting older for our absent-mindedness, but now experts are blaming our modern lifestyle. They say that we have become "the forgetful generation" and that day after day we overload our memories.

T 11.9 **The forgetful generation, part 2**

LeeAnn
Last year I graduated from college and I got a job in the same town. One day, for some reason, instead of going to work, which starts at nine o'clock, I took the bus and went to the university for an eleven o'clock lecture. I was sitting there, in the lecture room, and I thought to myself, "Why don't I know anybody?" Then suddenly I remembered that I'd graduated already and that I was two hours late for work!

Jerry
I live and work in Chicago. Last Christmas I packed my suitcase as I do every year and went to the airport to catch a flight to my parents' home for the holidays. While I was standing in line waiting to check in, one of the people from the airline came by to check my ticket. He looked at it and said, "Thank you, sir. Your flight to Kansas City leaves in about an hour." And suddenly I thought, "Kansas City? But I don't want to go to Kansas City. My parents live in Arizona!" You see, when I was a child I lived with my parents in Kansas City, but they moved to Arizona seven years ago. I couldn't believe it. I'd bought an airline ticket to the wrong city! How could I have been so stupid?

Keiko
A few months ago I got up to go to work. I got dressed and put on my nice blue suit because I had an important meeting. I'd been working at home the night before and preparing for a very important meeting the next day, and I remembered to put all the right papers into my briefcase. I got in my car and drove to work. When I arrived I looked down—I was shocked. I was still wearing my fluffy, pink bedroom slippers!

T 11.10 **The forgetful generation, part 3**

P = Presenter   A = Alan Buchan

P Stories of forgetfulness like these are familiar to many of us, and experts say that such cases as LeeAnn's, Jerry's, and Keiko's show that loss of memory is not just related to age, but can be caused by our way of life. Alan Buchan is a professor of psychology and he explains why.
A One of the problems, these days, is that many companies have far fewer employees. This means that *one* person often does several jobs. Jobs that before were done by many people are now done by a few. If you have five things to do at once, you become stressed and forgetful. I think many people in work situations, at a meeting or something, have the experience where they start a sentence and half way through it, they can't remember what they're talking about, and they can't finish the sentence.
P That's happened to me.

A It's a terrible feeling—you think you're going insane. I remember one lady who came to me so distressed because at three important meetings in one week, she found herself saying, mid-sentence, "I'm sorry, I can't remember what I'm talking about." This was a lady in a new job, which involved a lot of traveling. She also had a home and family to take care of *and* she'd recently moved. She had so *many* things to think about that her brain couldn't cope. It shut down.

P I can see the problem, but what's the solution? How did you help that lady?

A Well, part of the solution is recognizing the problem. Once we'd talked to this lady about her stressful lifestyle, she realized that she wasn't going crazy and she felt more relaxed and was able to help herself. But do you know one of the best ways to remember things, even in these days of personal computers and handheld computers?

P What's that?

A It's a notebook, or just a piece of paper! At the beginning of every day write yourself a list of things you have to do—and it gives you a really good feeling when you cross things off the list as you do them!

P Well, there you have it! Thank you very much Professor … uh … uh … ? Oh—Professor Alan Buchan!

T 11.11 **Informal English**

1. **A** What do you say we take a break for lunch?
   B Great idea. We can grab a sandwich at the deli.
2. **A** What are you up to?
   B Nothing much. Just sitting around, watching TV all weekend.
   A You're such a couch potato!
   B Hey, give me a break. I work hard all week. I like to chill out in front of the TV.
3. **A** Quick! Give me your homework so I can copy it.
   B No way! Do your own homework!
4. **A** Did you fix the TV?
   B Kind of. The picture's OK, but the sound isn't quite right.
   A What's on tonight?
   B Beats me. Did you look in the paper?
5. **A** What do you call that stuff that you use to clean between your teeth?
   B What do you mean?
   A You know! It's like string. White.
   B Oh! You mean dental floss.
   A Yeah. That's it!

Unit 12

T 12.1

E = Elliott   M = Martha
1. **E** How do you know Joel and Tara?
   M I studied at UCLA with Tara.
2. **E** Are you married?
   M Yes, I am. That's my husband over there.
3. **E** Where did you meet your husband?
   M Actually, I met him at a wedding.
4. **E** Have you traveled far to get here?
   M No, we haven't. We just got here yesterday. We flew in from Orlando.
5. **E** Do you live in Orlando?
   M Yes, we do.
6. **E** So, where are you staying in Atlanta?
   M We're staying at the Four Seasons Hotel.
7. **E** So am I. Can we meet there later for coffee?
   M Sure. I'll introduce you to my husband.

T 12.2 **Listen and check**

M = Martha   R = Ron
M I just met this really nice guy named Elliot.
R Oh, yeah?
M He was very friendly. Do you know what he said? First, he asked me how I knew Joel and Tara. I told him that I had studied with Tara at UCLA. Then he asked if I was married. Of course I said that I was!
R He asked you that?
M … and next he asked where we'd met. I told him that we'd actually met at a wedding.
R You told him that?
M Sure. Then he wanted to know how long we had been in Atlanta …
R Really?
M I said we had just gotten here yesterday, that we had flown in from Orlando.
R Uh-huh.
M He asked if we lived in Orlando, so I told him that we did.
R What else did this guy want to know?
M Well, he asked where we were staying in Atlanta and it turns out that he's staying at the Four Seasons, too.
R I see.
M Then he asked if I could meet him later for coffee …
R Mhmm.
M And I said we could and that I would introduce him to you.
R I'm not sure I want to meet this guy.

T 12.3 **What did Elliott say?**

R = Ron   M = Martha
1. **R** Elliot lives in Detroit.
   M But he told me he lived in New York.
2. **R** He doesn't like his new job.
   M But he said that he loved it!
3. **R** He's moving to Iowa.
   M But he told me he was moving to Florida!
4. **R** He stayed home on his last vacation.
   M But he told me he went to Paris!
5. **R** He'll be 40 next week.
   M But he told me he'd be 30!
6. **R** He's been married three times.
   M But he told me he'd never been married!
   R You see! I told you he was a liar!

T 12.4 **Listen and check**

1. The mail carrier told me to sign on the dotted line.
2. She asked him to translate a sentence for her.
3. She reminded him to send a birthday card.
4. He begged her to marry him.
5. He invited his boss to his wedding.
6. He refused to go to bed.
7. He advised him to talk to his lawyer.
8. The teacher ordered Joanna to take the chewing gum out of her mouth.

T 12.5 **Kathleen Brady**

OK. We argue sometimes but not *that* often. Usually we just sit quietly and watch TV in the evenings. But sometimes … sometimes we argue about money. We don't have much, so I get very upset when Kenny spends the little we have on drinking or gambling. He's promised to stop drinking, but he hasn't stopped. It's worse since he lost his job. OK, we were shouting, but we didn't throw a chair at Mr. West. It … it just fell out of the window. And I'm really sorry that we woke the baby. We won't do it again. We love children. We'll baby-sit for Mr. and Mrs. West anytime, if they want to go out.

T 12.6 **Ann West**

Every night it's the same thing. They argue all the time. And we can hear every word they say. During the day it's not so bad because they're both out. But in the evenings it's terrible. Usually they start arguing about which TV show to watch. Then he slams the door and goes down the street to a bar. Last night he came back really drunk. He was shouting outside his front door, "Open the door you … um … so-and-so." I won't tell you the language he used! But she wouldn't open it; she opened a window instead and threw a plant at him. Tonight she threw a chair at my poor husband. They're so selfish. They don't care about our baby one bit.

T 12.7 **Great Aunt Dodi's birth**

This story is told over and over again in our family. It's the story of how my Great Aunt Dodi was born twice. She was born on Prince Edward Island on January 16, 1910. She was the fourth of six children. It was January and really cold, freezing. The midwife only just managed to get there in time, through all the snow. When my great aunt was born she was blue, really blue, and she wasn't breathing at all and the midwife said, "Well, I'm terribly sorry, there's nothing we can do … I'm afraid the child isn't breathing."

But my great-grandmother stepped forward and she said, "Nonsense! Give me that child!" And she grabbed the baby from the midwife and ran downstairs into the warm living room and then … incredibly … she opened the door of the wood stove and put the baby into the oven. And what do you know, a few minutes later a great loud cry came from the oven and my great aunt had been born, or rather, born again.

So that's how my Great Aunt Dodi was born twice. She's still alive and she never tires of telling the story of her birth to her five children, eleven grandchildren, and two great-grandchildren.

T 12.8 See p. 95

T 12.9 "My Way"

And now, the end is near
And so I face the final curtain
My friend, I'll say it clear
I'll state my case, of which I'm certain
I've lived a life that's full
I've traveled each and every highway
And more, much more than this,
I did it my way …

Regrets, I've had a few
But then again, too few to mention
I did what I had to do
and saw it through without exemption,
I planned each charted course,
each careful step along the byway
And more, much more than this,
I did it my way …

Yes, there were times,
I'm sure you knew,
When I bit off
more than I could chew
But through it all,
when there was doubt
I ate it up and spit it out
I faced it all and I stood tall
and did it my way …

I've loved, I've laughed and cried
I've had my fill, my share of losing
And now, as tears subside,
I find it all so amusing
To think I did all that
And may I say, not in a shy way,
"Oh, no, oh, no, not me, I did it my way.
For what is a man, what has he got?
If not himself, then he has naught.
To say the things he truly feels
and not the words of one who kneels,
The record shows I took the blows
and did it my way …
Yes, it was my way …

T 12.10 Saying sorry

1. **A** Excuse me, what's that creature called?
   B It's a Tyrannosaurus.
   A Pardon me?
   B A Tyrannosaurus. Tyrannosaurus Rex.
   A Thank you very much.
2. **A** Ouch! That's my foot!
   B Sorry. I wasn't looking where I was going.
3. **A** Excuse me, can you tell me where the post office is?
   B I'm sorry, I'm a stranger here myself.
4. **A** I failed my driving test for the sixth time!
   B I'm so sorry.
5. **A** Excuse me! We need to get past. My little boy isn't feeling well.
6. **A** Do you want your hearing aid, Grandma?
   B Pardon me?
   A I said: Do you want your hearing aid?
   B What?
   A DO YOU WANT YOUR HEARING AID?!
   B I'm sorry, I can't hear you. I need my hearing aid.

Grammar Reference

Unit 1

Introduction to auxiliary verbs

There are three classes of verbs in English.
1. The auxiliary verbs *do, be,* and *have*
   These are used to form tenses, and to show forms such as questions and negatives. They are dealt with in this unit.
2. Modal auxiliary verbs
   Must, can, should, might, will, and *would* are examples of modal auxiliary verbs. They "help" other verbs, but unlike *do, be,* and *have,* they have their own meanings. For example, *must* expresses obligation and *can* expresses ability. (See Units 4, 5, 8, and 9.)
3. Full verbs
   These are all the other verbs in the language, for example, *play, run, help, think, want, go,* etc.

Note
Do, be, and *have* can also be used as full verbs with their own meanings.
do
   I **do** the laundry on Saturday.
   She **does** a lot of business in East Asia.
   What **do** you **do**? = What's your job? (The first *do* is an auxiliary; the second is a full verb.)
be
   We **are** in class right now.
   They **were** at home yesterday.
   I want **to be** a teacher.
have
   He **has** a lot of problems.
   They **have** three children.

Note
1. There are two forms of the verb *have: have* and *have got* with *do/does/did* for questions, negatives, and short answers.
      I've got a problem.
      Does she **have** a problem? Yes, she **does**.
2. *Have* and *have got* can carry the same meaning, but *have got* is used more in informal, spoken language.
   When we write, we normally use *have*.
3. We use *have*, not *have got* to talk about:
   a habit
      I always **have** lunch in the cafeteria on Mondays.
   the past
      I **had** a headache yesterday.   NOT I had got a headache yesterday.
      Did you **have** any pets as a child? NOT Had you got any pets …?
      I didn't **have** any money
         when I was a student.   NOT I hadn't got any money …

1.1 Tenses and auxiliary verbs

When *do, be,* and *have* are used as auxiliary verbs, they make different verb forms.

do

In the Present Simple and the Past Simple there is no auxiliary verb, so *do, does,* and *did* are used to make questions and negatives (except with *be*).
   Where **do** you work?
   I **don't** like my job.
   What **did** you buy?
   We **didn't** buy anything.

be

1. *Be* with verb + *-ing* is used to make Continuous verb forms.
   Continuous verb forms describe activities in progress and temporary activities.
      He**'s washing** his hair. (Present Continuous)
      They **were going** to work. (Past Continuous)
      I**'ve been learning** English for two years. (Present Perfect Continuous)
      I**'d like to be** lying on the beach right now. (Continuous infinitive)
2. *Be* with the past participle (*-ed*, etc.) is used to form the passive.
      Paper **is made** from wood. (Present Simple passive)
      My car **was stolen** yesterday. (Past Simple passive)
      The house **has been** redecorated. (Present Perfect passive)
      This homework needs **to be done** tonight. (Passive infinitive)
   There is an introduction to the passive on page 139.

have

Have with the past participle is used to make Perfect verb forms.
      He **has worked** in seven different countries. (Present Perfect)
      She was crying because she **had had** some bad news. (Past Perfect)
      I'd like to **have met** Napoleon. (Perfect infinitive)
Perfect means "before," so Present Perfect means "before now." (See Units 7 and 10.) Past Perfect means "before a time in the past." (See Unit 3.)

1.2 Negatives and auxiliary verbs

To make a negative, add *-n't* to the auxiliary verb. If there is no auxiliary verb, use *don't/doesn't/didn't*.

Affirmative	**Negative**
He's working. I was thinking.	He isn't working. I wasn't thinking.
We've seen the play.	We haven't seen the play.
She works in a bank. They like skiing. He went on vacation.	She doesn't work in a bank. They don't like skiing. He didn't go on vacation.

It is possible to contract the auxiliaries *be* and *have* and use the uncontracted *not*.
      He**'s not** playing today. (= He isn't playing today.)
      We**'re not** going to Italy after all. (= We aren't going to Italy …)
But
      I**'m not** working.   NOT I amn't working.

136   Grammar Reference 1.1–1.2

1.3 Questions and auxiliary verbs

1. To make a question, invert the subject and the auxiliary verb. If there is no auxiliary verb, use *do/does/did*.

Question

She's wearing jeans. You aren't working. You were born in Paris.	What is she wearing? Why aren't you working? Where were you born?
Peter's been to China. We have been studying.	Has Peter been to China? Have you been studying?
I know you. He wants ice cream. They didn't go out.	Do I know you? What does he want? Why didn't they go out?

2. There is usually no *do/does/did* in subject questions.
   Compare:

Who wants ice cream?	What flavor of ice cream **do** you want?
What happened to your eye?	What **did** you do to your eye?
Who broke the window?	How **did** you break the window?

1.4 Short answers and auxiliary verbs

Short answers are very common in spoken English. If you just say *Yes* or *No*, it can sound rude. We use short answers after Yes/No questions, and also to reply to statements. To make a short answer, repeat the auxiliary verb. In the Present and Past Simple, use *do/does/did*.

Short answer

Are you coming with us? Have you had breakfast? Kate likes walking. Mary didn't call. Don't forget to write.	Yes, I am. No, I haven't. No, she doesn't. She hates it. Yes, she did. You were out. No, I won't.

Unit 2

2.1 Present Simple
Form

Affirmative and negative

I We You They	work. don't work.
He She It	works. doesn't work.

Question

Where	do	I we you they	live?
	does	he she it	

Short answer

Do you live in Boston? Does he have a car?	Yes, we do. No, he doesn't.

Use

The Present Simple is used to express:
1. an action that happens again and again (a habit).
   > I **go** to work by car.
   > She **drinks** ten cups of coffee a day.
   > I **wash** my hair twice a week.
2. a fact that is always true.
   > Ronaldo **comes** from Brazil.
   > Some birds **fly** south in the winter.
   > My daughter **has** brown eyes.
3. a fact that is true for a long time (a state).
   > He **works** in a bank.
   > I **live** in an apartment near the center of town.
   > I **prefer** coffee to tea.

Spelling of verb + -s
1. Most verbs add *-s* to the base form of the verb.

wants	eats	helps	drives

2. Add *-es* to verbs that end in *-ss*, *-sh*, *-ch*, *-x*, and *-o*.

kisses	washes	watches	fixes	goes

3. Verbs that end in a consonant + *-y* change the *-y* to *-ies*.

carries	flies	worries	tries

   But verbs that end in a vowel + *-y* only add *-s*.

buys	says	plays	enjoys

Adverbs of frequency
1. We often use adverbs of frequency with the Present Simple.

   0%————————————— 50% ————————————— 100%
   never   rarely   not often   sometimes   often   usually   always

2. They go before the main verb, but after the verb *be*.
   Compare:

I **usually** start school at 9:00.	They're **usually** in a hurry in the morning.
I don't **often** go to bed late.	I'm not **often** late for school.
She **never** eats meat.	He's **never** late.
I **rarely** see Peter these days.	We're **rarely** at home on the weekends.

3. *Sometimes* and *usually* can also go at the beginning.
   > **Sometimes** we play cards.
   > **Usually** I go shopping with friends.

   Never, always, rarely, and *seldom* cannot move in this way.
   > NOT ~~Never I go to the movies.~~
   > ~~Always I have tea in the morning.~~
4. *Every day*, etc., goes at the end.
   > He calls me **every** night.

2.2 Present Continuous

Form

Affirmative and negative

I	'm 'm not	
He She It	's isn't	eating.
We You They	're aren't	

Question

What	am is are	I he/she/it we/you/they	doing?

Short answer

Are you going by train?	Yes, I am. No, I'm not.

Use

The Present Continuous is used to express:
1. an activity that is happening now.
   > Don't turn the TV off. I'**m watching** it.
   > You can't speak to Lisa. She'**s taking** a bath.
2. an activity or situation that is true now, but is not necessarily happening at the moment of speaking.
   > Don't take that book. Jane'**s reading** it.
   > I'**m taking** a French class this year.
3. a temporary activity.
   > Peter is a student, but he'**s working** as a waiter during the holidays.
   > I'**m living** with friends until I find a place of my own.
4. a planned future arrangement.
   > I'**m having** lunch with Glenda tomorrow.
   > We'**re meeting** at 1:00 outside the restaurant.

Spelling of verb + -ing
1. Most verbs add -ing to the base form of the verb.

going	wearing	visiting	eating

2. Verbs that end in one -e drop the -e.

smoking	coming	hoping	writing

   But verbs that end in -ee don't drop an -e.

agreeing	seeing

3. Verbs of one syllable, with one vowel and one consonant, double the consonant.

stopping	getting	running	planning	jogging

   But if the final consonant is -y or -w, it is not doubled.

playing	showing

Note
lie   lying

2.3 Stative verbs

1. There are certain groups of verbs that are usually only used in the Present Simple. This is because their meanings are related to states or conditions that are facts and not activities. This is a feature of the use of the Present Simple. The groups of verbs are:

   Verbs of thinking and opinions

believe	think	understand	suppose	expect
agree	doubt	know	remember	forget
mean	imagine	realize	deserve	prefer

   > I **believe** you.
   > Do you **understand**?
   > I **know** his face, but I **forget** his name.

   Verbs of emotions and feeling

like	love	hate	care	hope	wish	want	admit

   > I **like** black coffee.
   > **Do** you **want** to go out?
   > I **don't care**.

   Verbs of having and being

belong	own	have	possess	contain	cost	seem	appear
need	depend on	weigh	come from	resemble			

   > This book **belongs** to Jane.
   > How much does it **cost**?
   > He **has** a lot of money.

   Verbs of the senses

look	hear	taste	smell	feel

   > The food **smells** good.
   > We often use *can* when the subject is a person.
   > **Can** you smell something burning?
   > I **can** hear someone crying.

2. Some of these verbs can be used in the Present Continuous, but with a change of meaning. In the Continuous, the verb expresses an activity, not a state.
   Compare:

I **think** you're right.	We'**re thinking** of going to the movies.
(= opinion)	(= mental activity)
He **has** a lot of money.	She'**s having** a bad day.
(= possession)	(= activity)
I **see** what you mean.	Are you **seeing** Nigel tomorrow?
(= understand)	(= activity)
The soup **tastes** awful.	I'**m tasting** the soup to see if it needs salt.
(= state)	(= activity)

2.4 The passive

The passive is dealt with in Units 2, 3, and 7.

Form

The tense of the verb *to be* changes to give different tenses in the passive. This is followed by the past participle.

It	is was has been	fixed.
They	are were have been	

Notice the passive infinitive (*to be* + past participle)
    I'd love **to be invited** to their party.
and the Present Continuous passive (*is/was* + *being* + past participle)
    A party **is being held** by the Browns next week.

Use

1. The object of an active verb becomes the subject of a passive verb.
    Alfred Hitchcock **directed** *Psycho* in 1960.
    Psycho, one of the classic thrillers of all time, **was directed** by Alfred Hitchcock.
The passive is not just another way of expressing the same sentence in the active. We choose the active or the passive depending on what we are more interested in. In the first sentence, we are more interested in Alfred Hitchcock; in the second sentence, *Psycho* has moved to the beginning of the sentence because we are more interested in the movie.
2. *By* and the agent are often omitted in passive sentences if the agent:
    • is not known.
    My apartment **was robbed** last night.
    • is not important.
    This bridge **was built** in 1886.
    • is obvious.
    I **was fined** $100 for speeding.
3. The passive is associated with an impersonal, formal style. It is often used in notices and announcements.
    Customers **are requested** to refrain from smoking.
    It **has been noticed** that reference books **have been removed** from the library.
4. In informal language, we often use *you*, *we*, and *they* to refer to people in general or to no person in particular. In this way, we can avoid using the passive.
    They're building a new department store downtown.
    We speak English in this store.
5. Be careful! Many past participles are used like adjectives.
    I'm very **interested** in modern art.
    We were very **worried** about you.
    I'm **exhausted**! I've been working all day.

2.5 Present Simple and Present Continuous passive

The uses are the same in the passive as in the active.
    My car **is serviced** every six months. (= habit)
    Computers **are used** in all areas of life and work. (= fact that is always true)
    Sorry about the mess. The house **is being redecorated** at the moment. (= activity happening now)

Unit 3

Introduction to past tenses

We use different past tenses to focus on different moments and periods of time in the past. The tense we use depends on whether the action or event is a past habit or state, whether it is completed, the duration of an action or event, and the order we use to recall the action or events. Look at the diagram.

When Andrea arrived home at 8:00 last night,

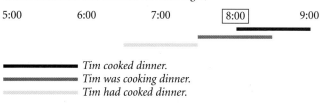

    Tim cooked dinner.
    Tim was cooking dinner.
    Tim had cooked dinner.

3.1 Past Simple

Form

The form of the Past Simple is the same for all persons.

Affirmative

I He/She/It We You They	finished left arrived	yesterday. at 3:00. three weeks ago.

Negative

I She They (etc.)	didn't	finish leave	yesterday. at 3:00.

Question

When	did	you he they	finish the report? get married?

Short answer

Did you enjoy dinner?	Yes, we did. No, we didn't.

Use

The Past Simple is used to express:
1. a finished action in the past.
    We **met** in 2000.
    I **went** to Boston last week.
    John **left** two minutes ago.
2. actions that follow each other in a story.
    Mary **walked** into the room and **stopped**. She **listened** carefully. She **heard** a noise coming from behind the curtain. She **threw** the curtain open, and then she **saw** …
3. a past situation or habit.
    When I **was** a child, we **lived** in a small house by the sea. Every day I **walked** for miles on the beach with my dog.
    This use is often expressed with *used to*.
    We **used to** live in a small house … I **used to** walk for miles …

Spelling of verb + -ed

1. Most verbs add -ed to the base form of the verb.

| worked | wanted | helped | washed |

2. When the verb ends in -e, add -d.

| liked | used | hated | cared |

3. If the verb has only one syllable, with one vowel + one consonant, double the consonant before adding -ed.

| stopped | planned | robbed |

But we write *cooked*, *seated*, and *moaned* because there are two vowels.

4. The consonant is not doubled if it is -y or -w.

| played | showed |

5. In most two-syllable verbs, the end consonant is doubled if the stress is on the second syllable.

| pre'ferred | ad'mitted |

But we write *'entered* and *'visited* because the stress is on the first syllable.

6. Verbs that end in a consonant + -y change the -y to -ied.

| carried | hurried | buried |

But we write *enjoyed*, because it ends in a vowel + -y.

There are many common irregular verbs. See the list on page 152.

Past Simple and time expressions

Look at the time expressions that are common with the Past Simple.

I met her	last night.
	two days ago.
	yesterday morning.
	in 2001.
	in the summer.
	when I was young.

3.2 Past Continuous

Affirmative and negative

I He She It	was wasn't	
		working.
We You They	were weren't	

Question

		I she he it	
What	was		doing?
	were	we you they	

Short answer

| Were you looking for me? | Yes, I was./No I wasn't |
| Were they waiting outside? | Yes, they were./No, they weren't. |

Use

We often use the Past Continuous in sentences with the Past Simple. The Past Continuous refers to longer, "background" activities, while the Past Simple refers to shorter actions that interrupted the longer ones.

*When I **woke up** this morning …*

This morning

… *the birds **were singing** and the sun **was shining**.*

The Past Continuous is used to express:

1. an activity in progress before, and probably after, a particular time in the past.
   At 7:00 this morning I **was having** my breakfast.
   I walked past your house last night. There was an awful lot of noise. What **were** you **doing**?
2. a situation or activity during a period in the past.
   Jan looked beautiful. She **was wearing** a green cotton dress. Her eyes **were shining** in the light of the candles that **were burning** nearby.
3. an interrupted past activity.
   When the phone rang, I **was taking** a shower.
   We **were playing** tennis when it started to rain.
4. an incomplete activity in the past in order to contrast with the Past Simple that expresses a completed activity.
   I **was reading** a book during the flight. (I didn't finish it.)
   I **watched** a movie during the flight. (the whole movie)

Note

The Past Simple is usually used to express a repeated past habit or situation. But the Past Continuous can be used if the repeated habit becomes a longer "setting" for something.
Compare:
   I **went** out with Jack for ten years.   I **was going** out with Jack when I first met Harry.

3.3 Past Simple or Past Continuous?

1. Sometimes we can use the Past Simple or the Past Continuous. The Past Simple focuses on past actions as simple facts, while the Past Continuous focuses on the duration of past situations and activities.
   Compare:

| **A** I didn't see you at the party last night. | **A** I didn't see you at the party last night. |
| **B** No. I stayed at home and watched football. | **B** No, I was watching football at home. |

2. Questions in the Past Simple and Past Continuous refer to different time periods: the Past Continuous asks about activities before; the Past Simple asks about what happened after.

> When the war broke out, Peter **was studying** medicine at medical school. He **decided** that it was safer to go home to his parents and postpone his studies.

What was Peter doing when the war broke out?	He was studying.
What did Peter do when the war broke out?	He went home to his parents.

3.4 Past Perfect

Perfect means "before," so Past Perfect refers to an action in the past that was completed before another action in the past.

Form

The form of the Past Perfect is the same for all persons.

Affirmative and negative

I You We (etc.)	'd (had) hadn't	seen him before. finished work at 6:00.

Question

Where had	you she they	been before?

Short answer

Had he already left?	Yes, he had. No, he hadn't.

Use

1. The Past Perfect is used when one action in the past happened before another action in the past.

> When I got home, I found that someone **had broken** into my apartment and **had stolen** my DVD player, so I called the police.
>
> Action 1: Someone broke into my apartment and stole my DVD player.
> Action 2: I got home and called the police.

> I didn't want to go to the theater with my friends because I'**d seen** the movie before.
>
> Action 1: I saw the movie.
> Action 2: My friends went to the theater to see the movie.

2. Notice the difference between the following sentences:

> When I got to the party, Peter **went** home.
> (= First I arrived, then Peter left.)
> When I got to the party, Peter **had gone** home.
> (= First Peter left, then I arrived.)

3.5 Past tenses in the passive

The uses are the same in the passive as in the active.

> The bridge **was built** in 1876. (Past Simple passive—finished action in the past)
> The bomb **was being defused** when it exploded. (Past Continuous passive—interrupted past activity)
> The letter didn't arrive because it **had been sent** to my old address. (one action before another action in the past)

Unit 4

Modal verbs 1

Introduction to modal verbs
The modal verbs are *can, could, may, might, must, will, would, should, ought to.* They are known as modal auxiliary verbs because they "help" another verb. (See also Units 1, 5, 8, and 9.)

> I **can** swim.
> Do you think I **should** go?

Form

1. There is no *-s* in the third person singular.
> She **can** ski.   He **must** be tired.   It **might** rain.
2. There is no *do/does/don't/doesn't* in the question or negative.
> What **should** I do?   **Can** I help you?   You **mustn't** steal!
> He **can't** dance.   I **won't** be a minute.
3. Modal auxiliary verbs are followed by the Simple form of the verb. The exception is *ought to.*
> You **must** go.   I'**ll help** you.   You **ought to** see a doctor.
4. They have no infinitives and no *-ing* forms. Other expressions are used instead.
> I can ski.   I'd love to **be able to** ski.
> I have to get up early.   I hate **having to** get up on cold, winter mornings.
5. They don't usually have past forms. Instead, we can use them with perfect infinitives:
> You **should have told** me that you can't swim. You **might have drowned**!
> or we use other expressions:
> I **had to** work hard in school.

Note

Could is used with a past meaning to talk about a general ability.
> I **could** swim when I was six. (= general ability)

Use

1. Modal verbs express our attitudes, opinions, and judgments of events.
> Compare:
> "Who's that knocking on the door?"
> "It's John." (This is a fact.)
> "It **could/may/might/must/should/can't/'ll** be John." (These all express our attitude or opinion.)
2. Each modal verb has at least two meanings. One use of all of them is to express possibility or probability.
> I **must** mail this letter! (= obligation)
> You **must** be tired! (= deduction, probability)
> **Could** you help me? (= request)
> We **could** go to Spain for our vacation. (= possibility)
> You **may** go home now. (= permission)
> "Where's Anna?"   "I'm not sure. She **may** be at work."
>   (= possibility)

4.1 have (got) to, can, allowed to

have to

Form

Affirmative and negative

I You We They	have to don't have to	work hard.
He She	has to doesn't have to	

Question

Do	I you (etc.)	have to work hard?

Use

Have to is used to express obligation. It expresses a general obligation based on a law or rule, or based on the authority of another person. It is impersonal.

> Children **have to** go to school until they are 16. (a law)
> Mom says you **have to** clean your room before you go out. (mother's order)

be allowed to

Form

Affirmative and negative

I You We They	are allowed to aren't allowed to	park here.
He She	is allowed to isn't allowed to	

Question

Am	I	
Are	you	allowed to park here?
Is	he	

can

Can is a modal verb. See the introduction to modal verbs on page 141.

Can and *be allowed to* are used to express permission. *Can* is more informal and usually spoken.

> You **can** borrow my bike, but you **can't** have the car. I need it.
> You **can't** come in here with those muddy shoes!
> You**'re allowed to** get married when you're 16.
> **Are** we **allowed to** use a dictionary for this test?

4.2 should and must

Form

Should and *must* are modal verbs. See the introduction to modal verbs on page 141.

Use

1. *Should* expresses mild obligation, suggestions, or advice. It expresses what, in the speaker's opinion, is the right or best thing to do. We often use *should* with *I think/don't think* ... .
   > You're always asking me for money. I think you **should** spend less.
   > You **shouldn't** sit so close to the television! It's bad for your eyes.
2. *Must*, like *have to*, expresses strong obligation. It is associated with a formal, written style.
   > All visitors **must** show proper identification. (sign in the lobby of an office building)
   > Books **must** be returned on or before the due date. (instructions in a library)

Note

1. *Must I ... ?* is possible, but question forms with *have to* are more common.
   > Do I **have to** do what you say, or can I do what I want?
2. *Have to* has all forms; *must* does not.
   > I **had to** work until midnight last night. (Past)
   > You**'ll have to** study hard when you go to college. (Future)
   > She's a millionaire. She's never **had to** do any work. (Present Perfect)
   > I hate **having to** get up on cold, winter mornings. (*-ing* form)
   > If you were a nurse, you would **have to** wear a uniform. (Infinitive)
3. *Should I/she/we ... ?* is possible. We often use *Do you think ... ?*
   > **Should I** try to eat less?
   > Do you think **I should** see a doctor?

4.3 Making requests: can, could, and would

1. There are many ways of making requests in English.

Can Could Would	you	help me, please? pass the salt, please?
Would you mind helping me, please?		
Can Could	I	speak to you, please? ask you a question?
Do you mind if I open the window? Would you mind if I opened the window?		

Can, *could*, and *would* are all modal verbs. See the introduction to modal verbs on page 141.

2. *Could* is a little more formal; *can* is a little more familiar.
   Could I ... ? and *Could you ... ?* are very useful because they can be used in many different situations.
3. Here are some ways of responding to requests:
   > **A** Excuse me! Could you help me?
   > **B** Sure.
   > Of course.
   > Well, I'm afraid I'm a little busy right now.
   > **A** Would you mind if I opened the window?
   > **B** No, not at all.
   > No, that's fine.
   > Well, I'm a little cold, actually.

4.4 Making offers: will and should

1. *Will* and *should* are used to express offers. They are both modal verbs. See the introduction to modal verbs on page 141.
2. The contracted form of *will* is used to express an intention, decision, or offer made at the moment of speaking.
   > Come over after work. I**'ll** cook dinner for you.
   > "It's Jane's birthday today." "Is it? I**'ll** buy her some flowers."
   > Give him your suitcase. He**'ll** carry it for you.

Don't worry about the bus. Dave**'ll** give you
   a ride.
Give it back or we**'ll** call the police!
In many languages, this idea is often expressed by a
present tense, but in English this is wrong.

I**'ll** give you my number.   NOT ~~I give you my~~
                                 ~~number.~~
I**'ll** carry your suitcase.   NOT ~~I carry your~~
                                 ~~suitcase.~~

Other uses of *will* are dealt with in Unit 5.
3. We use *should* to make an informal suggestion.
   What **should** we have for dinner?
   What **should** we do tonight?

Unit 5

Introduction to future forms

There is no future tense in English as there is in many
European languages. However, English has several
forms that can refer to the future. Three of these are
will, *going to*, and the Present Continuous.
Notice the different forms in these sentences:

I**'ll see** you later. (will)
We**'re going to see** a movie tonight. Do you want
   to come? (going to)
I**'m seeing** the doctor tomorrow evening. (Present
   Continuous)

The difference between them is not about near or
distant future, or about certainty. The speaker chooses
a future form depending on when the decision was
made, and how the speaker sees the future event.
There is more about this in **Use** below.

5.1 *will/going to* and the Present Continuous
Form

Affirmative and negative

I He They	'll won't	help you.
I'm/I'm not She's/She isn't We're/We aren't	going to	watch TV tonight.
I'm/I'm not He's/He isn't You're/You aren't	catching the 10:00 train.	

Question

What time	will you are you going to	arrive?
	are you meeting the manager?	

Note
We avoid saying *going to come* or *going to go*.
We**'re coming** tomorrow.
When **are** you **going** home?

Use

1. Decisions and intentions (*will* and *going to*)

will

Will is used as a modal auxiliary verb to express a decision, intention, or offer made at the
moment of speaking. We saw this use in Unit 4. (See page 142.) Remember that you can't
use the present tense for this use.

I**'ll** have the steak, please.   NOT ~~I have the steak.~~
I**'ll** see you tomorrow. Bye!   NOT ~~I see you tomorrow.~~
Give me a call sometime. We**'ll** go out for coffee.
"Jeff, there's someone at the door!"   "OK, I**'ll** get it."

going to

Going to is used to express a future plan, decision, or intention made before the moment
of speaking.

When I grow up, I**'m going to** be a doctor.
Jane and Peter **are going to** get married after they graduate.
We**'re going to** paint this room blue.

2. Prediction (*will* and *going to*)

will

The most common use of *will* is as an auxiliary verb to show future time. It expresses a
future fact or prediction. It is called the pure future or the Future Simple.

We**'ll be** away for two weeks.
Those flowers **won't grow** under the tree. It's too dark.
Our love **will last** forever.
You**'ll be** sick if you eat all that candy!

Will for a prediction can be based more on an opinion than a fact.

I think Laura **will** do very well on her test. She works hard.
I am convinced that inflation **will** fall to three percent next year.

going to

Going to can also express a prediction, especially when it is based on a present fact. There
is evidence now that something is certain to happen.

She**'s going to** have a baby. (We can see she's pregnant.)
Our team **is going to** win the game. (It's four to nothing, and there are only five
   minutes left to play.)
It **isn't going to** rain today. (Look at that beautiful blue sky.)

Note
Sometimes there is no difference between *will* and *going to*.

This government	will ruin is going to ruin	the country with its stupid	economic policies.

3. Arrangements (Present Continuous)

The Present Continuous can be used to express a future arrangement between people.
It usually refers to the near future.

We**'re going** out with Jeremy tonight.
I**'m having** my hair cut tomorrow.
What **are** we **having** for lunch?

Think of the things you might put in your planner to remind you of what you are
doing over the next few days and weeks. These are the kinds of events that are often
expressed by the Present Continuous for the future. The verbs express some kind of
activity or movement.

I**'m meeting** Peter tonight.
The Taylors **are coming** for dinner.
I**'m seeing** the doctor in the morning.

Remember that you can't use the present tense for this use.

We**'re going** to a party on Saturday night.   NOT ~~We go to a party on Saturday~~
                                                  ~~night.~~
We**'re catching** the 10:00 train.   NOT ~~We catch the 10:00 train.~~
What **are** you **doing** this evening?   NOT ~~What do you do this evening?~~

Sometimes there is no difference between an agreed arrangement (Present
Continuous) and an intention (*going to*).

We're going to get We're getting	married in the spring.

Unit 6

Introduction to *like*

Like can be a verb or a preposition.
Like as a verb has a person as the subject:
  I **like** modern art.
  I don't **like** the way he looks at me.
  Do you **like** fish?
  Would you **like** a drink?
Like as a preposition has an object after it:
  She's wearing a hat **like** mine.
  He's nothing **like** his father.
  That sounds **like** the postman.
  You're behaving **like** children.
  This new girlfriend of his—what's she **like**?

6.1 *What ... like?*

What is/are/was/were ... like? is used to ask about the permanent nature of people and things. It asks for a description or an impression or a comparison.
  What's the healthcare **like** in your country?
  What are the new students **like**?
Be careful!
1. With a description or an impression, we do not use *like* in the answer.
      What's London **like**?
      It's quite big, and it's very interesting.   NOT ~~It's like quite big ...~~

      What's Amanda **like**?
      She's tall, good-looking, and very funny.   NOT ~~She's like tall ...~~
2. With a comparison, we can use *like* in the answer. Here, *like* means *similar to/the same as*.
      What's London **like**?
      It's **like** New York, but without the tall buildings. (It's similar to ...)

      What's Amanda's daughter **like**?
      She's just **like** Amanda. (She's the same as ...)

6.2 *How ... ?*

How ... ? is used to ask about:
1. the present condition of something that can change.
   How's work these days?
   It's better than last year.
   How was the traffic this morning?
   It was worse than usual.

Note
To ask about the weather, we can use both questions.

How's the weather What's the weather like	where you are?

2. people's health and happiness.
   Compare:

How's Peter? He's fine.	What's Peter like? He's a nice guy. He's quite tall, has dark hair ...

3. to ask about people's reactions and feelings.
   How's your meal?
   How's your new job?

6.3 *How ... ?* or *What ... like?*

Sometimes we can use *What ... like?* or *How ... ?*, but they aren't the same. *What ... like?* asks for an objective description. *How ... ?* asks for personal feelings.
Compare:

How's the party? It's great!	What's the party like? It's very noisy, but there's lots to eat and drink.

6.4 Verb + *-ing* or infinitive

See Appendix 2 on page 153 for a list of verb patterns.

6.5 Relative clauses

1. Relative clauses are used to tell us which person or thing we are talking about. They make it possible to give more information about the person or thing being spoken about.
      The boy has gone to the beach. (Which boy?)
      The boy **who lives next door** has gone to the beach.
      The book is very good. (Which book?)
      The book **that I bought yesterday** is very good.
      This is a photo of the hotel. (Which hotel?)
      This is a photo of the hotel **where we stayed**.
2. We use *who* to refer to people.
      The book is about a girl **who** marries a millionaire.
   We use *that* to refer to things.
      What was the name of the horse **that** won the race?
3. When *who* or *that* is the object of a relative clause, it can be left out.
      The person **you need to talk to** is on vacation.
      The book **I bought yesterday** is very good.
   But when *who* or *that* is the subject of a relative clause, it must be included.
      I like people **who are kind and considerate**.
      I want a computer **that is easy to use**.
4. *Which* can be used to refer to the whole previous sentence of idea.
      I passed my driving test on my first attempt, **which surprised everyone**.
      Jane can't come to the party, **which is a shame**.
5. We use *whose* to refer to someone's possessions.
      That's the woman **whose dog ran away**.
6. We can use *where* to refer to places.
      The hotel **where we stayed** was right on the beach.

Unit 7

Introduction to the Present Perfect

The same form (*have* + past participle) exists in many European languages, but the uses in English are different. In English, the Present Perfect is essentially a present tense, but it also expresses the effect of past actions and activities on the present.

Present Perfect means "before now." The Present Perfect does not express when an action happened. If we say the exact time, we have to use the Past Simple.

> In my life, I **have traveled** to all seven continents.
> I **traveled** around Africa **in 1998**.

7.1 The Present Perfect

Form

Affirmative and negative

I We You They	've haven't	lived in Rome.
He She	's hasn't	

Question

How long have	I we you	known Peter?
How long has	she he	

Short answer

Have you always lived in Chicago?	Yes, I have. No, I haven't.

Use

The Present Perfect expresses:
1. an action that began in the past and still continues (unfinished past).
   > We**'ve lived** in the same house for 25 years.
   > Peter**'s worked** as a teacher since 2000.
   > How long **have** you **known** each other?
   > They**'ve been** married for 20 years.

Note
Many languages express this idea with a present tense, but in English this is wrong.
> Peter **has been** a teacher for ten years.   NOT ~~Peter is a teacher for ten years.~~

These time expressions are common with this use.

for	two years a month a few minutes half an hour ages	since	1970 the end of the class August 8:00 Christmas

We use *for* with a period of time and *since* with a point in time.
2. an experience that happened at some time in one's life. The action is in the past and finished, but the effects of the action are still felt. When the action happened is not important.
   > I**'ve been** to the United States. (I still remember.)
   > She**'s written** poetry and children's stories. (in her writing career)
   > **Have** you ever **had** an operation? (at any time in your life up to now)
   > How many times **has** he **been** married? (in his life)

The adverbs *ever*, *never*, and *before* are common with this use.
   > Have you **ever** been to Australia?
   > I've **never** tried bungee jumping.
   > I haven't tried sushi **before**.

Questions and answers about definite times are expressed in the Past Simple.
   > When **did** you **go** to the United States?
   > **Was** her poetry **published** while she was alive?
   > I **broke** my leg once, but I **didn't** have to stay in the hospital.
   > He **met** his second wife in the dry cleaner's.
3. a past action that has a present result. The action is usually in the recent past.
   > The taxi **hasn't arrived** yet. (We're still waiting for it.)
   > What **have** you **done** to your lip? (It's bleeding.)

We often announce news in the Present Perfect because the speaker is emphasizing the event as a present fact.
   > **Have** you **heard**? The prime minister **has resigned**.
   > Susan**'s had** her baby!
   > I**'ve ruined** the meal.

Details about definite time will be in the Past Simple.
   > She **resigned** because she lost a vote of no confidence.
   > She **had** a baby boy this morning. It **was** a difficult birth.
   > I **didn't watch** it carefully enough.

The adverbs *yet*, *already*, and *just* are common with this use.
   > I haven't done my homework **yet**. (Negative)
   > Has the mail come **yet**? (Question)
   > I've **already** done my homework.
   > She's **just** had some good news.

Final Note
Be careful with *been* and *gone*.
   > He's **been** to the United States. (= experience—he isn't there now.)
   > She's **gone** to the United States. (= present result—she's there now.)

7.2 Present Perfect or Past Simple?

1. The Present Perfect is for unfinished actions. The Past Simple is for completed actions. Compare:

Present Perfect	**Past Simple**
I've lived in Texas for six years. (I still live there.)	I lived in Texas for six years. (Now I live somewhere else.)
I've written several books. (I can still write some more.)	Shakespeare wrote 30 plays. (He can't write any more.)

2. We can see that the Present Perfect refers to indefinite time and the Past Simple refers to definite time by looking at the time expressions used with the different tenses.

Present Perfect—indefinite		Past Simple—definite	
I've done it	for a long time. since July. before. recently.	I did it	yesterday. last week. two days ago. at 8:00. in 1987. when I was young. for a long time.
I've already done it. I haven't done it yet.			

Be careful with *this morning/afternoon,* etc.

Have you **seen** Amy this morning? (It's still morning.)	**Did** you **see** Amy this morning? (It's the afternoon or evening.)

7.3 Present Perfect Simple passive

Form

has/have been + **past participle** (*-ed,* etc.)

It	has been	sold.
They	have been	

Use

The uses are the same in the passive as in the active.
Two million cars **have been produced** so far this year.
    (unfinished past)
Has she ever **been fired**? (past experience)
"Have you heard? Two hundred homes **have been washed** away by a tidal wave!" (present importance)

7.4 Phrasal verbs

There are four types of phrasal verbs.

Type 1
Verb + particle (no object)
    a. He put on his coat and **went out.**
    b. I didn't put enough wood on the fire and it **went out.**
In a, the verb and particle are used literally. In b, they are used idiomatically. *To go out* means to stop burning.
Examples with literal meaning:
    Sit down.
    She **stood up** and **walked out.**
    Please **go away.**
    She **walked** right **past** the store without noticing it.
Examples with idiomatic meaning:
    The marriage didn't **work out.** (= succeed)
    Our plans **fell through.** (= fail)

Type 2
Verb + particle + object (separable)
    a. I **put up** the picture.
    b. I **put up** my sister for the night.
In a, the verb and particle are used literally. In b, they are used idiomatically. *To put up* means to give someone food and a place to sleep usually for the night or a few days.
Type 2 phrasal verbs are separable. The object (noun or pronoun) can come between the verb and the particle.

| I **put up** the picture. | I **put up** my sister. |
| I **put** the picture **up.** | I **put** my sister **up.** |

But if the object is a pronoun, it always comes between the verb and the particle.

| I put **it** up. | NOT ~~I put up it.~~ |
| I put **her** up. | NOT ~~I put up her.~~ |

Examples with a literal meaning:
    The waiter **took away** the plates.
    Don't **throw** it **away.**
    They're **tearing** that old building **down.**
Examples with an idiomatic meaning:
    I **put off** the meeting. (= postpone)
    Don't **let** me **down.** (= disappoint)

Type 3
Verb + particle + object (inseparable)
    a. She **came across** the room.
    b. She **came across** an old friend while she was out shopping.
In a, the verb and particle are used literally. In b, they are used idiomatically. *To come across* means to find by accident.
Type 3 phrasal verbs are inseparable. The object (noun or pronoun) always comes after the particle.
    NOT ~~She came an old friend across.~~ or ~~She came her across.~~
Examples with a literal meaning:
    I'm **looking for** Jane.
    They **ran across** the park.
    We **drove past** them.
Examples with an idiomatic meaning:
    I'll **look after** it for you. (= care for)
    She **takes after** her father. (= resemble in features, build, character, or disposition)
    He never **got over** the death of his wife. (= recover from)

Type 4
Verb + particle + particle
    I **get along** very well **with** my boss.
    I'm **looking forward to** it.
    How can you **put up with** that noise?
Type 4 phrasal verbs are nearly always idiomatic. The object cannot change position. It cannot come before the particles or between the particles.
    NOT ~~I'm looking forward it to.~~

Unit 8

Introduction to conditionals

There are many different ways of making sentences with *if.* It is important to understand the difference between sentences that express real possibilities and those that express unreal situations.

Real possibilities
    If it **rains**, we**'ll** stay home.
    (*if* + Present Simple + *will*)
    If you**'ve finished** your work, you **can** go home.
    (*if* + Present Perfect + modal auxiliary verb)
    If you**'re feeling** ill, **go** home and **get** into bed.
    (*if* + Present Continuous + imperative)

Unreal situations
    You **would understand** me better if you **came** from my country.
    (*would* + *if* + Past Simple)
    If I **were** rich, I **wouldn't have** any problems.
    (*if* + *were* + *would*)
    If I **stopped** smoking, I **could run** faster.
    (*if* + Past Simple + modal auxiliary verb)

There are several patterns that you need to know to understand the variations. Note that a comma is usual when the *if* clause comes first.

8.1 First conditional

Form

if + Present Simple + *will*

Affirmative

> If I find your wallet, I'll let you know.
> We'll come and see you on Sunday if the weather's good.

Negative

> You won't pass the test if you don't study.
> If you lose your ticket, you won't be able to go.

Question

> What will you do if you don't find a job?
> If there isn't a hotel, where will you stay?

Note that we do not usually use *will* in the *if* clause.

> NOT ~~If you will leave now, you'll catch the train.~~
> ~~If I'll go out tonight, I'll give you a call.~~

If can be replaced by *unless* (= *if … not*) or *in case* (= because of the possibility …).

> **Unless** I hear from you, I'll come at 8:00.
> I'll take my umbrella **in case** it rains.

Use

1. First conditional sentences express a possible condition and its probable result in the future.

Condition (*if* clause)	Result (result clause)
If I find a sweater in your size,	I'll buy it for you.
If you can do the homework,	give me a call.
If you can find my purse,	I might buy you ice cream.
If you've never been to Wales,	you should try to go there one day.

2. We can use the first conditional to express different functions (all of which express a possible condition and a probable result).
> If you do that again, I'll kill you! (= a threat)
> Careful! If you touch that, you'll burn yourself! (= a warning)
> I'll mail the letter if you like. (= an offer)
> If you lend me $100, I'll love you forever. (= a promise)

8.2 Time clauses

Conjunctions of time *(when, as soon as, before, until, after)* are not usually followed by *will*. We use a present tense even though the time reference is future.

> I'll call you **when** I **get** home.
> **As soon as** dinner **is** ready, I'll give you a call.
> Can I have a word with you **before** I **go**?
> Wait **until** I **come** back.

We can use the Present Perfect if it is important to show that the action in the time clause is finished.

> **When I've finished** the book, I'll lend it to you.
> I'll go home **after I've done** the shopping.

8.3 Zero Conditional

Zero Conditional sentences refer to "all time," not just the present or future. They express a situation that is always true. *If* means *when* or *whenever*.

> If you spend over $50 at that supermarket, you get a five percent discount.

8.4 Second conditional

Form

if + Past Simple + *would*

Affirmative

> If I won some money, I'd go around the world.
> My father would kill me if he could see me now.

Negative

> I'd give up my job if I didn't like it.
> If I saw a ghost, I wouldn't talk to it.

Question

> What would you do if you saw someone shoplifting?
> If you needed help, who would you ask?

Note that *was* can change to *were* in the condition clause.

If I If he	were rich,	I he	wouldn't have to work.

Use

1. We use the second conditional to express an unreal situation and its probable result. The situation or condition is improbable, impossible, imaginary, or contrary to known facts.
> If I were the president of my country, I'd increase taxes. (But it's not very likely that I will ever be the president.)
> If my mother was still alive, she'd be very proud. (But she's dead.)
> If Ted needed money, I'd lend it to him. (But he doesn't need it.)
2. Other modal verbs are possible in the result clause.
> I **could** buy some new clothes if I had some money.
> If I saved a little every week, I **might** be able to save up for a car.
> If you wanted that job, you'**d have** to apply very soon.
3. *If I were you, I'd …* is used to give advice.
> **If I were you, I'd** apologize to her.
> **I'd** take it easy for a while **if I were you**.

8.5 First or second conditional?

Both conditionals refer to the present and future. The difference is about probability, not time. It is usually clear which conditional to use. First conditional sentences are real and possible; second conditional sentences express situations that will probably never happen.

> If I lose my job, I'll … (My company is doing badly. There is a strong possibility of being fired.)
> If I lost my job, I'd … (I probably won't lose my job. I'm just speculating.)
> If there is a nuclear war, we'll all … (Said by a pessimist.)
> If there was a nuclear war, … (But I don't think it will happen.)

would

Notice the use of *would* in the following sentences:

> She'**d** look better with shorter hair. (= If she cut her hair, she'd look better.)

***would* to express preference**

> I'**d** love a cup of coffee.
> Where **would** you like to sit?
> I'**d** rather have coffee, please.
> I'**d** rather not tell you, if that's all right.
> What **would** you rather do, stay in or go out?

***would* to express a request**

> **Would** you open the door for me?
> **Would** you mind lending me a hand?

Unit 9

Modal verbs 2

Modal verbs can express ability, obligation, permission, and request. They can also express the idea of probability or how certain a situation is. There is an introduction to modal auxiliary verbs on page 141.

9.1 Expressing possibility/probability

1. *Must* and *can't* express the logical conclusion of a situation: *must* = logically probable; *can't* = logically improbable. We don't have all the facts, so we are not absolutely sure, but we are pretty certain.
   He **must** be exhausted. He can't even stand up.
   Sue **can't** have a ten-year-old daughter! Sue's only 24!
   He's in great shape, even though he **must** be at least 60!
   A walk in this weather! You **must** be joking!
   Is there no answer? They **must** be in bed. They **can't** be out this late!

2. *Could* and *may/might* express possibility in the present or future. *May/Might + not* is the negative. *Couldn't* is rare in this use.
   He **might** be lost.
   They **could** move to a different place.
   Dave and Beth aren't at home. They **could** be at the concert, I suppose.
   We **may** go to Greece for our vacation. We haven't decided yet.
   Take your umbrella. It **might** rain later
   I **might** not be able to come tonight. I **might** have to work late.

Note the Continuous Infinitive
Must/could/can't/might + be + -ing make the Continuous form of these modal verbs.
   You must **be joking**!
   Peter must **be working** late.
   She **could have been lying** to you.

9.2 Expressing possibility/probability: the past

The Perfect Infinitive
Must/could/can't/might + have + past participle express degrees of probability in the past.

Past
   He **must have been** exhausted.
   She **can't have told** him about us yet.
   He **might have gotten** lost.
   They **could have moved** to a different place.

9.3 *So do I! Neither do I!*

When we agree or disagree using *So …/Neither … I*, we repeat the auxiliary verbs. If there is no auxiliary, use *do/does/did*. Be careful with sentence stress.

AGREEING		DISAGREEING	
So … I.			
I like ice cream.	• So do I.	I don't like Mary.	• I do.
I'm wearing jeans.	So am I.	We're going now.	We aren't.
I can swim.	So can I.	I can speak Polish.	I can't.
I went out.	So did I.	I haven't been skiing.	I have.
Neither … I.			
I don't like working.	• Neither do I.	I like blue cheese.	• I don't.
I can't drive.	Neither can I.	I saw Pat yesterday.	I didn't.
I haven't been to Paris.	Neither have I.	I'm going to have some coffee.	I'm not.

9.4 *too* and *either/neither*

We express that we have the same ideas as somebody else by using *too* and *either/neither*. With *too* we repeat the auxiliary verbs. If there is no auxiliary, use *do/does/did*.

"I like ice cream."	"I do, too." / "Me too."
"I have always studied hard."	"I have, too." / "Me too."
"I don't like working."	"I don't, either." / "Me neither."
"I can't play a musical instrument."	"I can't, either." / "Me neither."

Unit 10

10.1 Present Perfect Continuous

A note about Continuous forms.
Remember, the following ideas are expressed by all Continuous forms:

1. activity in progress.
    Be quiet! I'**m thinking**.
    I **was taking** a shower when the phone rang.
    I'**ve been working** since 9:00 this morning.
2. temporary activity.
    We'**re staying** with friends until we find our own place to live.
    We'**ve been living** with them for six weeks.
3. possibly incomplete activity.
    I'**m writing** a report. I have to finish it by tomorrow.
    Who'**s been eating** my sandwich?

Form

Affirmative and negative

I We You They	've haven't	been working.
He She It	's hasn't	

Question

How long	have	I you we	been working?
	has	she it	

Use

We use the Present Perfect Continuous to express:

1. an activity that began in the past and is still continuing now.
    I'**ve been studying** English for three years.
    How long **have** you **been working** here?
    Sometimes there is no difference between the Simple and the Continuous.

I've played I've been playing	the piano since I was a boy.

If the Continuous is possible, English has a preference for using it.
The Continuous can sometimes express a temporary activity, and the Simple a permanent state.
    I'**ve been living** in this house for the past few months. (= temporary)
    I'**ve lived** here all my life. (= permanent)
Remember that stative verbs rarely take the Continuous (see page 138).
    I'**ve had** this book for ages.
    I'**ve** always **loved** sunny days.

2. a past activity that has caused a present result.
    I'**ve been working** all day. (I'm tired now.)
    Have you **been crying**? (Your eyes are red.)
    Roger'**s been cutting** the grass. (I can smell it.)
The past activity might be finished or it might not. The context usually makes this clear.
    Look out the window! It'**s been snowing**! (It has stopped snowing now.)
    I'**ve been writing** this book for two years. (It still isn't finished.)
    I'm covered in paint because I'**ve been decorating** the bathroom. (It might be finished or it might not. We don't know.)

10.2 Present Perfect Simple or Continuous?

1. The Simple expresses a completed action.
    I'**ve painted** the kitchen, and now I'**m doing** the bathroom.
    The Continuous expresses an activity over a period and things that happened during the activity.
    I have paint in my hair because I'**ve been decorating**.
    Because the Simple expresses a completed action, we use the Simple if the sentence gives a number or quantity. Here, the Continuous isn't possible.
    I'**ve been reading** all day. I'**ve read** ten chapters.
    She'**s been eating** ever since she arrived. She'**s eaten** ten cookies already.
2. Some verbs don't have the idea of a long time, for example, *find, start, buy, die, lose, break, stop*. These verbs are more usually found in the Simple.
    Some verbs have the idea of a long time, for example, *wait, work, play, try, learn, rain*. These verbs are often found in the Continuous.
    I'**ve cut** my finger. (One short action.)
    I'**ve been cutting** firewood. (Perhaps over several hours.)

10.3 Time expressions

Here are some time expressions often found with certain tenses.

Past Simple
    I **lived** in Chicago **for six years**.
    I **saw** Jack **two days ago**.
    They **met during the war**.
    She **got** married **while she was in college**.

Present Perfect
    We'**ve been** married **for ten years**.
    They'**ve been living** here **since June**.
    She **hasn't been working since their baby was born**.

Future
    We'**re going** on vacation **for a few days**.
    The class **ends in 20 minutes**.
    I'**ll be** home **in a half an hour**.

Prepositions with dates, months, years, etc.

in	September 1965 the summer the 1920s the 20th century	on	Monday Monday morning August 8th Christmas Day vacation	at	7:00 the end of May the age of ten dinner time

Unit 11

Look at the following question words. Notice that *What, Which,* and *Whose* can combine with a noun and *How* can combine with an adjective or an adverb.

What kind of music do you like?
What size shoe do you wear?
What color are your eyes?
Which pen do you want?
Which way is it to the station?
Whose book is this?
How much do you weigh?
How many brothers and sisters do you have?
How many times have you been on a plane?
How much homework do you get every night?
How tall are you?
How often do you go to the movies?
How long does it take you to get to school?

11.1 Indirect questions

1. Indirect questions have the same word order as the affirmative and there is no *do/does/did*.

   Tom lives in California.

   I don't know where Tom lives .   NOT ~~I don't know where does Tom live.~~

   Here are some more expressions that introduce indirect questions:

I wonder I can't remember I have no idea I'd like to know I'm not sure	how long the trip takes.

   If there is no question word, use *if* or *whether*.
   I don't know **if** I'm coming or not.
   I wonder **whether** it's going to rain.

2. We often make direct questions into indirect questions to make them sound "softer" or more polite.

Direct question	**Indirect question**	
What time do the banks close?	Could you tell me Do you know Do you happen to know Have you any idea Do you remember	what time the banks close?

11.2 Question tags

Form

1. Question tags are very common in spoken English. The most common patterns are:
   affirmative sentence—negative tag
      You**'re** Jenny, **aren't** you?
   negative sentence—affirmative tag
      It **isn't** a very nice day, **is** it?

2. We repeat the auxiliary verb in the tag. If there is no auxiliary, use *do/does/did*.
   You **haven't** been here before, **have** you?
   You **can** speak French, **can't** you?
   We **should** take the dog out, **shouldn't** we?
   She eats meat, **doesn't** she?
   Banks close at four, **don't** they?
   You went to bed late, **didn't** you?

Note
For negative question tags with *I'm …* use *aren't*.
   I'm late, **aren't** I?   NOT ~~I'm late, am't I?~~
But,
   I'm **not** late, **am** I?   NOT ~~I'm not late, aren't I?~~

3. Notice the meaning of *Yes* and *No* in answer to question tags.
   "You're coming, aren't you?"   "Yes." (= I **am** coming.)
                                 "No." (= I'm **not** coming.)

Use

We use question tags to keep a conversation going by involving listeners and inviting them to participate.
The meaning of a question tag depends on how you say it.
A question tag with rising intonation is like a real question—it is asking for confirmation. It means "I'm not sure, so I'm checking." The speaker thinks he/she knows the answer, but isn't absolutely certain.

   Your name's Abigail, isn't it?

   You're in advertising, aren't you?

   You work in the city, don't you?

A question tag with falling intonation isn't really a question at all—it is a way of making conversation. It means "Talk to me." The speaker expects people to agree with him/her.

   Beautiful day, isn't it?

   It's wonderful weather for swimming, isn't it?

   That was a great concert, wasn't it?

   You haven't been here before, have you?

Note
We can also use question tags with negative sentences to make a polite request for information or help.

   You couldn't lend me your car this evening, could you?

Unit 12

12.1 Reported speech

Reported statements and tense changes
It is usual for the verb in the reported clause to move "one tense back" if:

1. the reporting verb is in the past tense (e.g., *said, told*).

   Present ———————▶ Past
   Present Perfect ———▶ Past Perfect
   Past ————————▶ Past Perfect

   "I'm going."   He said he **was going**.
   "She**'s passed** her test."   He told me she **had passed** her test.
   "My father **died** when I was six."   She said her father **had died** when she was six.

2. we are reporting thoughts and feelings.
      I thought she **was** married, but she isn't.
      I didn't know he **was** a teacher. I thought he **worked** in a bank.
      I forgot you **were coming**. Never mind. Come in.
      I hoped you **would** call.

There is no tense change if:
1. the reporting verb is in the present tense (e.g., *says, asks*).
   "The train **will be** late."   He says the train **will be** late.
   "I **come** from Spain."   She says she **comes** from Spain.
2. the reported speech is about something that is still true.
   Rain forests **are being destroyed**.
   She told him that rain forests **are being destroyed**.
   "I **hate** soccer."
   I told him I **hate** soccer.

Note
Some modal verbs change.

can ⟶ could
will ⟶ would
may ⟶ might

   "She **can** type well."   He told me she **could** type well.
   "I**'ll** help you."   She said she**'d** help me.
   "I **may** come."   She said she **might** come.

Other modal verbs don't change.
   "You **should** go to bed."   He told me I **should** go to bed.
   "It **might** rain."   She said she thought it **might** rain.
Must can stay as *must*, or it can change to *had to*.
   "I **must** go!"   He said he **must/had to** go.

12.2 Reporting verbs

There are many reporting verbs.
We rarely use *say* with an indirect object (i.e., the person spoken to).
   She said she was going.   NOT ~~She said to me she was going.~~
Tell is always used with an indirect object in reported speech.

She told	me the doctor us her husband	the news.

In more formal situations, we can use *that* after the reporting verb.
   He told her (**that**) he would be home late.
   She said (**that**) sales were down from last year.
Many verbs are more descriptive than *say* and *tell*, for example, *explain, interrupt, demand, insist, admit, complain, warn*.

He	explained complained	that he would be home late.
She	admitted	that sales were down that year.

Sometimes we report the idea, rather than the actual words.
   "I'll lend you some money."   He offered to lend me some money.
   "I won't help you."   She refused to help me.

12.3 Reported questions

1. The word order in reported questions is different in reported speech. There is no inversion of subject and auxiliary verb and there is no *do/does/did*. This is similar to indirect questions (see page 150).
   "Why have you come here?"   I asked her why she had come here.
   "What time is it?"   He wants to know what time it is.
   "Where do you live?"   She asked me where I lived.

Note
We do not use a question mark in a reported question.
We do not use *say* in reported questions.
   He said, "How old are you?"   He asked me how old I am.
2. If there is no question word, use *if* or *whether*.

She wants to know	whether if	she should wear a dress.

12.4 Reported commands, requests, etc.

1. For reported commands, requests, offers, and advice we use verb + person + infinitive.
   They **told us to** go away.
   They **asked me to** look after their cat.
   He **urged the teachers to** go back to work.
   She **persuaded me to** have my hair cut.
   I **advised the president to** leave immediately.

   Note
   Say is not possible. Use *ask, told*, etc.

2. For negative commands, use *not* before *to*.
   He told me **not to** tell anyone.
   The police warned people **not to** go out.
3. Be careful! *Tell* and *ask* can be used in different ways, but the form changes.
   We use *tell* for reported statements and reported commands.

Reported statements

| He told me that he was going. |
| They told us that they were going abroad. |
| She told them what had been happening. |

Reported commands

| He told me to keep still. |
| The police told people to move on. |
| My parents told me to clean up my room. |

We use *ask* for reported commands and reported questions.

Reported commands

| I was asked to attend the interview. |
| He asked me to open my suitcase. |
| She asked me not to leave. |

Reported questions

| He asked me what I did for a living. |
| I asked her how much the rent was. |
| She asked me why I had come. |

Appendix 1

IRREGULAR VERBS

Base form	Past Simple	Past Participle	Base form	Past Simple	Past Participle
be	was/were	been	lend	lent	lent
beat	beat	beaten	let	let	let
become	became	become	lie	lay	lain
begin	began	begun	light	lighted/lit	lighted/lit
bend	bent	bent	lose	lost	lost
bite	bit	bitten	make	made	made
blow	blew	blown	mean	meant	meant
break	broke	broken	meet	met	met
bring	brought	brought	must	had to	had to
build	built	built	pay	paid	paid
burst	burst	burst	put	put	put
buy	bought	bought	quit	quit	quit
can	could	been able	read /rid/	read /rɛd/	read /rɛd/
catch	caught	caught	ride	rode	ridden
choose	chose	chosen	ring	rang	rung
come	came	come	rise	rose	risen
cost	cost	cost	run	ran	run
cut	cut	cut	say	said	said
dig	dug	dug	see	saw	seen
do	did	done	sell	sold	sold
draw	drew	drawn	send	sent	sent
drink	drank	drunk	set	set	set
drive	drove	driven	shake	shook	shaken
eat	ate	eaten	shine	shone	shone
fall	fell	fallen	shoot	shot	shot
feed	fed	fed	show	showed	shown
feel	felt	felt	shut	shut	shut
fight	fought	fought	sing	sang	sung
find	found	found	sink	sank	sunk
fit	fit	fit	sit	sat	sat
fly	flew	flown	sleep	slept	slept
forget	forgot	forgotten	slide	slid	slid
forgive	forgave	forgiven	speak	spoke	spoken
freeze	froze	frozen	spend	spent	spent
get	got	gotten	spread	spread	spread
give	gave	given	stand	stood	stood
go	went	gone	steal	stole	stolen
grow	grew	grown	stick	stuck	stuck
hang	hung	hung	sweep	swept	swept
have	had	had	swim	swam	swum
hear	heard	heard	take	took	taken
hide	hid	hidden	teach	taught	taught
hit	hit	hit	tear	tore	torn
hold	held	held	tell	told	told
hurt	hurt	hurt	think	thought	thought
keep	kept	kept	throw	threw	thrown
kneel	knelt	knelt	understand	understood	understood
know	knew	known	wake	woke	woken
lay	laid	laid	wear	wore	worn
lead	led	led	win	won	won
leave	left	left	write	wrote	written

Appendix 2

VERB PATTERNS

Verbs + *to* + infinitive only

agree	
choose	
dare	
decide	
expect	
forget	
help	
hope	
learn	to do
manage	
need	to come
offer	
promise	to cook
refuse	
seem	
want	
would like	
would love	
would prefer	
would hate	

Notes
1. *Help* and *dare* can be used without *to*.
   We **helped clean up** the kitchen.
   They didn't **dare disagree** with him.
2. *Have to* for obligation.
   I **have to wear** a uniform.
3. *Used to* for past habits.
   I **used to smoke**, but I quit last year.

Verbs + *-ing* only

adore	
enjoy	
adore	doing
hate	swimming
don't mind	cooking
finish	
look forward to	

Note
We often use the verb *go* + *-ing* for sports and activities.
   I **go swimming** every day.
   I **go shopping** on weekends.

Verbs + *-ing* or *to* + infinitive
(with little or no change in meaning)

like	
love	
prefer	
hate	doing
can't stand	
begin	to do
start	
continue	

Verbs + *-ing* or *to* + infinitive
(with a change in meaning)

remember	doing
stop	to do
try	

Notes
1. I **remember mailing** the letter.
   (= I have a memory now of a past action: mailing the letter.)
   I **remembered to mail** the letter.
   (= I reminded myself to mail the letter. I didn't forget.)
2. I **stopped drinking** coffee.
   (= I gave up the habit.)
   I **stopped to drink** a coffee.
   (= I stopped doing something else in order to have a cup of coffee.)
3. I **tried to** sleep.
   (= I wanted to sleep, but it was difficult.)
   I **tried counting** sheep and **drinking** a glass of warm milk.
   (= These were possible ways of getting to sleep.)

Verbs + somebody + *to* + infinitive

advise		
allow		
ask		
beg		
encourage	me	
expect		to do
help	him	
need		to go
invite	them	
order		to come
remind	someone	
tell		
want		
warn (+ *not*)		
would like		

Note
Help can be used without *to*.
   I **helped** him **do** the dishes.

Verbs + somebody + infinitive (without *to*)

let		
make	her	do
help	us	

Notes
1. *To* is used with *make* in the passive.
   We were **made to work** hard.
2. *Let* cannot be used in the passive. *Allowed to* is used instead.
   She was **allowed to leave**.

Phonetic Symbols

Consonants			
1	/p/	as in	**pen** /pɛn/
2	/b/	as in	**big** /bɪg/
3	/t/	as in	**tea** /ti/
4	/d/	as in	**do** /du/
5	/k/	as in	**cat** /kæt/
6	/g/	as in	**go** /goʊ/
7	/f/	as in	**five** /faɪv/
8	/v/	as in	**very** /ˈvɛri/
9	/s/	as in	**son** /sʌn/
10	/z/	as in	**zoo** /zu/
11	/l/	as in	**live** /lɪv/
12	/m/	as in	**my** /maɪ/
13	/n/	as in	**nine** /naɪn/
14	/h/	as in	**happy** /hæpi/
15	/r/	as in	**red** /rɛd/
16	/y/	as in	**yes** /yɛs/
17	/w/	as in	**want** /wɑnt/
18	/θ/	as in	**thanks** /θæŋks/
19	/ð/	as in	**the** /ðə/
20	/ʃ/	as in	**she** /ʃi/
21	/ʒ/	as in	**television** /ˈtɛlɪvɪʒn/
22	/tʃ/	as in	**child** /tʃaɪld/
23	/dʒ/	as in	**Japan** /dʒəˈpæn/
24	/ŋ/	as in	**English** /ˈɪŋglɪʃ/

Vowels			
25	/i/	as in	**see** /si/
26	/ɪ/	as in	**his** /hɪz/
27	/ɛ/	as in	**ten** /tɛn/
28	/æ/	as in	**stamp** /stæmp/
29	/ɑ/	as in	**father** /ˈfɑðər/
30	/ɔ/	as in	**saw** /sɔ/
31	/ʊ/	as in	**book** /bʊk/
32	/u/	as in	**you** /yu/
33	/ʌ/	as in	**sun** /sʌn/
34	/ə/	as in	**about** /əˈbaʊt/
35	/eɪ/	as in	**name** /neɪm/
36	/aɪ/	as in	**my** /maɪ/
37	/ɔɪ/	as in	**boy** /bɔɪ/
38	/aʊ/	as in	**how** /haʊ/
39	/oʊ/	as in	**go** /goʊ/
40	/ər/	as in	**bird** /bərd/
41	/ɪr/	as in	**near** /nɪr/
42	/ɛr/	as in	**hair** /hɛr/
43	/ɑr/	as in	**car** /kɑr/
44	/ɔr/	as in	**more** /mɔr/
45	/ʊr/	as in	**tour** /tʊr/